POSSESSION, PURITANISM AND PRINT: DARRELL, HARSNETT, SHAKESPEARE AND THE ELIZABETHAN EXORCISM CONTROVERSY

Religious Cultures in the Early Modern World

Series Editors: *Fernando Cervantes*
Peter Marshall
Philip Soergel

Forthcoming Titles

Visions of an Unseen World: Ghost Beliefs and Ghost Stories
in Eighteenth-Century England
Sasha Handley

Diabolism in Colonial Peru, 1560–1750
Andrew Redden

www.pickeringchatto.com/religious

POSSESSION, PURITANISM AND PRINT: DARRELL, HARSNETT, SHAKESPEARE AND THE ELIZABETHAN EXORCISM CONTROVERSY

BY

Marion Gibson

MUNDUS
INTELLECTUALIS

LONDON
PICKERING & CHATTO
2006

Published by Pickering & Chatto (Publishers) Limited
21 Bloomsbury Way, London WC1A 2TH

2252 Ridge Road, Brookfield, Vermont 05036-9704, USA

www.pickeringchatto.com

BRITISH LIBRARY CATALOGUING IN PUBLICATION DATA

Gibson, Marion, 1970–
    Possession, puritanism and print : Darrell, Harsnett, Shakespeare and the
    Elizabethan exorcism controversy
    1. Darrel, John, b. ca. 1562 2. Exorcism – England – History – 16th century 3.
    Puritan movements – England – History – 16th century 4. England – Church
    history 16th century
    I. Title
    265.9'4'0942'09031

    ISBN-10: 1851968326

⊗

This publication is printed on acid-free paper that conforms to the American
National Standard for the Permanence of Paper for Printed Library Materials

Typeset by Pickering & Chatto (Publishers) Limited
Printed in the United Kingdom at the University Press, Cambridge

CONTENTS

ACKNOWLEDGMENTS

I would like to thank, for their help and encouragement, the wonderful staff of Nottinghamshire Archives; Nottingham University Library, Department of Manuscripts and Special Collections, especially Kathryn Summerwill; Derbyshire Record Office; the Record Office for Leicestershire, Leicester and Rutland; Staffordshire Record Office; the William Salt Library, Stafford; Lancashire Record Office; Exeter University Library; Exeter Cathedral Library; Lambeth Palace Library and Trustees; the National Archives, Kew; the clergy of the Church of St Peter and St Paul, Mansfield and St Helen's Church, Ashby de la Zouch; the Guild of St Mary's Centre, Lichfield; the British Library; the Bodleian Library; the Shakespeare Institute, University of Birmingham; Plymouth City Library and the staffs of all the libraries and record offices with whom I have corresponded.

For discussing the project with me, suggesting new ideas and in some cases reading entire chapters or blocks of chapters, thanks to: Jonathan Barry, Harry Bennett, Marilyn Clark, Patrick Collinson, Susan Doran, Thomas Freeman, Regenia Gagnier, Ronald Hutton, Nathan Johnstone, Diarmaid MacCulloch, Andrew McRae, Charlie Nicholls, Jim Sharpe, John Spurr, John Swain, Dawn Teed, Jan-Frans van Dijkhuizen, Alex Walsham, Tom Webster, Min Wild, Martin Wiggins, and Mark Pollard at Pickering & Chatto. Thanks especially to Harry, Hoppy and Mum and Dad.

This book is dedicated to my grandmother
Edith Anne Squire
(1906–2004).

INTRODUCTION

The Baker, the Bishop and the Baker's Son

On 29 October 1597 Joan Pie, a fortuitously-named baker from Nottingham, went to the house of her neighbours Thomas and Anne Porter to pay them a visit. But the object of her attention was unusual – Thomas's apprentice, a young man named William Sommers. Sommers had been a bad apprentice to Thomas Porter. He was the kind that masters dreaded, loafing in alehouses when he was supposed to be running errands, and coming home late and penniless. He even ran away for periods of several months. He had a low opinion of his master's abilities which he did not hesitate to share. But Joan Pie wanted to see this unhappy youth because he was reported to be possessed by the devil. She was one of the first, if not the first, visitors to Sommers – soon tens of others would follow, with one hundred and fifty people present nine days later on 7 November for Sommers's dispossession. Joan was ahead of the crowd and she took an active interest in Sommers's evolving condition. She visited in the mornings, evenings and at noon, keeping abreast of Sommers's behaviour and speeches in his fits.[1]

On 5 November, a preacher arrived in Nottingham hoping to dispossess Sommers. Although he had been sent for by the Mayor and local ministers, the first person to meet him was Joan Pie. She had left Sommers's bedside purposely to intercept him and give him the latest, sensational news. Joan told the minister, John Darrell, exactly what he must expect when he saw Sommers – which appeared to the godly (puritanically-inclined) onlookers to be the possessed boy's imminent death. Darrell was later to explain that Joan accosted him as soon as he dismounted from his horse: 'I was no soner light but tydinges was brought to me, by one of they[r] neighbour women Joahn Pye by name'.[2] Darrell discussed Sommers's case briefly with Joan, and she then escorted him to the house, entering triumphantly with the man that the assembled crowd hoped would cure William Sommers and cast out the devil from their midst.

1

The group commenced the pious investigation of Sommers's trouble, and that weekend they dispossessed him by prayer and fasting – the approved godly method, which avoided any 'popish' ritual and, they thought, drove out the devil by the force of Protestant faith expressed in sermons, self-denial and extemporary prayers.

Later, Joan Pie gave evidence to the ecclesiastical Commission appointed to investigate the events surrounding Sommers's dispossession by Darrell. Her evidence occupied two closely-printed pages of the pamphlet published by Darrell's supporters to spread the word about the success of his method. Joan's is one of the longest statements to survive, and is notable for its confidence and vividness. She reported that Sommers had convulsed extraordinarily, 'his bodie doubled, and his head betweene his legs: and then suddenly he was plucked round uppon an heape'. When Sommers was thus curled up, Joan described his body as 'like a greate browne loafe', a cottage loaf as we would now call it. Her simile was, of course, drawn from her own and her husband's trade. Later, she returned to the same accessible imagery to describe Sommers's starting eyes – like walnuts – and a strange mobile swelling in his body – like a '3 penie white l[o]afe'. Other similes concerned the kind of pests likely to be found in a baker's premises – a rat, and a black 'clock' or beetle. Her readers saw Sommers through Joan Pie's eyes, his body made of bread, his eyes of nuts, his substance invaded and preyed upon by vermin. This gingerbread boy, a creature from folktale, also had religious resonances, for Christ's own body was likened at Communion to bread, and his blood to wine. Sommers, in Joan's imagery, was thus both common and extraordinary. And Joan herself was both the streetcrier of this edible wonder, and a blessed apostle. Her evidence would be part of a communal meditation – an 'exercise' or 'prophesying', as the godly called them – on the significance of dispossession by prayer and fasting. And it would be printed and publicized across the nation.

How did the readers of Joan's words value this evidence, given by a woman who in describing matters of high religious importance spoke of little beyond her own mercantile world – who made no forays into the intellectual fields of medicine or theology and who did not speak the languages of those professions? For readers who identified with Joan, and perhaps particularly to illiterate or partially literate listeners to whom the pamphlet could be read out, her similes would have had a directness and familiarity that carried conviction. If an otherwise mysterious and inexplicable 'running lumpe' in the body could be likened to a man-made, priced and consumable item like a threepenny loaf, perhaps it could be grasped and believed as a wonder by ordinary Christians. Like the accessibility of Christ's parables and the stories of his miracles, which similarly spoke of seed and sheep, loaves and fishes, Joan's words may have appealed to the godly layman of the 'common sort'. But for sceptical and especially for educated readers, Joan Pie's similes might carry evidence of their own intellectual limitations.

Why, they might ask, was this ordinary woman being cited as an authority on the mysteries of demonology? Matthew Sutcliffe, Dean of Exeter, had written five years before of his disgust that in godly (and particularly presbyterian) circles ordinary people, 'Hick, Hob and Clim of Clough, yea, and Margaret and Joan too', judged ecclesiastical matters. 'It would be very ridiculous' he thought 'if the base sort of people, leaving the shuttle, the plough and the spade and shop board, should busy their heads in discussing matters of religion and government'.[3] Commonness and femininity were both disqualifications in such a field. Many of Joan Pie's fellow witnesses were of the same 'sort' or class of persons – a cordwainer (shoemaker), a locksmith, a tailor. That men of the cloth, like Darrell, and gentlemen also gave evidence was little comfort, and that the chaplains and agents of aristocrats should be present was even less so. It was worrying that such dissimilar people, drawn together only by 'puritan', or godly, sympathies, should be consorting in the bedroom of a provincial apprentice and then publishing their conclusions on what they had seen there. Their shared cultural community was one of which the established Church of England, of which the godly were a part, was very suspicious. That the preacher, the gentleman and the baker's wife thought alike was cause for concern rather than complacency.

This group in Sommers's bedroom, said Samuel Harsnett, chaplain to the Bishop of London, formed in effect a kind of presbyterian *classis*, or illegal conventicle.[4] Here untrained and half-trained theologians were making up their own doctrine, assisted by the illiterate and ignorant. They were dismantling the hierarchical organization of the established Church, where archbishops and bishops made decisions, ministers obeyed them, and laity obeyed both. Despite the Protestant Reformation, with its emphasis on individual paths to God through the understanding of his Word, lay people like Joan Pie had no business offering their own interpretations of religion. John Darrell, as an unbeneficed preacher, likewise had no right, nor did William Sommers, a musician's apprentice. In fact, no-one in Nottingham ought to be deciding Church doctrine. This was done at Canterbury, York, Lambeth and other seats of Church power, at convocation and in synod. Under the direction of the Archbishop of Canterbury Harsnett's employer, Bishop Richard Bancroft, had spent the last decade of his career attempting to put down such rebellious tendencies in his church, both in the courts and in print. Ironically, his chaplain Harsnett was the son of a godly baker, and made his name attacking precisely the kind of people that his parents had been, as well as destroying the career of their most celebrated exorcist, John Darrell.[5]

John Darrell and Dispossession by Prayer and Fasting

The godly did not particularly care what bishops and their chaplains thought of their dispossessions, because they believed that the gatherings were based on the best possible textual warrant: the gospels. In Mark 9:29, Christ had spoken to his disciples about a particular kind of demonic spirit that could possess human bodies. 'This kind' he said 'can come forth by nothing, but by prayer and fasting'.[6] Christ himself was able to cast out demons by simple command, since he was the son of God. His apostles had less power, but could achieve similar results because some of Christ's power had been given to them. But after the end of the Apostolic era, what power was left in the church to cast out devils? The Roman Catholic church had developed a complex rite that, they argued, drove out the demon by harassing him with hallowed objects, and charging him in God's name to leave. But after the Reformation, Protestants had no method of their own, because they found the idea of holy objects repugnant. They also thought it presumptuous to command the devil to do anything, since in providential theory the devil could do nothing without God's having willed it, and no Christian might presume to command God.

But Darrell, and a number of other godly ministers and lay people, became convinced that Mark 9:29 contained the solution of this problem. Here, they thought, Christ gave specific, if obliquely-expressed, instructions about how to drive out a devil by humbly *petitioning* God to intervene, 'therein secretly promising, that praier and fasting being used, evill spirites doe and shall goe out'. And so their godly group began to practice dispossession by prayer and fasting, arguing that it would show Protestantism to be the true church, and refute Catholic claims that only their priests could exorcize. Prayer and fasting was not a dispossession method invented, or even revived, by Darrell and his friends, however. As Keith Thomas has shown, it had been used by John Parkhurst, Bishop of Norwich, as early as 1574. Harsnett suggested that Darrell's models were two Kentish ministers, Roger Newman of Westwell and John Brainford of Kennington, who dispossessed a servant girl in October 1574, but they charged the devil rather than praying as Darrell prescribed.[7] Darrell was more familiar with the work of John Foxe the martyrologist, who used prayer without fasting, with his most famous exorcism being that of a law student, also in 1574. Darrell himself did not, apparently, fast or encourage others to fast in his own first dispossession. He simply prayed for the deliverance of the victim. Only later did he add fasting, because he came to believe it was advocated in the gospels, and he become known as the leading promoter of this method.

Ironically, in view of the Church of England's horrified reaction to Darrell's activities, there was no obvious theological objection to Protestant ministers performing dispossession by prayer and fasting, as Bishop Parkhurst's use of it shows. But it was not widely accepted that the scripture was sufficient warrant for dispossessions by minor godly clergy and lay people. This seemed likely to strip authority from the hierarchy and governmental structures of the national church, which could not be allowed, and to promote the political aims of the godly wing of the church, which – as we shall see – were widely regarded by the 'ungodly' as revolutionary. So, after his dispossession at Nottingham, and apparently much to his surprise, John Darrell was arrested. He was accused first of heresy and then of fraud, in particular of teaching his supposed patient William Sommers to simulate the symptoms of demonic possession, so that Darrell could become a godly celebrity when he 'exorcized' him. The minister was subjected to a lengthy trial by the ecclesiastical Court of High Commission in London, deprived of his ministry and imprisoned, with his fellow-minister George More, for eighteen months. When he was freed, he went into hiding and he and his friends engaged in a war of words with the church authorities that lasted until 1603 and produced at least fifteen books of up to two hundred pages in length. Darrell's dispossessing and publishing activities even changed the basis of church law on dispossessions, for in 1604 new canons forbade any exorcisms unless licensed by a bishop.

This book is about the struggle in the Church of England over dispossession by prayer and fasting, and especially the pamphlets and books written by Darrell, his godly friends, and their opponents. It is also about the other struggles for authority that were part of the bigger battle: broadly, between the marginal and the central, geographically, socially, in terms of age, authorial status, religious beliefs and political power.

'Puritanism' and the Church of England in the 1570s

The Darrell affair took place in the context of a much wider political debate, which we must explore in order to understand why he was represented as such a threat to good order in the Church and beyond. In the 1570s it had become clear to the governors of the Church of England (the Queen, her archbishops and bishops) that some English Protestants – 'puritans' – were so dissatisfied with the progress of reform in the church that they could be treated as posing a danger to it. To modern readers, this may seem an extremely surprising position for the church to have reached, especially so soon after the 'Elizabethan Settlement'. It has looked this way for some time: in 1819 Joseph Goadby prefaced his description of the difficulties inflicted on puritans by the Church of England with the necessary explanation that 'a spirit of intolerance abounded' and 'strange as it may seem, the clergy persecuted the clergy'. Goadby remarked serenely that in modern times 'if I differ from another, it may also be said another differs from me; and whoever he may be, he has no more right given him of God, to persecute me, than I have to persecute him'.[8] Goadby might have written differently later in his own century, but his basic perception was correct: that from the late seventeenth century onwards it became to most people curiously distasteful, perhaps even un-English, to brawl over religion.

Religious infighting had been one element of the Civil War, and came to symbolize stereotypically its causes: long after quarrels over taxes had been forgotten, the troublesome figure of the 'puritan' remained as the antithesis of the ruling 'cavalier'. The puritans preferred to think of themselves as 'the godly', but the stereotype of them as overly precise and uppity religious fanatics stuck. Few wanted to return to the debates of the 1570s. Dryden's poem *Absalom and Achitophel* made the point succinctly, using Israel as a metaphor for England:

> The sober part of Israel, free from stain,
> Well knew the value of a peaceful reign;
> And looking backward with a wise affright,
> Saw seams of wounds, dishonest to the sight:
> In contemplation of those ugly scars
> They cursed the memory of civil wars.
> The moderate sort of men, thus qualified,
> Inclined the balance to the better side.[9]

But Dryden's poem, despite its advocacy of moderation, also reworked the rhetoric that Elizabeth's government had deployed against the more extreme kinds of Protestant. For Dryden they were a 'host of dreaming saints', each filled with canting 'zeal to God and hatred to his King'.[10] Dryden agreed with contemporary historians of puritanism like Peter Heylyn: the godly, as they called themselves, were of 'rude humor and ungoverned Zeal' and 'Turbulencies and Seditions' were their legacy.[11] They actively fomented trouble against any type of authority, Dryden believed, as many of Queen Elizabeth's bishops had believed before him. Catholics were, more understandably he thought, just trying to preserve their ancient, well-established rights; but the godly wanted dangerous and anarchic innovation, a cranky individual liberty that was not allowable. He, Heylyn and subsequent historians inherited this view directly from the Elizabethan bishops John Whitgift and Richard Bancroft, among others.

The decision of the Queen and the leaders of her church that extreme Protestants were a threat, and the continued representation of them as such into modern times, is particularly striking given the context of Catholic activities in the latter years of Elizabeth's reign. Why attack fellow Protestants as 'greater enimies ... then the papists' when Catholics were a far more stereotypical 'fifth column',[12] backed by the outright threat of foreign invasion? The point was made by the godly courtier Sir Francis Knollys to Lord Burghley in 1584:

it grieves my heart to see the course of popish treason to be neglected and to see the zealous preachers of the gospel, sound in doctrine (who are the most diligent barkers against the popish wolf to save the fold and flock of Christ) to be persecuted and put to silence as though there were no enemies to her Majesty and to the state but they.[13]

Knollys had plenty of evidence to adduce. In 1569 the 'Northern Earls' of Westmorland and Northumberland had led a Catholic rising against Elizabeth. She had then been excommunicated by the Pope in 1570, giving *carte blanche* to anyone else who wanted to depose her on behalf of the Catholic church, but had been hesitating because the Queen was God's anointed monarch. If Elizabeth was assassinated, she might be succeeded by a Catholic, especially by her cousin Mary Queen of Scots, which would put an end to England's Protestantism; and there were a string of plots surrounding Mary. But the Queen and her government's harsh response to godly agitation is, in reality, partly explained by just this Catholic threat. No government wants to fight two battles at once, or feel that it being undermined by extremists from within its own party. The godly had chosen a particularly bad time to open their campaign for further church reform. They simply could not wait and refused to choose politically expedient moments for public and parliamentary action, because they believed that God's work should not be delayed. A time of national crisis such as that of the rebellion and excommunication was not the ideal moment for Thomas Cartwright, Lady Margaret Professor of Divinity at the University of Cambridge, to begin to argue publicly for a reformed system of Church government. But this was what Cartwright did in 1570. It was also clear that he 'said out loud what many of the most active laity and ministers of the Church had been thinking'.[14]

Cartwright and his sympathizers wanted, in modern terms, a flatter Church management structure, with greater equality for ordinary clergy and even laity. This meant abolishing the higher ranks of deans, bishops, archbishops and so on – which begged a question about the continuing status of the Church's supreme governor, the Queen.[15] Such parity would allow a move towards giving all clergy equal rights to form opinions, shape their own religious practice, and open up debate on knotty issues of divinity. Cartwright and his followers believed that this had been the original form of the Christian church, before Catholicism had corrupted it by introducing episcopacy. But this was the opposite of what the Church hierarchy wished to hear: as we shall see, their aim was to ensure stability, by moulding the new Church into conformity and uniformity based on obedience to superiors, and silence upon contentious subjects. Cartwright's speech and publications were thus a serious threat – and also an affront. The Queen was not to be lectured by mere clerics. Elizabeth thought, broadly, that reformation had gone as far as was desirable. She did not wish to persecute Catholics beyond what was necessary to ensure order and loyalty. She did not want to hear either that others wanted more power within her Church – through, for instance, Cartwright's presbyterian system in which each parish church would form a self-governing body – or that they thought existing arrangements popish. Parliament was also becoming overly interested in the regulation of religion, with bills on church law and the Prayer Book brought forward in the early 1570s. Publication was part of this campaign. A group of godly ministers led by Thomas Wilcox and John Field wrote and had printed an *Admonition* to Parliament which laid out their objections to bishops, hierarchy and certain ceremonies, and argued that presbyterianism was the form of Church government endorsed by the Bible. The ministers were jailed for this 'breach of courtesy to well-intentioned churchmen', and Cartwright was dismissed from Cambridge, but their opinions and especially their attitude would not go away.[16] This book will discuss many ministers and lay people who shared that attitude, refusing to remain silent, and insisting on their right to speak and publish their opinions.

The Queen was so determined to suppress godly dissent that when her new Archbishop of Canterbury, Edmund Grindal, attempted to defend some reforming practices, she had him placed under house arrest at Lambeth Palace. Grindal had defended so-called 'prophesyings' – meetings of ministers to preach complementary sermons and discuss doctrine in front of a lay congregation. The godly minister John Ireton, who was later one of Darrell's friends and advisors, called them 'universities of the pore ministers'.[17] But the Queen was suspicious of these meetings because she thought they might be, as Patrick Collinson put it, 'a first step in the partial delegation of the bishop's pastoral functions to permanent moderators of local synods'. Even first, partial moves towards such an outcome were anathema. Grindal, who was more sympathetic to godly arguments than his predecessor Archbishop Parker, had enjoyed good relations with the more assertive reformers in his previous Archdiocese of York – some of these would become key players in the exorcism controversy that is the focus of this book. His loss of authority and his death in 1583 meant that such people were deprived of a sympathetic ear, and the Queen lined up a successor who shared her views, and the views of the conformists within the Church. Grindal was replaced by John Whitgift, who was both conservative and disciplinarian. Although, as Diarmaid MacCulloch points out, Whitgift was unlike later Anglican conservatives in that he was not inspired by the older Church forms of worship, he valued them and intended that others should do so also.[18] With Whitgift at Canterbury, the Church shifted towards the complete suppression of godly nonconformity.

Whitgift and the Attack on the Godly

Whitgift had a list of three articles drawn up, to smoke out nonconforming clerics and make the government's position on Church matters crystal clear. Clergy were required to assent to these articles, subscribing their name to them in agreement. Most obviously difficult for puritan ministers to subscribe to was the second article, which asserted that the Church of England's Book of Common Prayer was consistent with Biblical instructions for worship, containing nothing contrary to them. A minister did not need to be a presbyterian to feel unease about the Prayer Book, although he might be labelled as such if he expressed it. In fact, ministers who thought of themselves as soundly conformist might have significant doubts about such matters as Biblical authority for the wearing of clerical vestments, or kneeling at communion. The ceremonies prescribed, and the dressing up, seemed inherently popish to a good number, who saw no reason to distinguish themselves and their activities as sacred in this way. Anything suggesting a mystical sacredness in communion smacked to them of the Catholic belief that it was more than a re-enactment of Christ's sacrifice. For Catholics, Christ, his body and blood, were really present. For Protestants, the communion service was simply a metaphorical act, where a concentration on objects and gestures was actually destructive of the inner processes and the words of the communicants. Whitgift tried to persuade the godly that such objects and gestures were 'things indifferent' or *adiaphora*, which might be performed quite harmlessly whether one thought them correct or not, but they could not agree. His articles brought the controversy to a head, and between three and four hundred ministers refused to assent to them. They were suspended from their posts.

This provoked uproar in their communities, in Parliament and at court, where the godly included in their number the Earl of Leicester, Sir Francis Walsingham and Sir Francis Knollys. Their protests were accompanied by challenges from lawyers to the Church's right to suspend and dismiss ministers for non-subscription. English justice was still based on several competing bodies of law – common, civil and canon – which conflicted with each other and with the Queen's prerogative to govern as she chose. Under common law – which those lawyers who practised it believed should be the basis of equitable government – the articles were not legally valid as a reason to deprive a man of his living. What about the right to trial by one's peers, and the right not to be deprived of one's freehold except by the judgment of such peers and by the law of the land?[19] Moreover, the Prayer Book prescribed in the articles was not the one named in statute, because when the key acts had been passed that established the Queen's supremacy in the Church and its right to enforce uniformity, the Prayer Book had been substantially different. Whitgift was thus violating common law, they argued, and his plan to enforce subscription through the church courts was also invalid because these were outdated anomalies, not consistent with common law. Ministers should be treated in the way that other subjects were treated: as common men not subject to special (and persecutory) jurisdiction. Every time a clergyman was deprived of his living and driven from his parish, Magna Carta was at stake, argued the common lawyers. There was an 'ideological parallelism' between godliness and the practice of common law in the pursuit of fundamental rights.[20]

This put Whitgift in an exposed position. It was his belief, as it was the Queen's, that it was perfectly lawful to demand whatever she wanted in the Church – it was her prerogative to do so. But the Queen should also be kept aloof from dangerous controversy, and her ministers and archbishops should ensure that conformity was obtained without recourse to her.[21] So Whitgift introduced a further test for those who would not subscribe. A series of interrogatories would probe the beliefs and practices of ministers beyond their mere assent to the prayer book. Did they wear the surplice and use rings in marriage, as required? Those interrogated had to swear '*ex officio mero*', a form of civil law oath, that they were telling the truth and answering each question fully. The *ex officio* oath had to be sworn before the minister had seen the questions that he would be asked, and bound him in effect to incriminate himself by his answers, since he could not remain silent or equivocate without breaking his oath. Neither could he refuse to take the oath without being punished. To some, like Lord Burghley, this seemed like the Catholic Inquisition, and to common lawyers it violated common law even more comprehensively – it was unlawful to require a man to incriminate himself.[22] In introducing the use of the *ex officio* oath, Whitgift thus opened up a new front in the battle with the godly. The oath was attacked in legal, moral and religious terms. The idea that ministers of the gospel might lie, or resort to Catholic techniques of sophistry rather than bearing witness truthfully, filled many with fury. But, more interestingly, what was in question was which set of laws governed England and her church. This was an attempt to extend Magna Carta to a new group of English subjects, not to defend ancient rights being eroded among those who had always enjoyed them. This meant a new equality under the law to be shared by ministers and laity – and although the case was not made and was unmakeable in the legal circumstances of its time, by implication there was the suggestion that everyone else, from the Queen down, should be equal under the law too.

Like many political disputes, this one ended in a fudge. Whitgift agreed to accept a limited type of subscription, in the form of a letter promising to observe the Book of Common Prayer and the orders of the Church, a formula suggested by the godly politician Sir Francis Walsingham. Such pressure prevailed enough to get a large number of ministers reinstated, so long as they subscribed to the basics of ministerial life and promised good behaviour. They could still, however, be followed up through the Church courts and ultimately deprived if found to be consistently nonconforming. And there was lasting damage: as the Church of England had become more repressive and demonstrated its unwillingness to reform further, so more and more ministers had become detached or semi-detached from it. From the suppressed prophesyings, where several ministers from different parishes would preach on the same text, developed a re-invention: 'exercises'. Now only one sermon would be heard in public and the rest of the event would be a private ministerial gathering – but a gathering at which anything might be said.[23] University graduation ceremonies provided another occasion for private meetings of the disaffected godly.[24] Some ministers attended decisively secret meetings, in effect the kind of little local synods on doctrine and church politics that had been feared. When organized by presbyterians, these were known as *classes*, but less radical participants preferred to think of them as 'conferences'. All these meetings operated outside the official Church structures, crossing the boundaries of parishes and dioceses, and this culture of travelling, gathering and debate was hard to attack.

Some organizations were almost impenetrable. The godly group which met at Dedham is particularly well known to historians, since it was formal enough to keep minutes, which have survived. But it was not discovered in its own time.[25] Equally notorious was the network of Northamptonshire ministers whose leaders were tried in the Star Chamber with the still-troublesome Cartwright in 1591. This *classis* too had formal structures of debate and governance, but they were only revealed when one of its members decided to expose its existence.[26] As well as keeping quiet about their activities, the godly argued in public that their meetings were simply away-days, intended to facilitate clerical education, abolish un-Protestant practices and allow ministers to share good practice. Often the meetings do seem to have been nothing more. But exercise shaded into conference shaded into *classis* in what Patrick Collinson has described as 'not … the private enthusiasms of a small faction of clergymen, but rather a religious revolution which was continuing to make impressive inroads on the upper ranks of lay society'.[27] These connections would become key in promoting another form of godly gathering, the dispossession fast and prayer meeting. And what made these dispossessions distinctive was that they were sometimes put into print. The godly did not publish the minutes of their *classes*, or the debate and table talk of their exercises. But they did sometimes offer a detailed report of a dispossession.

After 1588: The Suspension of Godly Agitation

In 1588, amid all this ferment deriving from Whitgift's policies and resistance to them, came four significant events which ultimately ended for several
decades the large-scale godly revolt within the church. The first, the defeat of
the Spanish Armada, ended the immediate threat of Catholic invasion, and
made it look as though, as MacCulloch put it, God approved of the Church of
England in its unreformed state. Then there was the death of the reformist Earl
of Leicester, and that of John Field the godly organizer in London – emphasizing that many of puritanism's traditional supporters were ageing and losing
power.[28] Field's death was especially significant for godly propagandist literature. Like all pressure groups and many persecuted sects, the godly hoarded
information and argument likely to be useful to their cause. Their passion for
documenting their own religious struggles was also a duty, and so they produced carefully-preserved records of appearances in ecclesiastical courts, and
the insult and difficulty heaped upon them by the church authorities. Field collected these as a 'Register' – Knappen calls it 'the puritans' Book of Martyrs'.[29]
He received them by hand and letter from all over England, and he kept them
alongside personal jottings and annotations of key texts. Field even kept religious poems in his collection, perhaps his own. He was not just an organizer
but a kind of literary agent and anthologist, all rolled into one. His loss left a
literary gap in the puritan movement. But it was filled by the fourth event of
significance to the godly in 1588: the appearance of the first in a long series of
pamphlets by a presbyterian calling himself 'Martin Marprelate'.

As his name suggested, the debate was moving into more extreme territory. Martin was not interested in reasoned debate about moderate godly issues
– kneeling at communion, or the sign of the cross at baptism – he was writing
to mar the prelates, attacking the whole idea of ecclesiastical hierarchy itself.
If the bishops were ejected from their palaces, Martin suggested, none of these
issues would be problematic. No-one would be expelled from the ministry.
God's Word could be directly interpreted by ministers, who had the best right
to do so. For Martin, the prelates thus stood between individual Christians
and true religion, primarily in the defence of their own troughs, filled with
tithe monies, fine wines and bejewelled robes. Works of theological argument
had never been hybridized before with the scurrilous witty pamphlets of the
kind produced by Thomas Nashe and other professional satirists. Cartwright
and others hastily distanced themselves from Martin, horrified by his collo-
quial directness and rudeness: the Dry Drayton preacher Richard Greenham
summed up their feeling when he said Martin made 'sin ridiculous, whereas it
ought to be made odious'.[30] Ironically, Martin damaged the godly consensus
on the inadequacy of the church, because most of the movement could not
bear to be identified with him, and he made them all look like extremists. But

what he did demonstrated beyond question the potential of the publishing industry for spreading uncensored opinion. Why argue about the *ex officio* oath in Parliament when you can reach everyone from the Earl of Essex to the man on the Clapham carrier's cart with one little pamphlet? The godly polemicists who came after Martin both benefited and suffered because of his example; John Darrell and his supporters in the exorcism controversy offering the closest parallel, and paradoxically meeting the most Marprelate-like opponent in Samuel Harsnett.

At the time of the Marprelate tracts, Harsnett's future patron Richard Bancroft was chaplain to Sir Christopher Hatton, the Lord Chancellor, but he was also making himself useful to Archbishop Whitgift. Rosemary O'Day neatly sums up the shared vision of the two men by referring to them as a single entity: 'Whitgift/Bancroft'.[31] Whitgift later wrote, in a 'reference' for Bancroft, that 'by his advice, that Course was taken, w[hi]ch did principally stop Martin and his Fellows' mouths, viz: to have them answered after their own vein in writing'.[32] Bancroft understood the decisive power of literature in such a contest between ideas, searching out Field's collections as well as Martin's pamphlets. Diarmaid MacCulloch describes him as having a 'passion for sniffing out the concealed', and he set about examining printers, publishers and ministers who might be sympathetic to Marprelate's cause.[33] Looking for secret presses and satirists was a useful excuse for a general assault on godly freedom of thought and association. By collecting evidence in raids on suspects, spying, intercepting letters and rigorously questioning the accused, Bancroft uncovered some of the secretive presbyterian organization. He brought some of its participants before the Court of High Commission that would one day try Darrell. Meanwhile, in 1588 a Royal Proclamation had been issued against seditious, schismatical books and libels, putting forward what the government thought to be erroneous doctrines and libels against individuals. A flow of people began to appear before the High Commission and Court of Star Chamber on charges related to Marprelate books and more general dissent. Large fines and imprisonment were the commonest punishments, but printers and authors accused of producing seditious works were found guilty of felony and sentenced to death. The most notorious was perhaps John Udall, who was convicted of felony for writing a book on Church discipline and died in prison appealing against his death sentence.

Most severely punished was John Penry, said to have written a number of the Marprelate books as well as others judged to be seditious. He was hanged in Southwark on 29 May 1592. But Penry was also being disposed of because he was a separatist, like Henry Barrow and John Greenwood, executed in the same year.[34] These men wanted to form a separate church, and they were prosecuted and executed under legislation designed to catch Catholic missionaries, which caused shock and anger among those who had framed it and voted it into law. What was especially disturbing was that moderate puritans could easily be accused of the same militant tendency, even when they actually abhorred such an idea. If the government was using legislation designed to suppress illegal publications and Catholics to harass and even execute Protestants whose views challenged the state church, the godly were in serious trouble. 'Puritans were terrified' says MacCulloch simply.[35] The more moderate godly were appalled at the government's action, but this draconian policy – and the inquisitions, torture and harassment that accompanied Bancroft's search for Martin – persuaded many to conform outwardly. The godly became inward-looking, turning away from presbyterianism, argues MacCulloch.[36] Certainly, the Darrell faction pay almost no attention to Church government in their books. Naive, principled or crazy as they were, only one of Darrell's writers paid the ultimate price for his beliefs. But all knew that the stakes were high, because godly people were now openly being treated as schismatics and heretics by a government and a Church that only twenty years previously they had hoped might support their desire for further Protestant reform. As the godly sagged into submission, Marprelate stopped writing, and most elements of the controversies he had fuelled cooled as the Whitgiftian party consolidated their position.[37]

A New Marprelate?

So did John Darrell and his friends, following the example of godly controversialists into print with their accounts of dispossessions, walk innocently into the vacancy left by Martin Marprelate? A recurrent question for readers is whether they were fully aware of the hostility and injustice that they would encounter if they expressed openly their views about dispossessing demoniacs. Contemporary estimates of Darrell's age suggest that he was born in about 1562, and it can hardly have escaped his notice that his world was saturated with religious controversy. Thirty years later, just before Darrell came decisively to public attention, the former Catholic John Donne was still lamenting 'Seek true religion. O where?'.[38] Since Elizabeth's accession to the throne about four years before Darrell's birth, every religious rite and associated Church practice, from the eucharist to bell-ringing, had come into question: was it acceptable to the new reformed Church? Was it sufficiently Protestant, or still tainted by whiffs of popery and superstition? Darrell went to Cambridge University in the 1570s, which was awash with discussion of further reform of the Church. It was whilst he was at Cambridge that the Queen's ability to destroy the authority of even her Archbishop of Canterbury, Grindal, became obvious. Darrell then spent a year in the mid-1580s in London studying common law at the height of the battle over subscription. Yet in his books he displays no interest whatever in Church polity. Did he not connect his dispossessions with the ongoing tension over these matters? Or was he brave or naive enough not to reflect on the consequences of entering the fray?

It seems that Darrell and his fellow godly believed that it would be possible to offer a sincere account of his activities without being drawn into the wider battle and regarded as schismatics. Whilst Whitgift, Bancroft and Harsnett saw the godly as dangerous rebels, following the trajectory of their notions of freedom of conscience into anarchy, they saw themselves as obedient and pious subjects, asking only for modest reforms. They thought that people would believe that Darrell was well-intentioned if he said so, and would treat his arguments fairly. They were, of course, wrong, and this book explores the literary and other consequences of their misplaced optimism. By the end of his trial Darrell, at least, was very well aware of the cultural context of his dispossessions in the government's battle with godliness and its different kinds of insurgent threat. But he still protested that there was 'no cause why these puritanes (as they call them) should be hated, despised, abhorred, and so shamefully intreated, as they were rather dogges, then men'. Astonishingly, he had even heard the godly called 'Sathanists' – perhaps because of their insistence on the devil's active presence in the world and his ability to invade even the human body. Radicalized rather than quieted by his representation as an unscrupulous fundamentalist, Darrell himself now believed that the devil had worked through the ecclesiastical authorities at Lambeth who had arrested and imprisoned him and More, and had had them deposed from the ministry. Harsnett, he said, was not really interested in the notion that Darrell and his patients had counterfeited possessions, which was the argument that he put forward in public. What he really wanted to question and destroy were godly works, and for this reason he was going straight to hell. He was 'one of those that will neither enter into the kingdome of heaven, nor suffer those that would'.[39]

Darrell, then, did not see himself as a new Marprelate, consciously trying to destabilize the Church of England in order to promote a particular political viewpoint. He argued that he was simply and earnestly doing God's work, that he had not sought publicity for his activities (a claim that this book endorses), and that he did not see why they were so problematic (which this book tries to explain). Like Malvolio, Shakespeare's puritan to whom we will return in Chapter 6, Darrell had had 'greatness' thrust upon him. He was represented by others as a deliberately seditious schismatic, writing and publishing illegal texts together with a disreputable band of other disaffected ministers and lay people. For all his denials, it was a view of him that has proved very persuasive until fairly recent times.

History, Literature and John Darrell

So who is right about John Darrell? What does the controversy over his activities and the texts produced by his group tell us about godly culture, about the methods and assumptions of his group of authors and their opponents, and the ways in which they and their works were perceived? It is part of the argument of this book that, in order to answer these bigger questions, more localized enquiries need to be made. Previous accounts of the Darrell exorcisms have established some of the facts of the cases, but have left largely unexplored the specific cultural context of individual dispossessions and the publications that came out of them. Literary scholars have ignored them almost entirely, and historians have not yet explored some of the archival deposits, with some in the past making large claims based on very limited evidence. The pamphlets about the case have more recently formed the basis for interesting reconstructions of Darrell's story, most successfully among many others by Corinne Holt Rickert, D. P. Walker and Thomas Freeman. But it has not seemed possible to me to offer a full reading of these works without intensive archival work to establish their genesis in the cultural climate of the English Midlands. Some of the sources I found most useful – St Peter's Parish Register, the Manorial Court Rolls of Mansfield, the Register of St Helen's in Ashby de la Zouch, for instance, where Darrell's marriage, the births of his six children, and his administration of an estate decisively establish a chronology for a part of his life contested in print for over four hundred years – had hitherto remained untapped, as had the wonderfully rich Nottingham Borough Records and until recently the mass of relevant deposits relating to Burton-upon-Trent, the location of another key dispossession.[40]

It is now possible to offer for the first time an analysis of all the surviving texts, taking into account the fact that they are very fragmentary, and emphasizing the importance of their local and regional origin in specific cultural circumstances. This book continues the 'school' of history initiated by Alan Everitt and his colleagues, and characterized by Patrick Collinson and John Craig as being 'the writing of national history as the history of the localities of which the nation consisted'.[41] This analysis is combined with the tools of literary criticism, and together these approaches help to explain why the impact on the national scene of the dispossessions of Darrell and his group, and the pamphlets written about them, was so varied and remains so contentious. Reading the pamphlets alone cannot solve the central mysteries of the Darrell case. Did he teach William Sommers to counterfeit? Did he try to use pamphlets about dispossession to gain a foothold in important Midland towns so that he could spread his godly message? What happened to him when he was released from prison? The works are so long and complex, scattering information about like confetti, that any reading looking for a ready and coherent narrative is doomed to repeat past mistakes. Only by a really close reading, examining each narrative or polemic in the context of other surviving texts and willing to accept unclarity, can Darrell's story be most fully told. This book therefore offers the most comprehensive biography of Darrell to date, establishing beyond reasonable doubt his innocence of the central crime with which he was charged, and tracing for the first time his family and the social and cultural context of his books as a vital background to understanding the writings of his godly group.

Another concern of this book is the texts that did *not* get written, did not survive or did not make it into print. We do not know anything concrete about Darrell's religious upbringing or his influences at university or in his early life as a minister. We do not have records of his birth or death and we know absolutely nothing of his life from 1599–1607, 1607–17 and after 1617. The manuscript account of Darrell's first dispossession is lost, as is a manuscript (or possibly a published pamphlet) on his exorcisms in Lancashire. His relationship with important godly figures like Richard Bernard, John Robinson, Alexander Reddish, Isabel, Lady Bowes, Henry Hastings, Earl of Huntingdon, Percival, Lord Willoughby of Wollaton and the second Earl of Essex is almost impenetrably obscure. The records of Darrell and his colleague George More's High Commission trial are lost, except for one document recently purchased by Lambeth Palace Library, and discussed here for the first time. Many of the important events of the case are obscured by controversy, but some are simply not discussed at all. It is important silences and absences, just as much as what does survive, that should shape our understanding of the Darrell affair. Why were some exorcisms more important than others? Why were some texts considered inflammatory, whilst others were not? How can we best explore the life and works of an early modern man who began his life in obscurity, provoked and then suffered a brief rise into textual exposure, and then – partly voluntarily – vanished back into silence? As Alexandra Walsham has suggested, written and published text was not the favoured medium of the godly – that was speech, and so it has not survived.[42] It leaves us with some thorny issues of reading what the godly did think it worthwhile to put in print, which can be usefully approached through literary criticism.

However, we can extrapolate from the works of Darrell and his fellow authors some insistent concerns and this book focuses in particular on extending Tom Webster's insights, in his book *Godly Clergy in Early Stuart England*, about the godly's emphasis on sociability and gatherings. It has been argued by literary theorists, following Stephen Greenblatt, that godly (as well as Catholic) exorcisms had many interesting homologies and direct connections with the cultural work going on in the Elizabethan theatre. Whilst this is true to some extent, it depends on how one looks at such dispossessions. The godly would not have seen them in this light, since the insight was one offered by their enemies. This book argues that they would have seen them as, firstly, occasions for speaking and for writing texts, rather than acting, and secondly as sociable matters – indeed, more specifically, through the imagery of family. This emphasis on gathering to speak and write can, I think, be seen in the form and content of the pamphlets written about the godly dispossessions involving John Darrell, as can an insistent anxiety about both defining their own 'family' structure and their place in the wider family of the English church.

1 A LITERARY GEOGRAPHY OF EXORCISM: 'FARRE FROM THE EYE OF JUSTICE'

Beginnings: Mansfield

When John Darrell was released from prison in London in 1599, he vanished, keeping his whereabouts secret for a period of eight years until he reappeared in the records of an ecclesiastical court, and was shown to be living at Teversal in Nottinghamshire. But although his disappearance was initially by design, for Darrell it was merely a return to the condition in which he was born and lived in his home town of Mansfield in the years *c*. 1562–75. The lives lived in Mansfield in the late sixteenth century were only written as they touched such bodies as the church, the civil administration or the courts. And many of these records are now lost. Darrell's story is one of an emergence into view, and then into text, because what he had been quietly doing and the beliefs that he had been quietly holding for over a decade had suddenly been raised to prominence by geographical, literary and political accidents. Darrell was noticed, and became an author, because other people perceived him – rather suddenly – as a threat and some began to write urgently about his activities, attacking or defending him. So we still have only these two views of his life – offensive and defensive, both from polemical angles. His history is thus the history of texts, of attitudes to writing and its purposes. And in Mansfield in the 1560s and 1570s there was literally nothing about John Darrell that anyone thought worthy of committing to paper for posterity.

Darrell was probably born in Mansfield in the early 1560s, the son of Henry Dorrell and his wife, who is not named in the records.[1] But there is no record of his baptism in the church of St Peter, and the silence about his early life is deafening. It is typical of its time and place, however. Mansfield was a small market town, far from the centres of power, and not the residence of any significant courtier or divine, governmental or educational institution. Darrell probably attended the Free Grammar School, which was founded in 1561 in a cottage near the church. His father leased property from the governors and seems to have been one of their number. Henry had in farm a watermill and windmill at Mansfield, the rent from which, with other mills, contributed thirty pounds a year to pay the schoolmaster and usher.[2] In the late 1570s he and his fellow millers were accused of impeding the water rights of William Cotton, lessee of the Queen's Mills at Mansfield, so that his name and business dealings were recorded in some detail. In the lawsuit is evidence of a violent, if confused, antipathy between the ways of a declining world of obligation and automatic deference and a new world of competition and upward mobility. Henry and his colleagues had been challenging the right of the Queen's Mills to mill all the corn of the manor of Mansfield, as had been the practice formerly, and they had made some powerful conservative enemies. Landowners could still sometimes behave like warlords and Sir John Byron (who would one day sit in judgment on Henry Dorrell's son John) had supported Cotton by sending some of his men to attack Henry's Memotte Mill. They had severed troughing and demolished a weir, according to several witnesses.[3] Like his son, Henry was in trouble for asserting new freedoms, which seemed to others an attack on order itself, justifying extreme repression. And like his son, his actions therefore created a textual trace.

The Darrells seem to have been ambitious, and John went to Queens' College, Cambridge, in autumn 1575. His life became interesting to record-keepers at this centre of power and learning. The College was also the choice of a number of fellow godly whose lives would intersect with his – the Earls of Huntingdon and their relatives the Hastings family, the Bowes family and the minister Richard Rothwell, whom Darrell must have known at Queens'. The Hastings or Bowes family might have helped to him to get a place: we do not know. But he went as a poor scholar, a sizar, which meant that his father did not have enough money to pay his fees, lodging and other costs and that he had no wealthy patron to do so. Sizars were boys supported by scholarship money from the College and by their own work – waiting on tables in the College, reading the Bible aloud during meals and running errands for fellows and the president. Darrell was one of some twenty sizars, in a community of about one hundred and twenty fellows and scholars at the College. He would have worked alongside College servants and his reputed egalitarianism may have begun then. He certainly would not have lived the high life like fellow-Queensman Anthony Byron, who in 1576 got into trouble for marrying illegally, and becoming simultaneously engaged to another girl.[4] Sizars were expected to behave impeccably, and since they were dependent on the College they tended to do so. The terms of Darrell's scholarship also meant that he had to take his Bachelor of Arts degree four years after his entry, which was then the earliest possible moment: this meant studying hard.

Undergraduates studied the *trivium*; grammar, rhetoric and logic, and the last two years of their studies also introduced them to moral, natural and metaphysical philosophy. It was a broad preparation for Darrell's life as a preacher and writer. Students' education was also supposed to continue in pious activities – sermons, with note-taking and discussions, and religious groups debating passages of scripture, such as that led by Laurence Chaderton at Emmanuel College. However, Darrell's religious radicalism does not seem to have had its origin at Cambridge. The presidents during his time at Queens' were William Chaderton and Humphrey Tyndall, both orthodox men. Chaderton in particular regarded the presbyterian controversies of the time as tantamount to rebellion, although he was sympathetic to moderate godliness. Of Cartwright's lectures on church government in 1570 he wrote:

> such errors and schismes openlie taught and preached, boldlie and without warrant, are latelie growne amongst us, that the good estate, quietnes, and governance of Cambridge, and not of Cambridge alone, but of the whole church and realme, are for great hazard unles severlie by authorities they be punished.

He did not change his view, and when he left Queens' in 1579, he became successively Bishop of Chester and Lincoln.[5]

Queens' enjoyed the attentions of the Earl of Leicester – Chaderton's and Tyndall's own patron but also the leading reformist at court – but there were only two fellows whose godliness was notable. Leicester had pushed his chaplain, Robert Some, into a fellowship and Some continued to attack Church governance throughout Darrell's period there. Another fellow, Edmund Rockrey, was expelled for similar views, but by the time of Darrell's arrival had returned, refusing to wear vestments, academic dress or to receive communion. Darrell must have been familiar with the controversies eddying around godly men at the University. But if he felt sympathy with them there is no evidence that he acted upon it. He completed his studies quietly, with a single interruption when plague broke out at the College in 1578, and took his degree (by participating in public disputations) in 1579. There is a discrepancy, however, in the dating of his return to the Midlands. He says in a book written in 1599–1600 (published 1600) that he left the University 'about eightene years past': thus, in 1581 or 1582. Did he take a Masters degree which is unrecorded and – even more unlikely – unmentioned during the controversy over exorcism? Did he begin study, continue as long as his funding lasted (three years after the BA) and then leave without taking the degree? The three years of MA study focused on arithmetic, geometry, music and astronomy. Perhaps Darrell found himself in academic, financial or other difficulty. If he had been in trouble for religious or behavioural reasons it would certainly have appeared in the later controversy, for Darrell said that Samuel Harsnett had made enquiries about him at Cambridge, with the intention of writing up and publishing anything discreditable. But he, and the records, again tell us nothing. Darrell was not interested in his own biography, except where it related to what he saw as the works of God.[6]

He certainly returned home to the Midlands, however, in the early 1580s and says that he lived at Mansfield and then Bulwell near Nottingham in the period to about 1584–5. On 24 January 1583/4, he married Joan (Johane) Gadsbery in St Peter's Church, Mansfield. Little more is known of his wife's family – the register-keeper even stopped recording the surnames of brides at one point, neatly demonstrating once again the selectivity of texts. Sometime after his marriage – in 1599–1600 he tells the reader that it was 'about fifteene yeares past' – Darrell went to London to study common law. But his period at the Inns of Court was unsuccessful. As he explains:

> the Lorde (who had longe before purposed to imploye me otherwise, and in the studye of an other [l]aw) did draw me another waye, by layinge his hande upon me, in causinge a strange and extraordinary sluggishnes to fall upon me.

He found that he wanted to work on men's souls, not their worldly goods and rights, and gave up study after a year. In 1599 Harsnett took a swipe at Darrell's allies during his trial, the common lawyers, by claiming that 'having begunne the study of law, he perceyved therein such great corruption, as he gave him selfe to the study of Divinity, that so hee might serve God, and keepe a good conscience'. Darrell denied that he thought lawyers corrupt: 'the common lawes I hold and ever did since I studied them, to be grounded upon the lawe of God and reason'. It is possible, however, that his beliefs were radicalized by the preachers at the Inns of Court. Richard Bancroft regarded them as 'Seducers' of law students, by whose means 'the flower of the Gentilitie of England ... [is] trayned up in a disobedient mislikinge of the present estate of the Churche'.[7] And shortly after Darrell's return from London he participated in the dispossession of Katherine Wright, which we shall discuss in this chapter. This suggests that his commitment to godliness was now a strong one. He was also ready to begin writing about it, although not in published form.

Meanwhile, Darrell's family began to grow. In 1584/5, on 8 February, John and Joan's first recorded child, Margery, was christened in Mansfield, on 30 July 1586 her sister Elizabeth, and on 18 January 1587/8 another daughter, Ellen. Sadly, either Ellen or Elizabeth died and was buried in summer 1587. The register is damaged and unclear: the month is not certain and the child's name may be Ellin or Ellis, which is elsewhere (although inconsistently) used as an abbreviation for Elizabeth. On 2 March 1588/9, Armada year, the Darrells' son, Thomas, was christened. This is the last entry in the Mansfield register relating to John Darrell. Another child must have been born elsewhere, probably at Bulwell where the register is now lost, for by 1599 Darrell describes himself as having five children (only two children are recorded as having later been born to the Darrells, one of whom died as an infant, as we shall see). Darrell's father and stepmother did not live long to enjoy their grandchildren, however. On 3 June 1589 Ellis (presumably Elizabeth), the wife of Henry Darrell, was buried, and Henry Darrell himself was buried on 15 August of the same year. John inherited his father's property, as the eldest or only son – no will or other paperwork has yet been found to offer clarification – and he continued his father's businesses. On 27 April 1591 a woman who was probably his mother-in-law, Joyce Walby alias Gadbury, died and he was granted administration of her estate by Mansfield manorial court.[8] He was also ordained soon after Henry Dorrell's death. There is no official record of this important event either, although Darrell would have had to produce a copy of his certificate and preacher's licence(s) if asked. It is infuriating to know so little about the crucial religious experiences that made him so controversial in later life, but entirely typical. Although spiritual autobiography was to become a godly genre, it is not yet in evidence in Darrell's world.

These previously unexplored records show that Darrell stayed in Mansfield until at least April 1591. There is also another text showing that his godliness was now evident, and was well received. William Horner Groves represents him in his 1894 *History of Mansfield* as 'minister of the Puritanical sect in the town', but his account makes unjustified assumptions and it is unlikely that Darrell held any such separatist-sounding position. He was, however, an occasional lecturer at the church, as its accounts show. He preached at St Peter's in 1589, and a gift of ten pence worth of wine and sugar to him is recorded among 'disbursments for the P'cher'. There was a preacher in residence, who lodged in a room belonging to the schoolmaster and received a wage of twenty shillings a year. But there were payments to a number of preachers other than Darrell in 1589, the only year for which accounts survive. In the 1580s, money was plentiful and the parish was very committed to a preaching ministry. This, with the establishment of an exercise at Mansfield, suggests that godliness was active there – although very sensibly an hourglass was also purchased out of the moneys allocated for preaching, to make sure sermons kept to time.[9] There are other indications of godly sympathies in the town: in 1574 two Mansfield men had been presented to the Archdeaconry Court for nonconformity, one of whom had remarked that 'M[aster] Archdeacon knoweth no more what a puritane is then his ould horse' and 'preached suche doctrine, that by goddes worde, yf [I] mette with him, [I] aught not to bidde him good morrowe'.[10] Later Mansfield would become a haven for the godly, like Darrell's fellow-exorcist Richard Rothwell, and Quakers. It is not hard to see why Darrell felt at home there, but he presumably also wanted further engagement with the spiritual life beyond his home town.

'In an Obscure Place': Eckington and Whittington

Darrell must have established a reputation in Mansfield as a godly man whilst still in his early twenties. This may be why, in about 1586, he was called upon to help dispossess a young woman of seventeen or eighteen years of age, Katherine Wright of Eckington in Derbyshire. Wright lived in the hamlet of Ridgeway Lane with her mother Cecily and stepfather, a 'poor' cutler named John Mekin. He had beaten her, she said later, and she had become ill as a result. Mekin was a controversial figure in Eckington, appearing in the manorial court records very regularly. In the period leading up to Wright's 'possession', he was fined for letting his animals stray (1579) and for his reluctance to use the lord of the manor's mills (1583, 1584), he settled a dispute with Philip Ibbotson (1581), was complained against for trespass and debt (1581, 1585), and complained himself against others (1582). Interestingly two of those accusing him of trespass, and being accused by him, were Thomas and Robert Wright, and although it has proved impossible to establish their exact relationships, it sounds as if there was dispute over the lands of Cecily Mekin, formerly Cecily Wright. Katherine's statements suggest that Mekin treated his wife badly as well as his stepdaughter. In 1587 the battle between the Wrights and the Mekins came to a head with two accusations of trespass and of debt made against the Mekins. The Great Court decided on 29 April 1588 that lands held by Cecily Mekin for her lifetime had been granted without the permission of the lord of the manor to Laurence Stansall in 1585, and as a result the lands were seized by the bailiff.[11] This ended the dispute in the court, but neither party can have been pleased with the outcome.

The Mekins' unofficial land transaction in 1585, which earned them an unspecified but sizeable sum, was against the background of the 1585 debt suit mentioned above. It was brought against John Mekin by William Hill; the Hills were tenants of land that Cecily Mekin leased. Mekin denied that he owed anything, much less the three shillings and four pence claimed. But on 31 January 1586 the Great Court found for Hill. They decided that Mekin owed him three shillings and three pence, with damages of one penny, costs of five pence and they imposed a further fine of two pence. It was just after this that Katherine Wright began to complain of illness, and beatings. She could not sleep, felt light-headed and began to swell, which she believed was caused, she later told Harsnett and his fellow-examiner William Pigott, by 'some stopping of humours, not unknowne to divers women'. As she was going to the well one morning, she said she saw a vision of a child without feet, and when she told her stepfather about this, he began to behave more kindly towards her. The visions stopped, but to keep Mekin's favour Wright continued to fake fits. She would scream and fall down, and (according to the pro-Darrell pamphlet *The Triall of Maist. Dorrell*) so often seemed about to fall into fire, water or the well that she was chained to a post. She also tried to cut her own throat. Drink spouted up to the ceiling when it was offered to her – said the author of *The Triall*, excitedly adducing evidence to prove that, whatever Wright later said, she could not have faked her symptoms. The High Commission, who in 1598 tried Darrell for teaching Wright as well as Sommers to counterfeit, was never going to accept that her possession was real, but her account of the abuse by Mekin bought her sympathy when they questioned her: her examiner Samuel Harsnett portrays Wright as living a pitiable life of toil and subjection in the back end of beyond.[12]

According to her own account, Wright had found a way of escape: her condition became known to her neighbour Edward Beresford of Cutthorpe-in-Brampton, and 'mooved in compassion', he took her into his home. Her father's house, Harsnett reports, 'was no fitte place to give entertainement to any that should come to helpe her'. Beresford seems to have considered a range of remedies, as it was usual to try other treatments before a possession was formally identified. He strongly believed in Wright's affliction. It may have been because of his involvement (and that of his brother John) that Gilbert Talbot, the seventh Earl of Shrewsbury, who knew the Beresfords well through shared interests in Chesterfield, later attended the proceedings of the High Commission against Darrell. During the trial, we know that Beresford attempted to create a new text about the case. He tried to write an account of Wright's symptoms and his proceedings, but Harsnett took away his paper: the last thing that he wanted was another godly memo, and he wanted his own account to prevail, which it did.[13] All we know of Wright's time at Beresford's house, therefore, is that she stayed for a month before she was sent to Mansfield to see John Darrell. During this time she was visited by a conjuror (presumably a healer or 'cunning man') who, the shocked author of a pro-Darrell pamphlet remarks, raised a devil and was immediately arrested by the command of John, Lord Darcy. Wright also journeyed to the home of the proactive godly gentle-woman Isabel Foljambe so that 'sundrye neighbour ministers' could visit her. It may be from this initial gathering of the godly that Darrell and his fellow-exorcist Thomas Beckingham first learned of her affliction.[14]

Darrell was not involved in any dispossessions before that of Katherine Wright: he tells us later that he saw ten demoniacs in his life, which is actually one less than the number of cases that he wrote about in his works. But he was described by Beresford as 'a man of hope, for the releeving of those which were distressed in that sort'. Beresford described Beckingham, however, as 'a man of note'. He had been the parson at Bilsthorpe, Nottinghamshire, since 1573 and must have established a reputation for dispossessions there. Darrell described him as 'an old man in the ministrie'.[15] However, Beckingham was not sure from Wright's symptoms that she was actually possessed, and Darrell was given responsibility for her treatment. Wright arrived in Mansfield to meet him on a Thursday sometime near Easter 1586, and by noon on Saturday the dispossession had been effected, in a meeting beginning at four o'clock in the morning. There was no fast, but Darrell told the High Commission that he had used some prayers 'conceived by himself', and some from Johann Habermas's prayer-book *The Enimie of Securitie*, which had been translated by the godly minister Thomas Rogers. The mix of extemporary and collected prayers – 'raw and undigested', said the Anglican Peter Heylyn, and nothing from the despised Book of Common Prayer itself – was typical of moderate godly choice. Darrell's fellow-exorcist George More was later to attribute some of the power of dispossession to using extemporary and not 'stinted' official prayers. So with Rogers's translation as a guide, Katherine Wright's dispossession was conducted in an experimental spirit. It was small-scale, for there were only a maximum of nine people present at any one time, and the number fell as low as four. The house in which the dispossession was carried out belonged to Edward Loades, the son-in-law or stepson of Beckingham, and probably also involved Henry Crosse and his wife Isabel, young friends of the Darrells.[16] It was a tentative, marginal event, kept very much within a small circle of family, friends and minister, that seems to have caused no ripples in the surrounding society.

Although he was still mired in obscurity, Darrell had already begun to challenge established authority, for he fell out with the beneficed and experienced Beckingham. They had differed over diagnosing Wright's sickness, and then things got worse. Beckingham, who had died by the time of the High Commission hearing itself, left an awkward accusation behind him, on which Harsnett pounced. This was that Darrell had lain on Katherine Wright's belly in a compromising manner: Beckingham had been so appalled that he had hauled Darrell off her by the heels, and thrown him out of the room. Darrell did not handle this accusation well, as Harsnett lip-smackingly relates. To begin with, he betrayed nervous anticipation, remarking 'ah ... I looked for this'. Then he said that he had read in the Bible of Elias and Paul, who recovered the dead by lying upon them, and 'being a yong student in divinitie, not past foure or 25 yeares of age, I did in a blinde Zeale (as I thinke) lie uppon the saide Katherine Wright'. When his answers were read back to him for assent, he wriggled, saying that he had lain on her side. Finally, three days later he asked to review the evidence again, and said that after talking with his wife (who had, he was careful to stress, been present during the incident with other people) he now believed that his reason for laying on Wright had been to restrain her. Loades had also lain on her and partly on Darrell himself, to add extra weight. Harsnett sneered that Darrell had 'made bolde with his oath' about this embarrassing matter. But the author of a later work defending Darrell offered another explanation. Regardless of what Darrell had thought he was doing, said the author of one of the sections of *The Triall of Maist. Dorrell*, the fact was that

Beckingham had subsequently gone mad. This pugnacious writer's suggestion was that the actions and words of 'this shameles lyer' – strong words about Darrell's fellow minister – were untrustworthy.[17]

Darrell could not keep away from controversy, however, and immediately set about antagonizing state as well as religious authority, in the form of the magistrate Godfrey Foljambe, of Walton near Chesterfield. Godfrey was the husband of Isabel Foljambe, who had been interested in Wright and was the patron of many godly preachers. Darrell should have been assured of a warm welcome from the Foljambes when Wright accused 'one Margaret Roper' of bewitching her, and Darrell tried to get Godfrey Foljambe to use his powers to commit her for trial. There was nothing unusual in his request, but, according to Harsnett, something went deliciously wrong for Darrell at the examination. Foljambe, 'disliking his course, threatned to send him to the Gaole'. This was a surprising outcome. Magistrates would sometimes refuse to commit suspected witches, in the same way that they would refuse to commit anyone else against whom there appeared to be no credible evidence. But it was not usual to threaten the complainant with prison.[18] In trying to smear Darrell, however, Harsnett has inevitably chosen the most damaging report of the examination that was available to him. There are in fact three different recorded stories from people present during the events of 1586. Darrell did not recall such a threat being made, saying that the magistrate was willing to commit Roper. He did not, however, offer an explanation of why Foljambe did not do so. John Mekin remembered that Foljambe, 'reproving the said Darrell for accusing the said woman, told him, that if he so demeaned himselfe any more, hee would send him to the Gaole'. Thomas Wright said simply that the magistrate 'examining the matter, found no cause in any sort to touch Margaret Roper, and forthwith discharged her'.[19] Foljambe himself died in 1595, three years before the proceedings against Darrell, and has left us no account of his decision.

Without a clear explanation, Harsnett's story of the rash young witchmonger reproved by the righteous justice prevailed in print, usually filtered through John Strype's slightly more charitable reworking of Harsnett in his *Life of Whitgift*. Anglicanism, triumphant, cheerfully buried its early opponent. Pocklington's *Altare Christianum* of 1637 portrayed Darrell ('with his miraculous power of possessing, dispossessing and repossessing and trouncing of devils up and down') as an almost demonic enemy of the church.[20] Brown's *Lives of Nottingham Worthies* (1882) turned Foljambe into a hero, 'cute enough to detect the roguery' of Darrell, and added inaccurately that Darrell 'represented [Foljambe's] demise as a judgement'. Darrell's entry in the old *Dictionary of National Biography* portrayed him as 'imposing on the credulity of the people'. Darrell's memory has gathered a thick dusting of abuse for the past four hundred years. John Nichols, county historian of Leicestershire, called him 'a fanatick ... turned priest because by his own confession he was fit for nothing else', adding (of his withdrawal from law school):

> it is hard to guess by what rule of Scripture, or sound reason, he could conclude that an extraordinary sluggishness was an indication that Providence designed him for a Divine.

He is echoed by his counterpart, Thomas Bailey, of Nottinghamshire:

> [Darrell] was designed by his friends for the profession of the law, but being of an indolent, yet fanatical, disposition, he pretended to a call, by the Holy Spirit, to take upon himself the office of a preacher of the gospel.

Historians have been equally unimpressed. R. A. Marchant, who did a great deal to uncover records of Darrell, nevertheless wrote that 'his abilities were mediocre. He had only one talent ... and only one message.' Barbara Rosen found him 'singularly unlovable'. Even his defenders, burdened with Enlightenment embarrassment, felt they had to account for his 'very peculiar sentiments' by divining that he was 'a weak, but zealous and honest man', as Brook says in his 1813 *Lives of the Puritans*, quoting (of all people) Strype. D. P. Walker was perhaps the mildest when he called the Foljambe incident 'a lesson from which [Darrell] failed to profit'.[21] But for Darrell the incident may have presented itself as a trial, or a correction, or both. He continued to work with Wright, but he did not dispossess again for ten years. Why? The lack of comment about Darrell's encounter with Foljambe is one of the key silences of the affair.

The episode is the more interesting because it does not seem that Foljambe's religion was remarkably different from Darrell's. As a magistrate, he enforced the laws against recusants rigorously, to the point of keeping his own grandmother under house arrest. This might have been the action of a merely moderate Protestant, but not only did he support his wife in her godly schemes, he also left the town of Chesterfield forty pounds *per annum* in his will to appoint a preacher. Being godly was not incompatible with circumspection on the subject of witchcraft, however.[22] Possibly Foljambe was disturbed by the growing interest in his locality in Darrell's activities. As we have seen, Wright's first dispossession was a private and largely unremarked affair, but when she became repossessed after Foljambe's dismissal of Darrell, the crowd at her dispossession was so large that one witness estimated there had been four or five hundred people present. Edward Beresford did not confirm this figure, but said there was 'a great number'. The whole matter had become more sensational: by her second dispossession Wright was claiming to be possessed with not one but eight devils. Roper was taken to her and an attempt was made to get Wright to scratch her – a countermagical 'cure' for bewitchment – although again

there is controversy over what happened. Mekin, who by 1598 was adopting a tone of disbelief about the whole matter, recalled simply that 'M[aster]
Darrell continued making of a wonder and a dinne' for three days before he
was convinced that Wright was once again dispossessed.[23] Magistrates generally believe that it is their duty to suppress 'dinne', and given their record in
the courts Foljambe may have regarded the dysfunctional Mekin-Wright clan
as troublemakers and Roper as an innocent victim. Perhaps he did not believe
in witchcraft as it was conventionally imagined. But possibly he was merely
alarmed by the prospect of a well-publicized witch-hunt in his jurisdiction.

It has also surprised historians that Darrell did not follow up his success
with Wright by publication, although this may be explained by his spats with
Beckingham and Foljambe. He presented a manuscript account of Wright's
dispossession to Isabel Foljambe, but there the matter ended: the account
was later lost. But Darrell may not have regarded publication as the holy grail
that academics tend to perceive it to be. Was Darrell interested in publicity?
It appears not. Why did he stop dispossessing after 1586? We do not know
– he regarded the episode as something of a youthful 'follie'. Perhaps there was
simply no demand. When the opposing factions later discussed Wright, it was
asked why anyone living 'in an obscure place' like Eckington would wish to
fake possession.[24] Both sides assumed that possessions – real *and* counterfeit
– tended to occur where they might be politically significant. This was not
always the case, of course, as Wright's possession seemed to prove. But generally it was assumed that when someone became possessed, something was
being demonstrated to the world. The godly would say that the sinful Babylon
of Nottingham or London or Chester was being ordered to reform by God
when he chose to allow a possession to take place there. When Darrell went to
Nottingham in 1597 he conceived of himself in explicitly geo-political terms as
God's 'Imbassador' or 'legate' to this ungodly town. On the other hand, godly
people might also see a possession in a town they regarded as 'theirs' as a special
providence of God, to test and mark out his own. The devil's assault on Joan
Jorden in Bury St Edmunds in 1599 happened in a town famed for its separatists and godly and was reported in London as such, as was the dispossession
at the Dutch church in Maidstone in 1572, and probably the case of Margaret
Herison at Burnham Ulph in Norfolk in 1586.[25] Burton-upon-Trent, where
Darrell participated in his next dispossession, was a godly community – as I
shall explore in Chapter 2 – and its inhabitants had every reason to welcome
a work of God in their town. Even so, the dispossession itself was held out of
town, in a way that suggests that the godly were not seeking publicity in the
way that might be imagined.

But there were, of course, ways of reading dispossessions geo-politically if
one was not godly – a reading which would be deployed against Darrell in the
future. The ungodly thought that by staging a dispossession in a big or godly

town the presumptuous precisians were attempting to push their cause where there was gain to be had: not just publicity but wealth and thus political leverage. Twelve years later Darrell answered such accusations made against him in an impassioned apostrophe of the people of Nottingham:

> Yea know yee, O Inhabitants of Nottingham … that iff I had not desired more you, then yours: the salvation of your soules, then your goods: I would not have bene your teacher … not for all your goods, though your towne be bigg, and many of you welthy.[26]

Certainly it was possessions and dispossessions in the larger and more significant settlements that most often attracted the repressive attention of the authorities of church and state. Those in small villages or individual gentry houses usually escaped censure because they simply mattered less. So did Darrell feel he had anything to prove in Mansfield and Whittington in 1586? Possibly not. He was interested in experimenting with dispossession and sharing his findings with Isabel Foljambe, an already godly reader, but there is no remaining evidence of what he expected her to do with his account. And there may not have been a particular application: Chesterfield and its environs (like Walton) were dominated by the Earl of Shrewsbury and preoccupied by the ongoing clashes between him and the townspeople, as well as by infighting among the Talbots and Cavendishes. Whatever the reasons – and there may be many no longer accessible – in 1586 no account of Katherine Wright's dispossession was published, and now only fragments of the story survive.

It could have been very different: the London case of Rachel Pinder and Agnes Briggs was a popular example of how a well-sited possession and a pamphlet or two could put a pin in the map for God or the godly, and it was cited by both sides. The case was publicized as a fraud by the authorities in an anonymous pamphlet, *The disclosing of a late counterfeyted possession by the devyl in two maydens within the Citie of London* (1574), which presented itself as answering both common reports and unlicensed printed books, which are now unfortunately lost. The Briggs and Pinder families lived in the heart of the city of London, at Galley Quay near the Tower and in Lothbury near the Royal Exchange. The daughters of both families claimed to be possessed, and they swelled and convulsed, spitting out hair, feathers, nails and pins accordingly. Rachel Pinder engaged in a dialogue with visitors to her bedside, in which she spoke in the devil's voice. John Foxe, the compiler of *Acts and Monuments*, was again the exorcist involved, and his helpers were members of the clothworking and mercantile community. It was hard to imagine a case more likely to attract attention and further the radical Protestant cause in the capital. The matter became so notorious that the Mayor, Alderman and Recorder of the City and the Archbishop of Canterbury, Matthew Parker, conducted examinations of the girls and then enforced their public confession of counterfeiting at Paul's

Cross – a humiliation also offered to Darrell in 1598.[27] For the city and church governors, whose account of the case was the one that prevailed, the affair was evidence of godly ambition that must be suppressed. Public attention must be relocated from fake wonders in the backstreets to authorized doctrine preached from the proper pulpit, and the city must be held against the cultural insurgency of the godly. Behind innocent-looking sick children were those who wanted to force the Queen into further church reform, and perhaps even question her right to rule: fingers pointed most often at the Earl of Leicester, and after his death at his stepson the Earl of Essex, who did indeed rebel in 1601 and expected the godly to support him.

As we shall see in Chapters 3 and 4, possessions and dispossessions often constituted a challenge to established authority, whether they were so meant or not. In many cases that authority was geographical (as well as political, generational, financial, educational and so on). It was unthinkable that tradespeople from the Thames wharfs or the ministers of obscure Midland parishes should presume to instruct the Queen and her chosen appointees at Lambeth, Westminster and Whitehall. One of Richard Bancroft's most heartfelt objections to the presbyterianism that he saw in such outbreaks of godly agitation was that the Queen 'must submitt herself and her Scepter to the fantasticall humors of her owne parishe governors'. Such people in such places should not aspire to national importance. But there was always a tension in such denunciations, especially in provincial grammar school boys like Harsnett (Essex) and Bancroft (Lancashire). These meritocrats knew that because the shires were 'farre from the eye of justice', as the Assize clerk Thomas Potts put it in 1612, they were also dangerous. People of genuine ability – one day to be the poet Thomas Gray's 'mute inglorious Miltons' – might be fomenting trouble there. And the bigger settlements in remote counties were in need of particular vigilance. Bancroft described what he perceived as the godly's

> pollicie … w[hi]ch in tyme maye growe to be daungerous, if it be not prevented … they bend not them selves to preache abroade in the contrye, and where there is greatest neede, but in the most populous places: as in Markett Townes, Shire Townes and Cities, where they knowe that strange devises and novelties, finding alwayes most frends, and best intertaynement, they might with lesse labor sowe theire contentions.[28]

Darrell's career shows clearly that an emergence from the margins into market and shire towns, and finally into print in London itself, was construed as a provincial revolt. The dispossession of Katherine Wright escaped attention for a decade because it did not break through into public consciousness in the manner of later exorcisms. But a revolt that began in a major town like Nottingham could easily sweep with it the London godly, and it must be combatted both in the shires and the capital. Darrell would soon discover just how frightened the authorities were by provincial 'contentions', and it was out of a desire to uncover the roots of these that they later excavated the Wright exorcism from its safe obscurity, publishing their findings.

Transition: Ashby de la Zouch

Whilst Darrell was in many ways content at Mansfield, as he later wrote, spiritually he was not satisfied. He was ordained in about 1589 and in 1592 he chose to migrate to a place where he would be at the heart of a powerful godly community. He moved to Ashby de la Zouch in Leicestershire. Harsnett later investigated his financial affairs at the time of this move, and said that his father's bequest to him consisted of 'two or three houses, and a little land in Mansfielde and else where'. He alleged that when Darrell sold this property, he then lived by usury off the proceeds, which Harsnett estimated at '(as one of his friendes sayeth) five or six hundreth poundes'. Darrell did not question the description of his inheritance, but he did dispute the use to which he put the proceeds of its sale. Whilst he says that he left a comfortable life for the sake of piety, he also suggests that his business was not flourishing. He did not renew the leases on the mills that Henry Darrell farmed:

> ... after certaine shorte leases which my father left me were expired, (which were worth yearely three times more to me then my land[)] I sould that little lande I had, as beinge not able of the annual rent there-of (spetially in those deare yeares) to mayntaine my selfe and familie, havinge 5. children. But it is as true, that presently with the same moneye I tooke a farme in Ashbie-delaZouch, and bought some store of sheepe, kine, horses, oxen, with other thinges appertayninge to husbandry.

If there was no interval between receiving the proceeds of the sale and reinvesting them, there could be no accusation of sinful usury. Darrell also said that, far from profiting from his dealings, he gave to the poor at least some part of his newly-liquid funds.[29]

Despite Darrell's uninterest in life-writing, this was important, because Harsnett's rhetoric of profit and loss was a key part of his attack on Darrell's religious beliefs. Like many anti-puritan writers he strove to represent the intangible and spiritual as material and worldly. If Harsnett could get his readers to see Darrell as a grasping place-seeker, then his move to Ashby and all his activities in Burton and Nottingham could be explained as an attempt to escape provincial poverty and get a well-paid office for himself in a bigger settlement. It was nothing to do with promoting God's glory: Darrell would be seen as a moneygrubber, his story one in the cony-catching genre of over-reaching tricksters. Accordingly, and contradictorily, Harsnett tried to present

Darrell both as a penniless place-seeker and as a secretly wealthy hypocrite. But neither image seems to have much foundation in fact. Darrell had a sizeable inheritance and, later in life, he could afford to employ a servant: he haughtily dismissed Harsnett's attempt to portray him as a poor nobody. And he was, according to even Harsnett's account, wealthy enough to indulge godly scruples. Harsnett retells what he has heard of Darrell: that he might once have had a parsonage, but would not confirm his desire for it lest this presumption should displease God. Accordingly, he did not get the post, and 'preached for the triall of his guifts, having no ecclesiastical living'. No attempt to make him look like a hypocrite would stick.[30] If he was going to refuse livings and earn his bread as a lecturer, however, Harsnett was right to suggest that Ashby was a good place to be.

There are two Ashby de la Zouches in the pamphlets about the Darrell case – John Darrell's Ashby and William Sommers's Ashby, a real one and a fictional one. Which is which depends on whether one believes that John Darrell or his patient William Sommers was lying about supposed contacts between the two in Ashby in the 1580s and 1590s. Sommers, whose dispossession in Nottingham in 1597 was Darrell's final exorcism, alleged that he had met Darrell in Ashby many years before, and there Darrell had taught him to feign the symptoms of possession in order to take credit for dispossessing him at a later date. He claimed to have met Darrell in an alehouse in the town. But the claim that Darrell orchestrated Sommers's possession seems patently false. Sommers's own letter to Darrell after his exposure as a fraud, quoted and requoted by both sides, suggests that he began faking the 'trickes' of possession after hearing from other people than Darrell what the symptoms were: 'those trickes that I did before you came, was through folkes speeches that came to me' he said. Darrell's friends also pointed out that as a godly minister 'Mai[ster] Darrell [is] known to be a man that haunteth no alehouses'.[31] But in the process of their conflict, each teller creates for the reader a different Ashby de la Zouch. Sommers's Ashby is a place of pleasurable escape from his master's household, where he might frequent alehouses, meet other boys and indulge in plotting to escape from his apprenticeship. For Darrell, Ashby is a place of duty and propriety, where he lived as part of a vibrant community of godly under the eye of first Thomas Widdowes and then Arthur Hildersham, successive vicars of Ashby, and beyond them under the patronage of 'the puritan Earl'. He could thrive in Ashby and earn a living as a lecturer in the church, supplementing the vicar's preaching.

Ashby de la Zouch was certainly a godly town. It is centred on the castle and was dominated in the 1590s by the its owner, the godly third Earl of Huntingdon, who was married to the Earl of Leicester's sister. Huntingdon had in his gift the living of the church, and in this capacity had become Widdowes's and Hildersham's patron. By extension, then, their fellow minister

Darrell moved to and lived in Ashby under his and their wings. No records of a direct connection between Darrell and the Earl have been discovered – Thomas Freeman suggests that Darrell was introduced to the Ashby godly by Isabel Foljambe – but Huntingdon's influence was inescapable there. His castle, the church and the grammar school he had begun were the heart of the puritan project, and he hoovered up promising godly men to teach and preach there. He began with the Genevan exile and pamphleteer Anthony Gilby, who 'planted Protestantism in the county'. Gilby was respected by the most radical presbyterians as well as the mainstream godly and was ironically described by John Aylmer, Bishop of London in the 1570s, as the 'bishop' of Ashby because of his ability to organize like-minded ministers. During the controversy over prophesyings, Gilby was defended by his bishop, Thomas Cooper of Lincoln, who stated flatly that 'true religion' was at home in Ashby 'above any other place'. Exercises quickly replaced prophesyings, and they lasted long after Gilby's death in 1585. Widdowes, Gilby's son in law, became the vicar and his successor as godly champion. The curate, and the school's master from 1600, was the equally puritanical John Brinsley.[32] So Darrell arrived in Ashby to see all around him godly 'edification' in action – in education, ministry and magistracy.

In 1593 Arthur Hildersham succeeded Widdowes as vicar. He had served as lecturer at Ashby before gaining the prize of the vicarage, and he and Darrell must have known each other from the early days of Darrell's residence. Hildersham was sent for by Huntingdon to take up ministry there during Widdowes's tenure in September 1587, and Darrell arrived in Ashby, he says, on Michaelmas day 1592. But here is another textual crux of Darrell's story: the date of his arrival in Ashby is angrily disputed. Harsnett, who was seeking to prove that Darrell had lived longer in Ashby than he would confess, estimated that he had lived there some eight and a half or nine years before he left for Nottingham in late 1597. He had lived in three different houses there, said Harsnett, the first owned by one Perrin, the second by John Holland, where Darrell had lived for about six years, and the last by William Swinson, where he had dwelt for about eighteen months. Darrell, said William Sommers, was living in a house by the school and near the churchyard when Sommers had met him and since this supposed meeting was over six years earlier, this must have been when Darrell was living at Holland's house. However, this neat little sum presupposes that Harsnett's information about Darrell's movements was correct, and that Sommers was telling some version of the truth. In fact, as we have seen, the christening of Darrell's son Thomas in 1588 in Mansfield, his lecture in the church in 1589 and his administration of Joyce Walby's will in 1591 together confirm for the first time that he was not in Ashby before 1592.[33]

Harsnett, said Darrell, was trying to prove that he had lived in Ashby for almost nine years precisely so that he could show Darrell's and Sommers's time there had overlapped. It was quite possible to prove that Sommers had lived at the house of Thomas Gray, Langley Abbey, near Ashby. He had gone from there to Mrs Gray's brother, Anthony Brackenbury, first at Bell Hall in Worcestershire, then at Holme near Newark, Nottinghamshire. In both households, he had been a servant. Brackenbury had employed him to look after a warren of silver-haired rabbits, whilst at Gray's his duties seem to have been more general, involving the running of errands into local towns. Sommers had run away from Gray back to his mother in Nottingham, and had then been sacked by Brackenbury for an early attempt at faking fits. Darrell believed that it was about 1589 when Sommers left Gray, although he said that the Grays had been pressured into confirming that it was 1592. He further said that he had positive proof that Sommers had been with Brackenbury by June 1591. Meanwhile, Darrell denied that he had ever lived in a house belonging to John Holland, and said that he had not even spent three years together renting any particular house in Ashby.[34] Darrell's chronology, his dated presences in Mansfield up to April 1591, and his constant offers to produce testimonials to the truth of his assertions are together convincing beyond reasonable doubt: he was not in Ashby to teach William Sommers to counterfeit in the late 1580s and early 1590s, even had he desired to do so. Sommers's and Harsnett's story of a four-year period of conspiracy between Darrell and Sommers can safely be dismissed as fiction, decisively clearing Darrell of guilt for the first time in over four hundred years.

It was not until 1593 that a text was created to establish Darrell's certain presence in Ashby. He was resident there when his second known son Andrew was baptized in the church on 29 July. This was a significant year for Ashby, for in October Hildersham became vicar and gave new leadership to the group of ministers there. They shared a vision of world governed by God's word and they expressed it during this time of ascendancy in complementary sermons and lectures. Their thinking – or at least one way in which it might be read – is exemplified by a report of one of Darrell's sermons. Harsnett recounts with the gleeful anger that is his speciality how Darrell preached in the church in November, probably of 1593, on the anniversary of the Queen's accession. In this sermon,

> he inveighed mightily against the people there, for ringing the bels as they do throughout all the realme, in signification of their joye, and thanksgiving unto Almighty God, for the beginning and continuance of her Highnesse most Christian and blessed government: and in his zeale, or rather furie, was so fervent therein, as hee tearmed their said ringing, to bee the prophaning of the sabbath, and said they were all in danger thereby of God's heavie displeasure.[35]

For the godly, church bells were for summoning the faithful, not for the announcement of holidays. But Darrell's views begged an obvious question.

If forced to choose, would he side with God or his Queen? It was a question asked repeatedly of the godly, and it was part of the allegation that they were inherently rebellious. Darrell, Hildersham and their ilk, thought Harsnett, slighted central government's rights on a regular basis, as their other unauthorized provincial activities (exercises, exorcisms) proved. Their connections with Leicester, and the fact that Huntingdon was a potential claimant to the throne should the Queen die, made their activities the more dangerous and seditious in his book.

The battle over which view of Ashby would prevail – as a haven for skivers and dangerous radicals, or a perfect protestant parish – continued in other texts. In a biography of Arthur Hildersham by the godly Simeon Ashe, and based on the recollections of Arthur's son Samuel, Hildersham is seen as leading the Ashby godly to the promised land regardless of his own tribulations. As lecturer at Ashby, he had already appeared (10 January 1588/9) before the High Commission for preaching without a license. In 1590 he was imprisoned, and suspended from preaching until 1592. In 1596 he so angered the judge Sir Edmund Anderson with a sermon preached at the Assizes that Anderson tried to have him indicted. In 1598 he was summoned by the High Commission, probably in connection with Darrell's trial, but there is no record of an appearance.[36] The godly reverenced such trials and their opinion is also expressed in another surviving text, his monument. It depicts an ideal minister, praising:

> his sweet and ingenuous disposition, his singular wisdome in setling peace, advising in secular affaires, and satisfying doubts, his abundant charities and especially … his extraordinary knowledge, and judgment in the holy scriptures, his painfull and zealous preaching together with his firme and lasting constancy in the truth he professed.

So is Sommers or Darrell right about Ashby? There is sufficient textual evidence to hazard a guess at the cultural climate during Darrell's residence, and it corresponds better with sincere godliness than with the seditious trickery that Sommers alleged he found there. When we look at the effect that the Ashby godly seem to have had on Darrell's career, it is one of strengthening his convictions (whether one agrees with them or not) rather than turning him into a plotter and charlatan. Hildersham, as vicar, was at the forefront of the godly project, and was Darrell's spiritual comforter and advisor: his probity was never questioned, although his zeal was reproved. He would offer Darrell his judgment about travelling to Lancashire to a dispossession there, take the leading role in the exorcism at Burton, and support him when everything went wrong at Nottingham. He would try to defend him before the High Commission. Hildersham had long experience of the kindness of mentors like John Ireton and Richard Greenham, and he now played that part for Darrell. His role was both professional and personal: he baptized another son of Darrell's in April

1597 and buried the same child, Samuel, on 18 June.[37] Drawn together by a shared religious and political faith, preaching from the same pulpit and sharing the trials of everyday life, Darrell and Hildersham seem to have reinforced each others' sincerity and confidence. It seems likely that the experience of Ashby allowed Darrell to become the assertive thinker and writer that he was by the end of the 1590s.

Burton-upon-Trent's *Most wonderfull and true storie*

The godly coterie at Ashby was the perfect supportive environment for Darrell and his time there also reintroduced him to dispossession, in 1596. He was an assiduous attender of exercises at Ashby, Burton, Packington and other places. Some sixteen ministers attended these and it was probably through this godly networking that William Walkden, the parson of Clifton Campville in Staffordshire, heard about the now decade-old case of Katherine Wright. Walkden's grandson, Thomas Darling, had been showing the same symptoms as Wright and Darrell agreed to go and visit the boy on 27 May 1596. He recognized in Darling what he had seen before, and offered a diagnosis: Darling was possessed. It was clear what had to be done, and he advised a dispossession by prayer and fasting. But, interestingly, Darrell was worried about his own motives for wanting to take part in another exorcism. He was afraid that others thought that he was seeking personal glory in such stunts. So fretful was he about this that he would not even be present at Darling's dispossession, which occurred on 28 May. He said that he would pray for Darling in his absence, and let his godly colleagues demonstrate the Lord's power instead of him. So a group of godly lay people numbering only nine or ten in total, and with no minister present, dispossessed the boy without him.[38] The dispossession happened at Darling's uncle's house at Caldwall, outside Burton and in a private home, which also kept its local notoriety to a minimum.

Later it was alleged, including by Thomas Darling himself, that Darrell did not believe him to be possessed, or had significant doubts about it. A dispossession in the town had been planned, said Darling, but the group of ministers had rejected the idea, seeming to have some misgivings.[39] But Darrell always said quite clearly that he did believe Darling. It was precisely because of his conviction that a work of God was being performed at Burton that he was so wary of seeking personal attention there. His shyness of publicity extended to writing about the case too. He played a minimal role in offering corrections to an account of the dispossession written and edited by others, as we shall see. The collaborative work about Darling's case, *The most wonderfull and true storie* (London, 1597), was the first account of one of Darrell's exorcisms to reach print, and it deserves a chapter to itself (Chapter 2), as do the significant events of which it was a part. But Darrell apparently wrote nothing himself, not even a manuscript account of the kind he had produced to chronicle Katherine Wright's dispossession. Later he was to say that he regretted missing the deliverance of the 'Boy of Burton', but at the time it, and his print silence, kept him free from the kind of notoriety that he feared, and so from the kind of official displeasure that pursued Hildersham throughout his career.

But the lure of trying his gifts and seeking assurance of his faith proved too strong for Darrell, and when the next opportunity arose to take part in a dispossession he was unable to refuse. It would lead him eventually to ignominy and imprisonment, but as a first step he chose wisely in the location of his endeavours: not a town centre in the Midlands, but a gentry household in Lancashire, which produced few records and attracted little attention at the time.

Back to the Margins: Cleworth

When Darrell went to Cleworth, in Lancashire, to the house of Nicholas Starkie where – spectacularly – seven people appeared to be possessed, he was still shy of authorship. So although he did eventually write an account of his dispossessions at there, it was not until 1599 or 1600. We have, therefore, no contemporary account of the case. There are two reports of the Cleworth exorcisms, one by Darrell and one by his fellow-minister George More but, significantly, both were delayed until several years after the event. In Darrell's case we have already seen that he had a motive for silence. As he revealingly argued in his later work *An Apologie or Defence*, if he had desired fame and vainglory, why had he made so little haste to the printing press? But his fellow-exorcist More's text, the other work of 1599–1600, was hardly more forthcoming. Both books are particularly tardy and cursory-looking when compared with the forensic attempts to record the chain of events in Nottingham later in 1597. We know that More's account of the events at Cleworth had been delayed at the printers for several months, because when the text did reach print it contained an apology to that effect. But even so, it was written and sent to the publisher well after the events it described. So why were both the books on the Lancashire dispossessions so late in coming? Why was the narrative of events there so oddly brief, and left largely uncontested by Harsnett and other doubters? Clearly something unusual happened during the publicizing of this case: on top of Darrell's desire to avoid vainglory, something else seems to be going on.

The lack of controversy over the case was a matter of comment by both sides in the bitter debate about Darrell's other dispossessions. George More noted that Harsnett 'finds great fault with some of our friendes, for that they spake so much of the dispossession of Summers [*sic*] in a little treatise or two, but nothing of the dispossession of those 7 in Lancashire and of some others'. Darrell, meanwhile, wrote that Harsnett's accusations that other demoniacs were counterfeit could be read as 'intimating to all men, that the 7 in Lancashire were such', but that the High Commission 'let them alone' and was 'winkinge' at them. Why, he asked 'was not M[aster] Starchy and some other about them, being so many, fetched to London by Pursevants or warrants?'. Why were no questioners sent to Lancashire? Why had Bancroft and Harsnett 'shuffled and slubbered over' this matter? The prefacer of *The Triall of Maist. Dorrell* referred to 'the Bishops ... deepe silence' about the matter. Both he and Darrell suggested that this was out of fear that the Lancashire seven might be genuine demoniacs, but Darrell also thought that Harsnett was reluctant to accuse Starkie because he was a gentleman. However, this does not seem to have held Harsnett or Bancroft back in other cases. Edward Beresford, Thomas Gray and even Mrs Gray were all subjected to intensive questioning by Harsnett, and Bancroft threatened Mr Bainbridge of Calke with imprisonment simply for his assertion that Derbyshire people believed that Darrell and More's dispossessions were genuine.[40] So what was different about the Lancashire case which meant that Nicholas Starkie was exempted from the sort of trouble encountered by his fellow gentry, and the events in his house went unpublicized for three years?

Firstly, it may be that both Darrell's and More's texts of 1600 are based upon an earlier account which is now lost. If this is true, the missing version is perhaps that which is repeatedly referred to by both men: an account called 'The History of the 7 in Lancashire'. This was written by John Dickons, preacher of Leigh (the Lancashire parish in which Cleworth lay), who had assisted at the dispossession. In early June 1597 the printer John Oxenbridge was apparently waiting in vain for it or another account to reach him so that he could print it. At last, on 29 August 1597, nearly three months after the publication of the story of the Boy of Burton in *The most wonderfull and true storie*, the publisher Raffe Jackson paid the usual fee of six pence to the Stationers' Company for the right to publish 'A true declaration of 7. persons whiche in ye parishe of Cleworth in Lancashire were strangly and really posessed of Sathan and of their delivery by praier and fastinge'. But there was a difficulty: the book (which had no named author) was entered into the Register with the proviso that it be printed 'when it shalbe Laufully Aucthorised'. There is no further indication of authorization being either forthcoming or refused, and so the text's status remains unclear. Harsnett says in 1599 that a book written by Dickons, and 'justified from point to point by M[aster] More' – presumably in the hearings – 'runneth from hand to hand', which suggests that in 1599 it was still a manuscript being circulated. Perhaps, then, permission was refused. One copy was certainly given to Harsnett, for More reports that he was examined closely about its contents, and Darrell says that he too had a copy.[41] This ghostly text may be an explanation for the delaying of the other two: an account had been written and was known to be being published by others less wary of self-publicity, so there was no need for anyone else to write one.

But Dickons's book seems to have been handed over to the ecclesiastical authorities and there stalled. It was probably never published, so that in fact there was a further need to provide an account of what had happened in Cleworth. More's claim for the importance of his book, written from prison in 1599, suggests that it will be the first eyewitness account of the case available to the public. He explains that the stories of Sommers and Darling are 'put in print' and he will now 'adde to these two the storie of those in Lancashire'.[42] In fact, his book seems like a reply to Harsnett's acute observation that Darrell and his friends had not adequately promoted the Lancashire case. Like Darrell, More was a reluctant author. His text has an awkward sincerity. He opens his pitch to the reader with the dutiful sense that he ought to follow existing conventions: 'it is the manner of men that set foorth any storie … to give a Reason for their purpose therein'. His main aim, he accordingly tells us, is to clear Darrell, not only of the slur of counterfeiting, but also of Harsnett's allegation that he had been the ringleader of the ministers at the Cleworth dispossessions. 'Pollicie' says More 'hath preferred him to bee principall, when in deed they [the High Commission] know hee is not'. More's book exists to claim both his own rightful share of martyrdom and also the right to defend his collaborator, for he explains that he and Dickons took the lead in the prayer and fasting, that both of them did so sincerely, and that both believed quite rightly in John Darrell's innocence.[43] If Dickons's book on the case had reached the shelves of the bookshops, More would not have had to write his account, but as it is he presents it as the only fair report available of the case of the 'Lancashire seven'. Again, the loss of Dickons's book thus partly explains the delay in publishing More's *True Discourse* and Darrell's *True Narration*.

More was right, incidentally, to doubt his place in the history of the exorcism affair and its writings. He is almost invisible in what becomes, thereafter, the story of Darrell's authorial career. He is always referred to as a secondary figure, a co-defendant whose offence was 'bearing witnesse' to and 'justifying' Darrell's dispossessions. Harsnett says that he had 'otherwise greatlie misbehaved himselfe' also, but still portrays him as secondary to Darrell. At least *A True Discourse* establishes that this was not the whole story. Like his contemporaries Arthur Hildersham, Richard Bernard, John Dickons, Robert Balsom, Richard Greenham, John Foxe, Richard Rothwell and others, More was a godly clergyman perfectly prepared to lead a dispossession attempt in his own right. He was the minister at Calke in Derbyshire, which was a 'peculiar' – outside of some of the usual church controls – and later served by the equally godly friend of Hildersham, Julines Herring. More was part of the group that gathered at the exercises at Ashby, which was how he became involved with Darrell. He was sent to Lancashire as a kind of minder, charged by both Darrell and the Ashby godly with keeping Darrell out of trouble and away from personal vainglory. More explains that 'it was … thought fit, that I also should go with him, as a companion in the journey, and a witnes to all his proceedings according to his owne request'.[44] *A True Discourse* can be precisely defined as his discharge of part of this duty in print. He also tried to help Darrell by giving evidence to the Ecclesiastical Commission at Nottingham, but was forbidden. Other than that, the fact that he was released from prison sometime before 1602, and that he was married, nothing has yet been established about his life.[45]

More's book deals only with the Lancashire dispossessions. But the other account, Darrell's, raises further questions about the importance of the Lancashire dispossessions to the case for the defence of the two ministers. Darrell's story of the Cleworth demoniacs forms only half of the first, very brief, part of a treatise titled *A True Narration of the Strange and Grevous Vexation by the Devil of 7 Persons in Lancashire and William Sommers of Nottingham*, whose longer second section is a work of demonological theory devoted to 'The Doctrin of the Possession and Dispossession of Demoniakes out of the Word of God'. By the time his book was written, Darrell was probably a free man, and he might simply have offered his own version of More's or Dickons's text and appended it to his demonological treatise. He certainly wrote both parts himself, but his treatment of the Lancashire case shows that it is the less important and original section. He repeats almost word for word his own arguments in other works, and distinctive phrases used in More's work, *A True Discourse concerning the certaine Possession and Dispossession of 7 persons in one Familie in Lancashire*. 'A dumpishe heavie countenance' is used by both to describe a possession victim, for example. Although More was in the Clink at Southwark whilst Darrell was in the Gatehouse at Westminster, and both were initially in 'close' confinement, it may also be that the two men had corresponded about their recollections, since it is clear that later on in their imprisonment each received visitors, books and writing materials. The relationship between their two texts is opaque, but it is apparent. The two books seem to cling together for mutual support. But this literary oddity actually reflects quite fairly the experience of the Lancashire dispossessions, at least as they are described by More and Darrell. The episode was a traumatic one for both men, and it demonstrated that not all parts of England were like Burton-upon-Trent: yearning for a godly happening followed by a godly pamphlet. This is a further reason why the case of the 'seven in Lancashire' was of less interest to both sides in the controversy over dispossession, as we shall see.

The story of the Lancashire seven is a convoluted one, full of unspoken tension between Protestant and Catholic, and with hints of an untold story of highly-politicized feuding, which the ministers did not know or chose not to relate. Nicholas Starkie, father of some of the possessed and guardian, kinsman or employer of the others, had married a widowed inheretrix, Anne Barton née Parr.[46] Some of her relations were extremely bitter about the loss of her inheritance. They were Catholics, and More says that they prayed for the deaths of any issue resulting from the Starkie marriage. Four of the children of Nicholas and Anne died, and when Anne was told that her family were praying against her she attempted to avert the danger by willing her land to her husband and his heirs in the event that her own children should die. She and Nicholas then had two healthy children. In February 1594, however, when the children were about ten and twelve, their daughter Anne began to seem melancholy. Meanwhile her brother alleged that he found himself compelled to shout constantly. Both children then began to have fits, for which Starkie tried many remedies. He spent, More relates, two hundred pounds on medical treatments. He went to a Catholic priest. His final resort, to Edmund Hartley, 'a witch' or cunning man, was also 'popish', and counterproductive. Hartley recited charms and used herbs to treat the victims and they were well for a year and a half as a result. But this was merely an illusion, implies More, staged by the devil to lead the family and their cunning man deeper into error.[47] What was needed was a godly dispossession – but Starkie received no good advice on the matter for two years, so lacking was his locality in proper Protestant feeling.

His errors became more obvious when Hartley began to demand large sums of money, a house and land for his services. Then, on a visit to Starkie's father Edmund's house, he discovered that Hartley had made a magic circle on the ground, which he required Starkie to rub out. Hartley was beginning to make threatening remarks, and seeing this and 'many other bad qualities in this fellow', Starkie at last sought help in the right place – although perhaps not for the right reasons. He went to Dr John Dee, the lay Warden of Manchester College, who was famous for his own magical knowledge. But Dee was a magician of a different kind from Hartley, at least in his own conscience. His interest was in angels, and he was intent on keeping out of trouble of the kind that had partly motivated his removal from London. He said that he would not meddle with the case. Instead he urged Starkie to call in some godly preachers, and sent for Hartley in order to reprove him for his practises. The 'witch' was in an increasingly exposed position: in January 1596 John began to have fits again, and they spread to other children in the house, three girls whom Starkie was bringing up and educating with his own children, Ellen Holland, Margaret and Elinor Hardman. Strange fits also afflicted the family's maidservants and a visiting relative from Salford, Margaret Byrom. Hartley now seemed more likely to be the cause of the fits than their cure, and the supposed victims came, by a poorly documented process, to believe that he had bewitched them by kissing them.[48] Hartley now told Byrom that he could not cure the fits, but only two or three men at prayer could do so.

According to Dee's advice, therefore, his curate at Manchester, Matthew Palmer, was called in with some clerical colleagues.[49] They almost immediately suspected Hartley. He attempted to pray with them, but they rejected his efforts: 'Pray? quoth one, why man thou canst not pray'. When Hartley insisted that he could, he proved to be unable to recite the Lord's Prayer, a classic diagnostic test for witchcraft. 'They then thought him to be a witch' says More with characteristic brevity, 'and caused him presentlie to be apprehended, and brought before 2 Justices of peace'. These may have been James Assheton, who later wrote to Darrell inviting him to Cleworth, and Edmund Hopwood, who soon visited the possessed to take testimony from them. Both men knew Dr Dee, with Hopwood borrowing *Malleus Maleficarum* and Johann Wier's *De Praestigiis Daemonum*, among other demonological books, from him in 1596–7. Hopwood was also well-known for his godliness and would have been a natural local choice as examining magistrate. Once interviewed, Hartley was committed to Lancaster prison in late January or early February 1597, to await trial at the Assizes.[50] At the Lent Assize trial in early March, he was convicted. He would have been sentenced to a year's imprisonment because, although he had been found guilty of witchcraft, he had not killed anyone. With apparent disappointment, the court concluded that 'they could finde no lawe to hange him'. But Nicholas Starkie would not accept this outcome – apart from the motive of vengeance, it was presumably thought in this conservative country that Hartley's enchantments could not be lifted until he was dead – and he recalled the incident of Hartley's drawing the magic circle, which he recounted under oath to the court. This was conjuration, the court decided, which carried the death penalty automatically. With questionable legality (a new indictment ought to have been drawn up, and the matter tried) Hartley was sentenced and hanged, having penitently confessed when the rope broke during the first attempt.[51]

Having 'proved' that the demoniacs were bewitched by Hartley, More's account, by far the fuller of the two, turns to the more difficult matter of the dispossession. In seeking help for this, Starkie was lucky, because Dee's butler was Richard Walkden – the cousin of Thomas Darling, whom Darrell's friends had so recently dispossessed at Burton. According to Darrell, Walkden told Starkie of this success and Starkie then sent for Darrell. Harsnett says that Dee also wrote to Darrell. And after three pleas for help he consented to go, taking More with him.[52] Having secured the local cooperation of Dickons, Darrell and More set out into territory 'where we never came in our lives before'. This phrase is partly an assertion that neither man could previously have instructed the demoniacs, but the undercurrent of adventure and of risk was a common response of travellers to Lancashire. It seemed a wilderness. Lancashire 'lay at the periphery of the structure of the early Tudor Church', and was routinely portrayed as 'a vaste place' of 'evil' journeys, 'unbridled and bad', its inhabitants prone to 'theft, violence and sexual laxity' as well as religious 'blindness'. Leigh had been the scene of 'great misorders' in the church over the choice of a new curate, and some ministers went about armed. The county was also notorious for stories of sorcery and grave-robbing, such as those told of Dee's former scryer Edward Kelley in the 1570s.[53] Lancashire was, in contemporary imagination, the embodiment of otherness and incivility. The wrath of the church authorities seems to have been the least of the godly ministers' worries as they travelled north: their texts were produced in response to that wrath, but that was three years later. At the time, both accounts suggest, Darrell and More simply felt that a dispossession in such an inherently devilish place would have many risks.

Accordingly, when Darrell and More arrived at Cleworth on 16 March, they were prepared to be shocked – and they were not disappointed. The Starkies, although not actually recusants, had no idea, Darrell said, of what reformation meant. Their children were called and began to convulse as expected, but they then began to abuse and physically attack the ministers, and had to be carried out.[54] This had not happened before. Darrell and More retreated to discuss with Starkie what to do, and prayer and fasting was quickly agreed upon. But on their return to prepare the demoniacs for their delivery, they were met with a barrage of threat, insult and 'horrible blasphemie'. Says More soberly

> We durst not proceede but gave over ... forced to give place to the Devil ... the trueth is, we were greatly discouraged at that time, not knowing wel what to doe.

There is a powerful sense in both More's and Darrell's accounts of Cleworth of claustrophobia and cultural isolation. The ministers are a beacon of Protestant decorum in the Catholic, witch-ridden wilderness, with their very headquarters horribly invaded by demonic attack, and their authority rejected by those they had come to help: they had nowhere else to go but the garden. Cleworth was a large and comfortable house, but it was full of screaming demoniacs and their dispossession took all of the next day and several hours of the day after, exhausting the ministers' precious preaching voices. Forty people were present. Each minister prepared and delivered a sermon, against a background of shrieking and writhing, and each worked individually with several patients, offering prayers, crying with compassion, and trying to engage the victims in their own cure. They were successful, but Darrell and More had no desire to linger after the dispossessions on 17 and 18 March 1597. Darrell was later invited to come to Manchester and offer a defence against Catholic attacks on his work, but he did not go.[55] And nor did either of the ministers apparently want to write up and publish the matter.

The location of Cleworth in the wild, papistical 'north parts' may thus be another reason why the dispossessions there received no immediate coverage in print, and also why they were not central to the High Commission case against Darrell and More – which, of course, reinforced their neglect by Darrellite writers. From the Midland godly's point of view, despite its success and relatively large size, this was an event in a distant hamlet with no obvious usefulness to a godly community locally. For Darrell and More it seems to have caused considerable culture-shock: there is a feeling of reserve about the case which is not fully explained by any known fact. There was some pressure to publish, but not until after *The most wonderfull and true storie* – a dispossession in a better-known and more godly community, as we shall see in Chapter 2 – had been worked up. Darrell remained chary of writing about his work, and More was effectively under orders to prevent him from becoming a celebrity. That left Dickons, and his account seems to have been quietly suppressed. Finally, the matter was decisively buried by the progress of events at Nottingham. And so the story of the Lancashire seven remained (and remains) obscure.

The dispossession of the Boy of Burton was to be seen by Darrell and More's prosecutors as far more important, and even the Wright case, over a decade old, was investigated by Harsnett. But he did not question Nicholas Starkie even when he came to London and visited George More in the Clink: all that was required of him was a letter certifying that he believed the Lancashire case was genuine. It is likely, therefore, that there was simply far more cultural capital to be won for both sides in the Midlands. From the perspective of the church authorities, Nottingham, Burton and even, eventually, Eckington had to be fought for. Lancashire was a county where any Protestant activity was likely to be welcomed, and was not lightly to be undermined.[56] The response of the northern archdiocese to Darrell's activities, even in controversial Nottingham, was later to be a resounding endorsement. Even godly Burton was in a county renowned for its recusancy, and the dispossession there went unchallenged by any authority. But the Burton exorcism is important for a number of reasons; because of the godly community in the town, and to see why Darrell began to emerge from anonymity into first celebrity and then authorship. It is therefore time to return to the dispossession of the Boy of Burton, and to the book that publicized it, *The most wonderfull and true storie.*

2 'A BOOKE DECLARING THE FEARFULL VEXATION': SPREADING THE WORD

Soon after More and Darrell returned to the Midlands from their struggle in the North, the published account of the dispossession of the 'Boy of Burton', Thomas Darling, appeared in print. It was entered in the Stationers' Register on 6 June 1597, apparently seeming innocuous to its censors – who must have felt foolish when their colleague Samuel Harsnett was excoriating the book in the High Commission hearings ten months later. It was not through oversight that they passed it for publication, however. Its authors and publisher, John Oxenbridge, had been equally (and rightly) convinced that the book ought to be processed through the usual channels and could be published legally without fuss. It was a type of publication that had been seen and allowed before and it did not seem to them, as it did not seem to its licensers, subversive. Yet the official Anglican histories of the Darrell case – Strype, Heylyn and so on – regard such publications as *The most wonderfull and true storie* as transparently sinister propaganda, created and issued as part of a plot to pervert English culture and convert the nation to presbyterianism by stealth. Were they right? Why might such a book have been licensed, and only later denounced as seditious, recalled and its printer imprisoned? An examination of the story of the 'Boy of Burton' can help explain.

A Society of Friends: The Burton Godly, Paget and Essex

On Saturday 27 February 1596 a wealthy clothier from Burton-upon-Trent named Robert Toone went hare-hunting in a wood across the Trent, taking his thirteen year old nephew, Darling. Winshill Wood was not far from Toone's home, where his nephew also lived, and so when the two became separated Darling decided to walk home. However, he soon began to be sick, and was put to bed. His relations concluded that he had an ague but later Darling began to accuse a local woman, Alice Gooderidge, of causing his sickness by witchcraft. He had met her in the wood on the way home, had happened to fart in her presence and she had cursed him. He gave every indication that she had sent a spirit into him: screaming, writhing, blaspheming, vomiting and rejecting (by relapsing into fits) any religious activity. Two elements of his story made it plausible. It was likely that Darling had met Alice Gooderidge on his way home. She is probably the Alice Wright who with her mother Elizabeth Wright leased land at Stapenhill, Scalpcliff and Winshill, and a cottage for Elizabeth at Stapenhill, in the 1570s, and these arrangements had probably not changed much twenty years later after her marriage to Oliver Gooderidge.[1] Moreover, Elizabeth was known as 'the witch of Stapenhill', because she provided treatment for farm animals. It was later alleged that she had cured a cow by making the sign of the cross and praying. The town's former patron saint, St Modwen, was sometimes depicted with a red cow, and Elizabeth Wright may simply have been invoking the help of the saints in a traditional Catholic fashion.[2] For her godly accusers, however, Catholicism was one step along the road to witchcraft and whatever Elizabeth was up to, her daughter Alice was a fit subject for suspicion. Thomas Darling's story, despite attempts to challenge it, stuck.

Darling's family was godly, as Darrell and others later testified. They were also powerful and well-connected in Burton and the surrounding area. It is now possible to situate them precisely in local society, politics and Burton's economy. Robert Toone, apart from his cloth interests, also had in farm the water corn mills at Winshill (Burton or Lower Mills) and a horse-driven malt mill in Burton's Market Place. He leased Kitchener's Hay, land by the Trent formerly assigned to the kitchener of Burton Abbey, and also fishing rights on the river. The Toones had leased Burton Mills since the early sixteenth century, Henrys alternating with Roberts until the present Robert had succeeded his father upon his death in about 1568. The mills were Saxon in their origin and continued, in fact, to mill corn until the early 1990s – they are currently being restored. As well as this major holding, Toone had a large house. It and the mercantile arm of his business were both situated in the heart of the town. He leased premises on the Market Place and a house on the north side with a garden across the square, adjoining the school in Church Lane. These were all prime sites with rents to match, and Toone's nephew Thomas later made a boast of the centrality of his uncle's house, and the fact that it was built of stone.[3] All the properties that Toone is known to have rented were leased from the Paget family, the Barons Paget of Beaudesert, who possessed most of Burton as lords of the manor – with one significant interruption, to be discussed presently. And as if this affluence were not enough, Toone had strengthened his position in the town and county society by marrying the daughter of the bailiff at Stapenhill, another Paget manor across the river in Derbyshire, in 1584. He was thus a respected member of mercantile society and on excellent terms with local gentry and nobility.[4]

Despite their importance and respectability, however, the Toones did not rush to accuse Wright and Gooderidge, in order to 'explain' their nephew's appalling behaviour. They initially took a medical approach, and they had a proper godly scepticism about magical intervention. Robert engaged a young man as 'keeper' to Darling, to stop him throwing himself from the gallery or window, and his wife Elizabeth tended to him herself, but they believed him to be ill, not bewitched. It may have helped that Alice Gooderidge was not, as is often thought, a stereotypical witchcraft suspect. Her land holdings in the 1570s amounted to at least ten separate parcels, leased from the Pagets, and although she was about sixty years old she was married, with remaining family connections in the town. She was not, apparently, especially poor or isolated, and her accusation would be a serious matter. It was not until early April, therefore, that Gooderidge was sent for by the boy's grandmother, the wife of William Walkden, vicar of Clifton Campville in Staffordshire, and his aunt, the wife of Thomas Saunders of Caldwall.[5] These outsiders are portrayed in the written account of the case as taking the lead in beginning investigation of the suspect, and John Darrell confirmed later that he was sent for by Walkden and not by Robert Toone or one of the Burton godly. As we have seen, Walkden sent for Darrell because he had heard of his success in dispossessing Katherine Wright.[6] From this initial contact, the godly group of Burton tradespeople of which the Toones were part gradually came to be convinced that Thomas Darling really was possessed by the devil.

The supposed origin and progress of Darling's possession are thus clear, and the story of his encounter with the 'witch' is not unusual. So what about the accusations that his illness was part of a godly plot? It is certainly true that Burton had a substantial godly presence in the 1590s. However, when the townspeople of Burton were asked to sign a statement supporting Darling's claim to have been dispossessed, they were also being asked to defend his and his family's good name. This raises some questions about how much, relatively speaking, godly or worldly sympathies influenced their assent. The Toone household mobilized forty signatories for the minister John Denison, who took the testimonial to London, and the impression given is of a tightly-knit community of 'puritans'. But it can now be seen that some of the signatories, even if they shared the Toones' godliness, were also tied to them by business connections, friendship, kinship and obligation. Robert Toone's father-in-law Thomas Dutton signed, as did one of the constables of Burton, Thomas Hasten, to whose daughter Elizabeth Toone was godmother, and Thomas Saunders, Edward Wightman and Jesse Bee, all relatives by marriage. William Caldwall, an equally wealthy fellow clothier and lessee of a fulling mill built by his grandfather and Henry Toone, signed too. He had been a witness at Robert and Elizabeth Toone's wedding, and was Robert's cousin. Two members of the Clark family, also clothiers, signed the testimonial, and the Clarks were a step-family of the Caldwalls and thus also cousins of the Toones.[7] There must be many other, now invisible connections, which might have influenced signatories. But the level of support, and its social breadth, is still surprising for a small town, and does seem genuinely indicative of a strong godly grouping with a belief that God had shown special favour to Burton through His possession and dispossession of Thomas Darling.

Those socially superior to the Toone-Darling family, equals and dependants offered their backing. Accordingly they had the support of Peter Eccarshall, the curate of Burton (which had a lay rector), the innholder and surgeon Jerome Horabin, the barber Robert Hyde, the alehouse-keeper John Simpson, the victualler, butcher and alehouse-keeper William Woodcocke, and the chandler Humphrey Wakefield. A separate supportive statement was signed by the magistrates Thomas Gresley and Sir Humphrey Ferrers, who committed Gooderidge to prison upon her accusation by Darling. The Gresleys of Drakelow were solid Protestants who had assisted in the custody of Mary Queen of Scots at Tutbury. Thomas's second wife Katherine, who had died only the year before, was one of the Walsinghams, kin to the leading godly politician Sir Francis.[8] Hastings Gresley, brother of Thomas, was a visitor to Darling during his possession, as was Oliver Rampaine, Burton's schoolmaster. Edward Cokayne came from Ashbourne in Derbyshire to visit. Prominent men from Stapenhill, William Gregory and John Cockes, also joined in the activity surrounding the prosecution of their neighbour Gooderidge. Cockes and Gregory both leased a substantial amount of land at Stapenhill from the Pagets.[9] But involvement with the prosecution does not necessarily imply godliness: the non-godly were also engaged by the case. Visitors to Darling included Elizabeth Dethick, the wife of Humphrey Dethick of Newhall, who would later marry Sir Humphrey Ferrers. The Dethicks were wealthy, with interests in expanding industries such as coal mining, and they possessed the impropriate tithes of the rectory of Stapenhill. But Elizabeth was not godly. She was 'a woman of great spirit, and a resolute Papist', who had used to dine and probably celebrate mass at the manor house in the days of the Catholic third Baron Paget.[10]

Elizabeth Dethick's interest was still valuable to the godly, however. Elizabeth was a well-connected woman in godly circles. Her son Francis was about to marry Katherine, daughter of Thomas Gresley and named after her Walsingham mother. Equally importantly, Elizabeth Dethick's own daughter Catherine had already married Alexander Reddish of Reddish, Lancashire. Both marriages were into strongly Protestant families, but the Reddish connection would prove particularly significant to the godly. Alexander Reddish was the 'bosome Friend' of Arthur Hildersham, and he and his wife Catherine were later to be celebrated for their patronage of the definitive 'puritan' William

Bradshaw, author of *English Puritanisme*. From the early seventeenth century the Reddishes housed and maintained Bradshaw at Elizabeth Dethick's former home, Newhall, which Alexander inherited as part of Catherine's dowry. Here Bradshaw promoted godly causes and solidified English puritan identity, adopting the name with pride.[11] He was significant in the Darrell story in a narrow as well as a wider sense, for before his own authorship began, he would get into trouble at Cambridge for distributing Darrell's pamphlets. There were strong Reddish connections in Lancashire too, where Darrell would (as we have seen) dispossess his next patients. The visit to Darling of Alexander Reddish's formidable Catholic mother-in-law was thus, paradoxically, evidence of the presence of a very important patron, both of the Burton godly and the wider national community.[12]

The lords of the manor, the Pagets, were conspicuous by their absence, but their connection with Burton is a further (although never before explored) element in the Anglican allegation that Darling, Darrell, Oxenbridge and the Burton godly were part of a puritan plot. The Pagets were absent because in 1596 their estate was in Crown hands. The Catholic third Baron had been suspected of participating in the Throckmorton plot with his brother Charles: his lands were confiscated and he fled abroad. His name may have been on the leases, but the manor was no longer his. By 1596 he was dead, but the estate had not yet been restored to his Protestant heir: the fate of the godly party in Burton hung in the balance. An unsympathetic lord of the manor and patron of the rectory could be disastrous, and in the absence of the Pagets they had received support from the Earl of Huntingdon, head of the town's feoffees and a much more congenial patron than the third Baron. But Huntingdon had died in 1595, leaving an unfilled gap. The fourth Baron was at least Protestant, and in 1596 he was – the other reason for his absence – preparing to sail with Essex to fight the Spanish at Cadiz. This was an exploit that earned him part-restoration of his estate two years later. The connection with first Huntingdon then Essex, and Paget's marriage into the Knollys family (to whom both Sir Francis Knollys and Essex's mother Lettice belonged), are precisely the kind of associations that led Heylyn to suggest the puritans were plotting to install a Dudley, Hastings or a Devereux on England's throne. The orchestration of events such as dispossessions and the publication of treatises on God's favouring of the godly was all part of this aim. Here was a story coming from Essex's own back yard. Chartley, his country seat, was just twelve miles away, and one of the visitors to Darling was either the gentleman of his household Anthony Bagot or Anthony's brother Walter. Anthony took part in Essex's rebellion, his sister was married to another of Essex's household, whilst Paget was one the 'frequenters of the Earl of Essex' in Staffordshire who was 'suspected of complicity or at least sympathy with his rebellion'.[13] Had Heylyn known these facts, he would have had a field day with them.

Essex rebelled in February 1601, marching through the city of London with three hundred men who egged on the citizens to join them. Their objective was to see the sheriff, and ask for his assistance against the enemies of the Earl and, by extension, the realm. Essex's supporters had been in ferment for weeks, leading up to a Privy Council hearing on 7 February, which the Earl was supposed to attend to discuss continuing concerns about insubordination, both during his military service and in more recent and widely-rumoured schemes to seize the Tower, city or the court itself. Since the early 1590s, he had been perceived as a threat: portrayed as a champion of godliness, pestering the Queen for money and men to fight Catholicism, making himself unpopular with important people precisely because of his popularity with the godly. The voyage to Cadiz was part of his efforts to commit England to an expansive policy of challenging the Spanish and supporting Protestantism wherever it needed help – in France and Ireland in the 1590s. Unable to accept that the Queen wanted peace and prosperous stability, Essex drifted out of favour and in 1598 had left court after a dramatic showdown with Elizabeth. He tried to redeem himself at war in Ireland, but simply repeated earlier mistakes. When he was hailed as a hero and surrounded by godly preachers showering him with praise – amid military failure, allegations that he had disobeyed orders in returning home and financial disaster – he was a marked man and was soon accused of treason. Desperation pushed him into open conflict with his enemies and he was executed within three weeks of his revolt.

Although it has been shown that Essex was not in fact a particularly forthcoming patron, or even consistently godly in his associations and policy, as the successor of Sir Philip Sidney, the Earl of Huntingdon, and the Earl of Leicester as a figurehead for the godly cause he had an enormous reputation. Essex House buzzed with godly preachers in the years before the rebellion, and the godly throughout the land magnified his name. Even the most innocent actions, which seemed products of both good Protestant thinking and stout loyalty to the Queen, became suspect, with growing anxiety on both sides. In 1599, during his illness after his disobedient return from Ireland, preachers across London were examined about their having prayed for the Earl's recovery, despite their protestations of the conventionality of their good wishes.[14] Thomas Darling's 1596 dispossession was part of the same pattern – innocuous-looking yet able to be read as sinister by someone like Bancroft, who became Bishop of London in 1597, and was soon aware of Darrell's activities. It was Bancroft who had *The most wonderfull and true storie* recalled and who questioned Oxenbridge. The political context of the dispossession must have seemed to him very threatening, and Darrell was to suffer for it even though he was not present at the time.

Darling was dispossessed on 28 May 1596 at the house of his uncle Saunders at Caldwall, with the aid of that favourite text, Rogers's translation of *The*

Enimie of Securitie. Shortly afterwards he was repossessed and re-dispossessed. Under great pressure, he later admitted that he had faked his possession so that 'god should be glorified and his worde the better thought of'. But despite all the subsequent hostile investigation of his possession, and his own admission that he had counterfeited (which he later retracted) he retained his godly convictions, as we shall see. Harsnett, Heylyn and others were in some ways right to see the independent-mindedness of the likes of Thomas Darling and John Darrell as a threat.[15] But there was a tendency to overreact when their beliefs and activities connected so well with national and local political tensions as, with hindsight, they could be seen to do at Burton. This was why *The most wonderfull and true storie* was recalled and why Darrell and Darling later came under great pressure to confess counterfeiting at Burton: because seen in a certain way the dispossession there looked dangerous. The Burton godly were not a revolutionary puritan cell, but their thought did contain inherently libertarian elements, which, as this chapter will argue, can be seen as much in their writings as in their actions. But had Darrell and the godly been treated differently, they might not have developed into the problem that Bancroft was busy creating for himself and the nation.

Trouble at t'Mill: Economic Tensions in Burton

Apart from the desire for godly reform, there were in fact a range of other, more intangible, factors that made it desirable for a boy in Burton to pretend to a possession by Satan. The Anglican historians were not interested in these, but it does not mean that they were not important. *The most wonderfull and true storie* was produced by the group of people who were most affected by them, and not by Darrell or even Arthur Hildersham. These factors were economic. In the 1590s Paget lands at Burton and Stapenhill were being managed by a steward, with intervention by the feoffees, Gresleys, Bagots and Crown officials. Audits and surveys of income and boundaries troubled tenants, whilst investment and the promotion of the town's economic development suffered. On Paget's restoration he petitioned the King to grant Burton another annual fair, protesting that in his absence, trade had been woefully neglected. The implication was that no-one had been minding the shop for Burton's tradespeople. It was not clear in 1596 if or when Paget would be restored, or how he would behave if he were, and the period was thus one of uneasy vacuum. The town's trade, weights and measures regulation, tolls, legal affairs and rents were all tied to the manor, its lord and its court – were businesses and homes really secure in a situation so liable to change? In fact the fourth Baron never lived permanently at Burton, and was not restored to the full possession of his estates until 1603.

In the meantime, the town was awkwardly poised economically, between the manorial past and a self-governing future as a borough.

Burton was not an especially troubled community but it was in the process of decisive economic change. The manorial system creaked as new enterprises grew and traditional practises declined. Since the introduction of hops into English brewing, it had been discovered that Burton's water had properties allowing the brewing of better beer than elsewhere. Its chemical content allowed the absorption of more hops, giving beer more flavour and promoting fermentation. There was already a market for drink in Burton, but this opportunity was irresistible. The godly, like the ungodly, began to brew on a large scale, and to open alehouses and outlets whatever their moral reservations. Many of Darling's supporters brewed in the winter alongside their other trades, and sold ale. Eventually the centre of Burton would be occupied by giant breweries like Bass and Coors, and the late sixteenth-century saw the start of this religiously-problematic bonanza.[16] And as new industry began, traditional trading changed. Just like Mansfield (and Eckington, Driffield, Bolton and Grantham, to name just a few), Burton experienced tensions over milling rights.[17] Must Burton people mill their grain at Burton Mills, or not? Was it lawful for other millers to undercut existing businesses? Toone's milling business was the established one, and he had to fight off the local equivalent of Henry Dorrell to maintain his right to charge the traditional toll. There had been dissent over milling rights in the 1550s and, like other disputes, this resurfaced in the period of drift after Paget's flight.[18] In the early 1590s, therefore, Toone sued John Parleby in order to establish his right to take one sixteenth of the grain that he ground as toll. The interrogatories administered to witnesses in the case asked them to confirm that Toone's rent and charges for maintaining weirs were substantial, that his mills were subject to danger of flood and freezing, that his measures were just, that people from Burton had always ground their corn, malt and grain at the Toone mills, that they could be fined if they went elsewhere, and that the toll had always been one sixteenth. Toone gathered witnesses from as far afield as Coventry, including his father-in-law and his relatives Christopher Toone and Richard Clark, to make his case.[19] Clearly he was anxious to maintain his monopoly and income, in the face of challenges to both from competitors.

Alongside and part of this economic strain was a religious one. Burton's shrine, and the lucrative cult of St Modwen, had been destroyed as part of the government's attack on the abbey in 1538. In some ways this was welcome: immediately the parish had begun keeping extremely detailed registers, suggestive of a godly enthusiasm for chronicling the religious experiences of the laity, and following Thomas Cromwell's instructions. But economically the dissolution was dislocating. The gap it left in Burton life was expressed physically in the church. The Burton laity had used the west end of the abbey church for services and after its dissolution in 1539 they began to take over the building, possessing it completely upon dissolution of the college (which had succeeded the abbey) in 1545. Gradually the chancel fell down, and there were no funds to repair it. It was walled off, leaving the congregation in the truncated nave – an unsatisfactory and symbolic semi-ruin.[20] The extent to which religion and local economic and political conditions were interlaced in Burton can also be seen in the history of the Pagets and their interaction with the godly. After the dissolution, the church's advowson was granted to the Pagets, lay rectors charged with maintaining a curate and preacher. Sir William Paget, the first Baron, was Protestant, and the future looked rosy. But he soon dispensed with the preacher and devoted his salary to the curate. In 1563 the estate fell to his Catholic son Thomas. He occupied the lordship for twenty years, stifling innovation. Only his flight and attainder, so economically problematic, could help the godly, and the Crown's efforts to strengthen Protestantism in Burton went rather too well. By 1585 Peter Eccleshall was the new preacher, and from 1587 the curate, and in 1588 he was indicted at the Quarter Sessions for not using the Book of Common Prayer. He gathered likeminded godly around him. The pamphleteer Philip Stubbes, author of *The Anatomy of Abuses*, came to live in Burton briefly in the early 1590s. He must have found the increasingly godly atmosphere congenial. There was an exercise, part of a string of related meetings in Ashby, Appleby, Packington and Repton.[21] The schoolmaster was godly and apparently insisted on entering his children's baptisms (including the puritanically-named Livewell) in the Parish Register personally. Oliver Rampaine taught Darling, and reinforced in him the godly culture of the small world in which he lived.

It suited this godly world, under interlinked economic, political and religious pressure and filled with a zealous longing for self-assertion, to utter a cry of passionate faithfulness in 1596. It suited Darling personally to assert intense godliness, because it placed him at the centre of his community's concerns, and it suited them to believe him. The loss of Huntingdon, the uncertainty over Paget's future role and convictions, the excitement over Essex, and the building head of steam resulting from the exercises all point to a desire to mark the special status of the Burton godly. It further bolstered their cause to record Darling's experiences and words, and to publish these in print. By laying claim to an extraordinary event, at once a chastisement and a blessing, the godly of Burton were claiming not only that they were favoured religiously, but that in political terms they were God's chosen people too. No matter what the Queen, episcopacy or an incoming lord of the manor might do, God had spoken in Burton, marking its townspeople – and perhaps its aristocracy – as His own. Towards the end of his possession, Thomas Darling's devils were heard to cry out 'wee cannot prevaile, wee cannot prevaile, their Church increaseth'.[22] The community that desperately wanted their church to increase and prevail found in Darling's struggles a sincerely felt affirmation, but also a convenient forum for expressing some of their less optimistic anxieties.

Anglican historians' general argument that the Burton dispossession and the publication of *The most wonderfull and true storie* were part of a movement motivated by national politics is thus only partly correct. The Essex, Walsingham and Knollys connections established here may be one reason why *The most wonderfull and true storie* was the first of Darrell's pamphlets to be pushed forward to publication by friendly (though now invisible) parties, and also the first to be suppressed. Someone conveyed the manuscript to London, talked with Oxenbridge about its publication, and flagged up to him that this dispossession was one of several involving John Darrell which might find a market. But wider cultural factors (economic and locally political to Burton) which did not manifest themselves so obviously in print, also need to be taken into account. The dispossession was something the community themselves, tradespeople and merchants, wished to publicize. However, to argue that high politics influenced them and may have promoted their writing is not to suggest that their (or Darrell's) activities were insincere, revolutionary or devious.

For the authors of *The most wonderfull and true storie*, intangible cultural forces came together, which in retrospect looked threatening to the church authorities but were apparently not intended to be so. The literary form which their self-expression took springs directly from the spirit of kinship and shared enterprise among them. It unites high politics with local factors, in a characteristically godly form. It was not just the godly's supposedly unified and transparent politics of national and church government that enraged Samuel Harsnett when he came to consider their work. It was also the cultural politics of their authorship, which he represented – unsurprisingly – as being just as problematic.

A Community of Authors: Bee, Saunders, Wightman, Denison, Darrell

The book about Darling's possession was written as a collaborative enterprise to an extent that is at first remarkable. It was a family affair, and the text on which the book *The most wonderfull and true storie* (1597) was based was composed entirely by relations of the possessed. Darling's relative by marriage, Jesse Bee, and his uncle Saunders took notes of the boy's fits.[23] Being godly, words were vitally important evidence to these men and much of the action centred on the reading of scripture and noting down its effect. Bee and Saunders also recorded many apparently verbatim exchanges between Darling and his visitors, and Darling and 'devils'. Bee took the lead, but had to go on a month-long trip to London towards the end of the possession, and Saunders took over his work in this period, passing his short notes to Edward Wightman, another of Darling's uncles who was related to the Caldwalls by marriage, to write up. Neither note-taker or Wightman made their involvement known in the book, but Bee appears as one of the main protagonists, since he read the Bible to Darling when required. It is hard to imagine how he could both read and write at the same time as observing fits, and the ever-vigilant Harsnett revelled in destroying the impression of accuracy given in the text that Bee and his relatives produced. Their collaborative authorship is portrayed as misrepresenting, by its very multi-vocality, the events at Burton – a game of Chinese whispers, where shared assumptions combined with poor communication and downright lies in a text that was a patchwork of falsity. It is through Harsnett that we know *The most wonderfull and true storie* was written by committee.

Much of its credibility, however, hung on Jesse Bee as the main 'witness', in both the spiritual and legal senses of the word, and so it was Bee who was Harsnett's first target. In the introduction to *The most wonderfull and true storie*, John Denison, a minister who edited Bee, Saunders and Wightman's notes for the proposed publication, took pains to establish Bee's credentials. Denison said (without naming him) that Bee was

> with the boy almost in all his fits, [and] did both take notes at the present of all that was doone and spoken, and conferred also afterwards with the witnesses of best judgement and credit, that he might be sure of that which hee had set downe.[24]

This latter process was represented as being important, for Bee was not a divine or a well-educated gentleman, but a saddler. Denison did not disguise this, and even foregrounded it, calling Bee a 'man of trade'. Whilst he implied that Bee's consultations had ensured that his account was checked and approved by others, he also established Bee as a plain artisan, with the suggestion that the implied readers might trust such a narrator. Bee was also qualified in that he was 'a private Christian', and therefore a self-selected professor of true religion. Denison's description of Bee suggests that his intended readership was likely to favour the testimony of a man not bound to the establishment or corrupted by holding ecclesiastical office, and a man who grounded his truth-claim not in education or worldly connections, but in a direct experience of God. Naturally, none of this impressed Harsnett or the High Commission – Bee was exactly the kind of man most offensive to them, with strong beliefs that had foundation only in his own religiosity and poorly-educated reasoning.

Harsnett was very careful, however, not to attack openly Bee's social standing or education. He was himself the son of a baker, and his *Discovery* is notable for its avoidance of rhetoric likely to offend readers of low or middling status – the kind of people in Burton and elsewhere to whom his godly opponents were thought to be making a targeted appeal. Although he had decisively rejected his parents' position, and even substantially changed his name, Harsnett did not want to alienate this key readership in his writing against Darrell. So he simply announces Bee's occupation and allows it to speak for itself to the anti-precisian party. Elsewhere, these people were far less restrained, and the godly snapped up and disseminated their snobbish comments as effective propaganda demonstrating the elitism of prelates. 'It is a common thinge now for every pragmatical prentise to have in his head and mouth the government and reformation of the church' said one conformist, whilst Bancroft thought it 'unseemelie' that princes should commit their God-given authority to 'the common sorte ... Mr. Pastor and his ignoraunt neighbours', or that Christ's kingdom might be found where 'riff raff, tag and rag', half a dozen shoemakers, tinkers and tailors gathered with a preacher to 'rule the whole parish'. Matthew Sutcliffe derided 'ignorant merchants, clowns and men of occupation', questioning how those who sold mustard or oatmeal or worked for sixpence a day could govern a church.

The godly, however, were sometimes guilty of the same rhetoric. They were egalitarian only as far as it suited them to be so – although at Darrell's exorcisms at least they seem more genuinely welcoming of the 'common sort' than Christopher Hill suggested when he argued that the godly were, in effect, the *bourgeoisie*. However, there was an established rhetoric against the common godly which was understood by all, even where it was not shared. In attempting to get approval for exercises on the condition that 'the vulgar and secular sort' be excluded, one anonymous puritan agreed that it may have been right to ban prophesyings because:

> the poore vulgar people, whome it was fitter to have bene at the their labours and occupations, leaving their ordinarie parishes, resorted thither ... to heare matters and points of divinitie disputed and decided farre unfit for their capacitie.

The abuse was reversible (as are so many of the binary tropes used in early modern controversy). Whilst often defending the role of 'Tradesmen and artificers' within their own wing of the church, the godly derided their opponents, the 'dumb dogs' or non-preaching ministers, as the poorly-educated leftovers of Catholicism: 'popish priestes, Tailors, whelewrights, Fletchers, servingmen ... coblers, cooks' and so on. Each side, therefore, stereotyped the other as uneducated upstarts and each side recognized the power of such language. Harsnett had no need to deploy it – the word 'saddler' was enough. But if the middling Bee was stereotypically dangerous in this rhetoric of social hierarchy, he and his fellow-authors' collaborative mentality was equally so, in a way that was seen as unique to the godly. *The most wonderfull and true storie* was a kind of written conventicle, and thus detestable.

The fact that the godly operated through networks of friendship, kinship and introductions seems to have been regarded by the anti-precisians as particularly threatening. It did not seem to occur to them that such networks were a common feature of early modern life, and that they themselves corresponded and met in remarkably similar ways. But there was one difference: they could do so openly, whilst the godly networks had been driven completely or partially underground. *Their* sociability thus seemed suspicious. In two extraordinary passages in his unpublished notes on the precisians, Bancroft wrote of them:

> Item though they dwell an hundreth myles asunder, and one never saw the other, yet they knowe of one anothers doinges, and their opinions that they holde … There be no Precisians in England, though by greate distaunce of place they be severed, but they knowe by reportes one another (I have herd the lyke of witches).[25]

That such men congregated and had 'private conferences, for the better agreeinge in their opinions' was bad enough – to be likened to magic and devil-worship, in fact – but that they wrote together was far worse. Accordingly, Harsnett's attack focused on the communication within the team of authors, and their consultation with external editors, one of whom was John Darrell.

First Bee and then others were forced into a grovelling recantation of their part in the production of the offensive text. When Bee was questioned by the High Commission's officers, Harsnett records that he said:

> Darling having many fits in my absence, sometimes I was informed of them by worde of mouth … and sometimes I received some short notes … And when I was present my selfe at his fits, I tooke the notes … which notes (when I came home) I joyned together, as my memory would serve me: alwaies studying rather to write them in better order, then the boy spake them, then in worse: and rather binding my selfe to the sence of the boyes words, then to the wordes themselves, I also confesse, that the boyes speeches were oftentimes delivered so fast one upon another, as I not being able to write the briefe notes of them, one man would tell me one peece, and an other some other peece: which when I came home, I did still joyne together … But I am not sure, that eyther they told mee the truth directly, or that I have therefore written every thing as I shoulde have done …[26]

Bee is shown to have reported hearsay and lies because of his trust of fellow-godly's words and his confidence in his literary abilities. There is more, in the same abject, self-incriminating vein, which caused Heylyn to label Bee 'a Religious sad Lyar'.[27] Did Bee really condemn his own work in such extreme terms? His words as recorded have precisely the flavour that Bancroft's demonological imagery leads us to expect: that of a witchcraft examination. Here, leading questions such as 'Did the Divell never come unto you since you were in prison? speake the truth, as you will answer unto almighty God' could produce the written, although almost certainly not *verbatim*, response 'The Divell never came unto me since I was in prison, nor I thanke God, I have no motion of him in my minde, since I came to prison, neither doe I now feare him at all'.[28] Such answers checked all the boxes required by the examiner: self-incrimination, affirmation of state power, church power, and so on. Bee's words similarly have all the thorough, unambiguous usefulness for Harsnett's purpose that his examiners could have wished.

This was the kind of document routinely produced by the church courts for signature by the unfortunate accused, if he was willing to submit. Here is the document prepared for Arthur Hildersham's signature by the High Commission in 1588:

> I confesse here that I have rashely and undiscreetly taken upon mee the office and function of a preacher … nether beinge admitted into orders, nether licensed by any authoritie, and contrarie to the orders and lawes of this church of England, contrary to the example of all antiquitie in the primitive churche, and contrary to thexample and direction of the apostles … and thereby have given great and juste offence unto manye. And this rashnes I have made more greveous and offensive in that I have uttered in my foresaid sermons and prechinges certaine impertinent and very unfitt speaches for the auditory, as moveinge their mindes rather to discontentment with the state, then tendinge to any godly edification. For which my presumption and undiscreetnes, I am very hartily sorye …[29]

Hildersham sent this document to the collector of the godly's Register of their sufferings, with a note explaining that had refused to assent to it, and was accordingly suspended from his fellowship. He was bound also to appear before the High Commission at Easter if he did not read it out publicly before this date. Bee's words, then, and those of his fellow accused, should not be seen as a straightforward account of his or their methods or activities. His account is one extracted under extreme pressure and written by another, which offers a caricature of godly culture, highlighting all the elements most obnoxious to the questioner. It almost certainly does represent actual godly gatherings in Burton and the shared authorship that came from them. But it is also a selection from the pre-existing identikit features most likely to confirm the stereotype created in the public mind of the lowly and ignorant religious controversialist, meeting with his fellows in secretive conference and then foisting his nonsense on the unsuspecting reader.

Harsnett's secondary targets were Bee's fellow note-takers Saunders and Wightman, but there is no record of their having been questioned. Saunders perhaps escaped by being a substantial man of the wider county, and not as readily accessible as a Burton tradesman. The failure to question Wightman is less explicable, especially in the light of his later unorthodox beliefs (see below). Perhaps, although Wightman figured in Harsnett's text as part of a dangerously unorthodox gathering, in 1596–7 no-one could have imagined the course that his spiritual life would take. Wightman was just a godly uncle of

Darling, a thirty-year-old businessman, with drapery, mercery and the ubiqui-
tous alehouse-keeping among his occupations.[30] He had been married for three
years to Frances Darbye and they had a young family.[31] His wife was noted by
Harsnett to be as godly as he, attending the prayer and fasting and attracting
the attention of her nephew by her piety. In one of his last fits, Darling cried
out in the voice of his devil 'there is a Woman earnest at prayer, get her away'.
A marginal note is handwritten in the Lambeth Palace Library copy of *The most
wonderfull and true storie*, almost certainly made during the High Commission
prosecution, identifying this woman as Frances Wightman.[32] But Harsnett did
not apparently pursue her or her husband beyond identifying and scorning
them.

His real interest, after Bee as the chief note-taker, was in the editorial figures
who reworked the ragbag notes. The next examination was thus of the minister
John Denison who, unsurprisingly, spoke in exactly the same vein as Bee about
his editorial work. He described his practice as reading two or three leaves of
notes, after which

> I did set down the sum of them as my memory wold serve me, leaving out many
> things, and adding somtimes of mine own according to the general sence, as I
> imagined … I did in the contracting of the saide booke, very willingly amplifie
> the boyes commendation … and I did bende my selfe to make many thinges
> appeare more probable then they were in the written coppie.

Denison said that he omitted contradictory matters, and from his answers it
appears that his questioners had before them both his book and the notes of
Bee, Saunders and Wightman, which they compared in an act of searching
literary criticism. They also forced Denison to compare the two:

> by reason that I did so much trust my memory in the contracting of this booke,
> I perceive by comparing it with the written coppie, that I have disordered some
> of the fits, and likewise the circumstance belonging unto them … as also some
> points of the boys supposed speeches to sathan are mistaken by me, and some
> displaced, altering the sence.

Denison was made to confront particular phrases and passages in detail:

> where it was in the written coppie (at large) the boyes torments and afflictions in
> his fits were no doubt meere illusions: I judging those words to crosse the whole
> intent and meaning of the booke, did of purpose leave them out.[33]

His statements make it appear that he was not only misguided and dishonest,
but that he was a poor scholar, bumblingly unable to attain the most basic
standards of accuracy in his composition. Harsnett's glee as he deploys once
again the stereotypical image of the ignorant, schoolboyish, arrogant precisian

controversialist playing far out of his league is palpable. This was what happened when a minister allowed himself to be led astray by godly lay people, and
run into print before he could walk. This was what happened when the godly
gathered to write by committee.

But, of course, John Darrell was the ultimate and most important focus of
Harsnett's attack on *The most wonderfull and true storie*. He had looked over
Denison's final draft, and Harsnett held him responsible therefore for all of
Bee's, Saunders's, Wightman's and Denison's errors and for Denison's composi-
tional technique. Darrell was predictably outraged. Why should a mere reader
be responsible for a book not a word of which was penned by him? He had not
even been present at the dispossession. Responding to Harsnett, he explained
that he had indeed perused the book, but had then returned it to Denison with
a letter, in which

> I did sett downe the summe of that I speake [*sic*] to Darling and his frends,
> desiering that that being the truth might be published, and that the other lines
> which were penned (and now printed) wherein these said untruthes are con-
> tayned, might be left out.

But Denison did not follow Darrell's advice. When Darrell later defended
'the substance' of *The most wonderfull and true storie* to Harsnett as accurate,
Harsnett omitted this qualifying phrase from his account of the book in his
Discovery, forcing upon Darrell an identification with every word of the text.[34]
Yet whilst holding Darrell ultimately responsible – as if he were the sole author,
in fact – Harsnett was also stressing the faulty methodology of the authorial
team. His questioning of them and writing-up of their confessions mercilessly
delineates their inaccurate communication, their mutually-reinforced delusion
and their lack of accountability as co-authors. Harsnett was particularly adept
at combining contrary positions and attacking an opponent from both, having his cake and eating it. He could state that the book had been produced by
conspiratorial brethren, *and* that Darrell alone should accept culpability for its
errors.

Harsnett was not entirely wrong in suspecting that something other than
ale was brewing at Burton in 1596, however. Edward Wightman increasingly
professed anabaptist and anti-trinitarian views and, most disturbingly, by 1611
was claiming to be a new messiah. His fellow godly, as Ian Atherton and David
Como's recent article shows, tried privately to reclaim Wightman, but could
not. He began to write treatises, and accost people in order to read extracts
to them and in 1611, fatally, he presented a petition to the King. His bishop
Richard Neile, and Neile's chaplain William Laud (who could not have been
more likely to inflame Wightman) also attempted to confer with him, but after
some inconclusive hearings at the High Commission, Wightman was sent to
Lichfield for trial in the consistory court on charges of heresy. He was con-

victed. On 9 March 1611/12, he was taken to a stake in Lichfield's Market Place to be burned, and the fire was lit. According to witnesses he cracked, crying that he would recant, and the crowd rescued him. But Wightman found himself unable to conform. When he was brought to the court to repent of his former views, he refused and 'blasphemed more audaciously than before'. So he was once again taken to the Market Place. This time he did not recant, and the fire consumed him. He died just before Easter, 1612, the last person to be burned for heresy in England.[35] The shadow of this potential is precisely what lies across Harsnett's attack on the co-authors of *The most wonderfull and true storie*.

But although there was some foundation for his fears, and those of Bancroft and Whitgift, the process of confrontation initiated by the ecclesaistical authorities hardened both sides into stereotype as they struggled to define their differences and score points. The godly were pushed down the path of asserting freedom of conscience at all costs, whilst their opponents found themselves cast in the role of tyrants. Rhetorics were appropriated and reappropriated, and as part of this process two opposed constructions of the purpose and act of writing and publication can be seen in development. They reflected the different cultural worlds of those involved. These competing poetics were to define future writings in the Darrell affair.

The Word, Truth and Sociable Authorship

On one side stood the enforcers of conformity, here led by Samuel Harsnett. Harsnett's great strength as a writer lay in his close reading of texts and ability to critique them to maximum effect. In modern terms, he occupies the position of literary critic: autocratic, individual and judgmental. His brutal deconstruction of the assumptions of authors was a skill honed in his role as censor, picking over the texts of items submitted to the Company of Stationers for approval, together with a team of fellow chaplains and eminent churchmen. Ironically, whilst he was busy with the Darrell affair in late 1598 and early 1599, he slipped up badly in passing for publication John Hayward's book *The First Part of the Life and Raigne of King Henrie IIII*. It was dedicated to Essex and dealt with Henry IV's deposition of his predecessor Richard II – widely read at the time as a precedent for Essex should he wish to dethrone Elizabeth. He might have learnt from this experience how easy it was to look subversive even if one was utterly innocent. Nevertheless, he was usually extremely clear about the importance of close reading and the responsibility of an author for his (occasionally her) text. In his professional view at least, writing had a usefully unproblematic relationship with its author: to deconstruct one was to reveal, and if necessary destroy, the other. And the godly's literalist insistence on every detail of a text led them to share – indeed, intensify – these professional assumptions and so play at least part of Harsnett's game for him. Like many differences between the godly and the proto-Anglican, the obsession with language was a matter of differing intensity rather than differing views. The godly's version of 'Protestant biblicism' was based on 'integrating the most arcane linguistic and grammatical skills into a vision of true religion'.[36] It was a highly trained and astonishingly nit-picking response, and it presupposed that texts did not just reveal their authors but were part of a religious experience in their own right. More than any other grouping, for the godly the word *was* God, and their own words should strive for the same irreproachable purity. So Harsnett was right when he thought that deconstructing their texts would be an attack on the cultural heart of godliness.

But Harsnett's practice (especially in the *Discovery*) teases out his position further. On the one hand, the words of texts under examination must be read with scrupulous care, for through the word one can straightforwardly access the author and his meaning, even if hidden within the words. But words are also deeply corrupted tokens that may be bent and twisted, deployed as decoys in the service of a higher truth than their immediately apparent referent: the need to preserve order. There is nothing sacred or transparently truthful about the way they are used in the *Discovery*, for example. The cynicism of Harsnett's reading and writing does therefore, in a twisted conflation of art and artifice, reflect his proto-Arminian views. For Harsnett, the truth of religion lay in image as well as word, and in ceremony, action and emotion as much as in text. He preached against the narrowness of Calvinism, and as soon as he arrived as Bishop of Norwich he put down anomalous occasions for preaching, and erected crucifixes and a high altar in his church. As F. W. Brownlow insightfully notes, he had 'a conviction of the mystery of things' and 'makes a virtue of the intellectual simplicity that will not juggle with texts ... "God is love" is all he really has to say'.[37] Privately, then, Harsnett's faith was a mystical entity, visible but almost silent and so shielded from the kind of scrutiny to which he mockingly subjected the Bible-bashing puritans. Their text-fetishizing culture was convenient for him, allowing him to fight on their territory: he could tear apart their books so easily and cheerfully in part because he did not believe that text was, or should be, aesthetically or spiritually central to religious experience. Peter Lake notes that Bancroft, Harsnett's mentor, 'almost entirely expunged the language of spiritual enthusiasm or active piety from his vocabulary' because after baptism and communion there was little need to be interested in doctrine.[38] Harsnett shared Bancroft's style and assumptions that there was nothing inherently sacral about text. So whilst he is the close reader *par excellence* when it comes to the godly, his own works suggest a cavalier and opportunistic habit of writing. What was practically useful would be written, rather than what the author believed to be spiritually true. What mattered was the deeper, already-established truth of authority, which might have only a distant relationship with actual *adiaphoric* words.

For Harsnett's opponents, authorship was very different. It was a passionately committed and rather experimental activity centred on the embodiment of truth in text, and nothing about it could be a thing indifferent. There was an element of anxiety about committing spiritual experiences to print, as Alexandra Walsham points out.[39] Just as the scriptures offered direct revelation of God's intention and being, so ought godly texts to represent transparently godly truths, and writing must be done properly if it was to come close to the central godly experience of hearing the word preached. Bee, Saunders and Wightman took notes because they wanted to record every last detail of that truth, right on the spot – an intention that Harsnett's concentration on their delays, miscommunications and errors designedly obscures. Such godly writing involved a sharing of utterance – not inevitably, but often – which mirrored the relations between those involved. In the case of the Burton godly, their ties were those of business, family and church: and in the same way that they gossiped about each others' children and took out shared leases, they collaborated in the enterprise of writing. Their image of authorship in *The most wonderfull and true storie* was not that of a single authoritative man in a study – a man in ecclesiastical office like Harsnett, for instance – but a sharing of witness and theological dialogue in which individual voices became part of a multi-vocal experience, just like a prophesying or exercise. The seamless transition from oral to written involved in turning a collaborative fast exercise into a co-authored pamphlet may have helped to overcome the reluctance that the godly traditionally felt about replacing the experience of actual gatherings and the hearing of sermons with a printed equivalent. Their truth about the dispossession at Burton was a shared truth hammered out in exegetical discussion, and it might justifiably and profitably be embodied in a co-authored text.

Tom Webster has characterized godly culture as particularly 'sociable', adding that exorcisms provided an additional stimulus to combination and conference among self-identifying godly.[40] The evidence presented here suggests that their writing about such events was often also sociable. Writing and record-keeping was a key godly response to repression, and it was done communally: Field's Register collections, the compilation of godly martryrologies and biographies in such works as the *Acts and Monuments* and Clarke's *Lives*, to which many godly contributed, and such shared works as the *Admonition* demonstrate this clearly. *The most wonderfull and true storie* and the works that followed it in describing Darrell's activities and defending them are generically similar. Of course, godly ministers and laity could and did write highly idiosyncratic treatises in the traditional monograph mode. George Gifford's work on witches, and – to take an example related to Burton – Philip Stubbes's *Anatomy of Abuses* appear to be such works.[41] This was relatively easy if one was in the position of most theological writers: men with 'several years' schooling and … a spell at university, followed by a teaching post … or an assistantship or curacy, and then a full-time living or salaried preaching post'.[42] But for those not in positions of self-validating authority, by background or office, or those unsure about the justification for their authorship, sharing the burden and risk of writing and publication was a natural step. It was also a choice that authors might make under pressure and bring to pass in a variety of ways: Darrell and More, each in a separate prison, seem to have collaborated in some way to offer a reworking of the words of a third author many miles away, John Dickons. The author of *A Brief Apologie*, one of the first accounts of Darrell's exorcisms, published an edited version of Darrell's own work (which would eventually be published as *An Apologie or Defence*) without his knowledge whilst he was imprisoned, with the intention of helping his cause.

We need not look far for other examples of sociable godly authorship. *The Triall of Maist. Dorrell* (1599), published during Darrell's trial at the High Commission, was written in a remarkably complex fashion, according to one of its co-authors. An internal editor, probably the unknown 'A. Ri.', told readers that its text had been written by someone who had collected materials in Darrell's defence, maybe the author or editor of *A Breife Narration*, 'G. Co.', or his collaborator. But this person had been reticent about publishing his own work, and it appeared that he had involved others in his decision to keep quiet.

> Because sundry supposed these Collections might be offensive to the Lord Chief Justice of England and the Prelates: the Author (though after diligent paines therein taken) would not publish them. They comming to my hand by occasion, I thought it great injurie to suppresse them, and so the godly to be deprived of that benefit which no doubt may come by them.[43]

The 'Editor' had decided not only to publish the 'Author's' attack on the injustice of Darrell's trial, but to add a narrative of a witchcraft case in Sussex. Here the Lord Chief Justice, Sir John Popham, had presided over the conviction and sentencing of a woman for, the editor said, causing in her victim symptoms very like those that Darrell's patients had exhibited. It was not clear whether the editor himself, or the original author, had attended this Assize, or if they had been sent the report by someone else. But the editor did claim to have been present at Lambeth at the High Commission hearing of Darrell's case on Whitsun Eve (26 May 1599). Here he had seen Popham looking troubled over Darrell's treatment, and his purpose in publishing *The Triall of Maist. Dorrell* with the account of the Sussex case was to demonstrate to Popham the inconsistency of his behaviour in cases involving the supernatural, and awaken his conscience so that he might give Darrell a fair hearing. He also wanted to answer the book that he had heard was being written by Richard Bancroft against Darrell – which would reach the press as Samuel Harsnett's *Discovery*, licensed 15 November 1599 – and he dated his editorial 3 September 1599.[44]

Both the author and editor of *The Triall of Maist. Dorrell* seem to have moved in the same circles: London godly life, meetings of Cambridge alumni, and events of interest to the legal and clerical professions. The author also gave an account of Darrell and More's Whitsun Eve hearing, which suggested that not only the editor but the author too had attended it. The author did not know personally the events in Nottingham, describing only what he had heard from others, so he was probably someone who became involved in the case only when Darrell reached London under arrest.[45] During his account of the Whitsun Eve hearing, the author also referred to the Cambridge graduation ceremony that he had subsequently attended. Here, the Archbishop of Canterbury's chaplain William Barlowe had received his doctorate, and in his oration had attacked Darrell. The author also knew gossip from Oxford about Dr Thomas Crompton, who was another adversary of Darrell at the High Commission, and he had some knowledge of what Darrell had said or was going to print in his own defence – the claim, for instance, that when William Sommers was arrested, Darrell had been away visiting his family in Ashby de la Zouch.[46] He also knew details of the behind-the-scenes manoeuvrings at the trial, describing how the registrar of the court had wanted to give Joan Darrell copies of her husband's answers, but Bancroft had forbidden him to do so, and how Thomas Darling had tested William Sommers's assertion that he had visited Burton to see Darling's fits.[47] The author cited Magna Carta and many statutes in Darrell's defence, making it likely that he was a common lawyer of the kind often helpful to puritans in trouble with the ecclesiastical courts.[48]

At the end of *The Triall of Maist. Dorrell* the editor, now calling himself A. Ri., resurfaces. He explains that the promised report of the Suffolk trial was for some reason not sent to the printers with the main body of the author's text. Apparently neither had, therefore, yet been published – the perils of illegal authorship. Time had run on, and Harsnett's *Discovery* had been finished and published, requiring yet more defences on Darrell's behalf. Now A. Ri. also referred to the Cambridge graduation address of Dr Barlowe, discussing its detail and political motivation, and mentioned the recent publication of Abraham Hartwell's account of a fraudulent French demoniac.[49] Hartwell was Whitgift's chaplain, and his book was politically motivated, as A. Ri. knew. He also seemed to know that a more substantial defence of Darrell, probably Darrell's own *Detection*, was being prepared, and he referred the reader to it. Finally, he described his attendance at a jail delivery in London (the metropolitan equivalent of an Assize trial), eight days before writing, where he had seen the case of the accused witch Anne Kerke, tried for afflicting a girl with possession-like symptoms. Richard Bancroft had also been there, and had suggested that the symptoms might be faked – after which, to confirm A. Ri.'s opinion of

him as scandalously ungodly, he had argued for the freeing of an atheist on trial
for his beliefs. A. Ri. had written or obtained a report of the allegations against
Anne Kerke, and he appended this to the *Triall*, which was finally published in
this extremely complex multivocal form.[50]

The process of multiple authorship described here echoes the composition
of *The most wonderfull and true storie* two years before, this time backed by the
collective resources of the London godly. Beyond the author and A. Ri. are
also a further range of contributors, for the author describes how he brought
together his arguments from

> printed bookes, written reportes of sundry faithfull and discret brethren present
> at the pleading on Whitsuneve, and out of certaine Apologeticall answers of
> M[aster] Dorrell himselfe and other.[51]

The creation and deployment of archival materials in support of the godly
cause, elevated to the status of an art form by John Field, was a practice which
Darrell and his Midland supporters, and then the London godly who came
to his defence, followed (literally) religiously. There was an element of self-
consciousness about their co-operative writing, and the processes of conference behind it, as can be seen again in their later organization of testimonials
to the events they described. There was greater safety and conviction in num-
bers, and forty heads were better than one. And as we shall see in Chapter 5,
one of Darrell's attacks on his post-Harsnett opponents Deacon and Walker
focused on the implausibility of *their* claims about joint authorship. The detail
in which they describe this process is indeed suspicious: but they give so much
detail because it is part of their claim to be godly that they have engaged in
earnest ministerial conference about their subject, which is reflected in their
text. Asserting a godly identity meant, for Deacon and Walker, also claiming to
use godly methodology, and even to write in a genre that echoed the favourite
articulations of godly culture – like A. Ri., Jesse Bee, Edward Wightman and
others before them.

Puritans, Plotting and Printing

To Peter Heylyn, writing against godliness in the 1660s, the story of the Boy
of Burton would have slotted naturally into the international presbyterian
plot that he described. For Heylyn, the godly were revolutionaries: the Earl
of Leicester was behind it all and his choices to replace Queen Elizabeth were
firstly the Earl of Huntingdon (his brother-in-law), and secondly Paget's friend
the Earl of Essex (his stepson). As we have seen and shall see, Darrell's career
intersects noticeably with those of Heylyn's usual suspects. Surely, said Heylyn,
under the protection of over-mighty godly of this kind, Darrell had watched

with interest the campaigns of Cartwright, Field and Marprelate, 'powerful Practises … then on foot in favour of the Presbyterian Discipline'. When these had failed, he took up the 'Project' that he had laid by 'till all others failed him': exorcisms and publication of their results. Was Darrell, then, promoting the puritan cause in strategic locations and at crucial times through a shared programme of subversive writing? Heylyn thought that by the end of 1597 he had achieved his aims: 'growing famous' and then catching the most obvious 'Fish for which he angled', a lectureship at Nottingham.[52]

With its new evidence about the Burton godly and their connections with Huntingdon, Paget and Essex, this book might thus choose to expand on his theory. Was it a coincidence that the Dudleys and their kin were lurking in the background at Ashby and Burton – craving the throne, as Heylyn thought? Was it innocently explicable that *The most wonderfull and true storie* was said to have been 'seen and Allowed by Hildersham (one of the principal sticklers in the Cause of Presbytery)'? Was all this not part of a revival of the Arian heresy with its 'Oppositions to Monarchical and Episcopal Government'? Wightman's life and writings offer a striking confirmation of Heylyn's associaton of the godly with revolutionary unorthodoxy – he was specifically charged with Arianism. And Atherton and Como's work on Wightman has already anticipated one of my conclusions: that his emergence from the world of the middling and moderate godly into heretical notoriety shows how truly 'corrosive to established order' godliness *could* be in its assumptions about the liberty of individual spirituality. I am certainly not arguing that Darrell was part of an overt and self-identifying godly plot, led by the three earls: there is no evidence of this at all. But, as this chapter has suggested, there are some important synergies between the little group of Midlands godly and the wider national picture, between godly sociability and writing and the rhetoric of revolutionary plots, especially if one looks at them from the position of Bancroft and Harsnett.

Yet Heylyn's conspiracy theory is just that: he attributes far too much forethought and cohesion to the supposed masterplan, and Bancroft and Harsnett did too. Like other Anglican historians since, they conflated puritan and presbyterian in a way that was intended to damage the godly party of their own generations, and in Heylyn's case to demonstrate English progress away from enthusiastic fanaticism in religion. The dissenting minister Daniel Neal, defending the godly against this onslaught in 1732, said that reading Strype and Heylyn, 'one would think here was a Plot of some cunning designing Men, to conjure the People into the Belief of the Discipline'. Interestingly, he chose a term associated with exorcism – conjuration – to sum up the laughable nature of the idea that the godly were revolutionary in their endeavours. He did not believe there was a puritan plot or that Darrell and his associates were involved in the attempt to create one.[53] When they wrote and published books, it was for the godly edification of others and not because they favoured anarchy and rebellion *per se*. Neal's construction of the godly is both a conservative one (as decent and orderly subjects, reformers of manners and morals) and a radical one (desiring further reformation). We can now imagine with Neal that the godly wanted both piety and political power and believed that the two were mutually and respectably attainable, without charges of hypocrisy or sedition having to be levelled against them.

Godliness held in tension the forces of conservatism and radicalism. When a Darrell or a Wightman emerged from the essentially respectably godly mainstream and was identified by the authorities as a dangerous revolutionary, it was certainly not an accident. Neal's defence of the godly is not one of stolid orthodoxy or indifference to politics. They expected their publications to go out into a world where they might win powerful political backing, and might be regarded as sedition. When 'the Earl of Essex his business [rebellion] was ... on foot', William Bradshaw knew that the only way to avoid trouble over his simultaneous distribution of Darrell's pamphlets was to go and stay hidden with friends. He wrote that he knew the books might very well be read as being 'against the State'. But *he* did not think that they were. He was not interested in subverting the government, but at the same time and for some of the same reasons as Essex, he was interested in changing the public mind.[54] The same can be said of Darrell and his group generally. And reform began at home, in a bedroom in Burton or a study in Ashby. The concerns of the godly were often local and individual – introverted matters of their own conscience, attempts to purify their own town, or turn to godliness a local magnate. It was only when these local politics threatened to mesh with national politics that suspicious attention was attracted to their actions and writings. As Patrick Collinson wrote, 'godly magistracy and ministry were naturally conservative forces, somewhat unnaturally and fortuitously converted into a force for revolutionary change'.[55] But the conversion occurred first in the minds of the non-godly.

At a national level it is therefore rather surprising that *The most wonderfull and true storie* was received and licensed as an uncontroversial text. The dispossession of the Boy of Burton and *The most wonderfull and true storie* did share certain motifs and trajectories with Essex and his rebellious friends. But when it was authorized for publication Essex was not giving nearly as much cause for concern as he would do within a few months. Neither was Bancroft yet Bishop of London, and sharply on the look out for any text that might represent godly agitation emerging into the open. Once Bancroft looked at *The most wonderfull and true storie*, it is a fair bet that he saw all the classic godly failings that the case of the Boy of Burton shared with the Earl: an inability to submit, to shut up and conform. Seen this way, Darrell's emergence into print in the important godly town of Burton and his relocation to the bigger and strategically vital county-town of Nottingham did form a pattern. *The most wonderfull and true storie*, which had appeared so innocent, was the first pin in the map – the first public announcement of godly mustering. No wonder, then, it was soon recalled, as part of concerns over Darrell's continuing activities.

But something that has not been explored before is how this concern came as much from the civil and ecclesiastical authorities at Nottingham as from Bancroft and his allies. They saw the same synergies as did the Bishop of London, and they saw them additionally in the form of a popular revolt. The texts produced at Nottingham and in the period of Darrell's trial and imprisonment are therefore the key to understanding how he and his works were propelled to national attention. Not only is Essex important, but so are the glovers, bakers and aldermen of Nottingham. Had events there developed differently, notice might never have been taken of *The most wonderfull and true storie* and the Darrell group's other publishing plans – and his own works would never have appeared. As we can see, he seems to have had no desire to publish anything before he found himself under attack in Nottingham and then 'traduced' in print, as Clarke put it.[56] He has been regarded as a man of boundless publishing and political ambition but John Darrell the author was, paradoxically, a creation of his enemies. His writing was a defensive response, furthered by others, and even after four dispossessions in Mansfield, Whittington, Burton and Cleworth he still had nothing to say in print himself. Events in Nottingham in late 1597, and the cultural warfare which they reflected and intensified, turned Darrell into a pamphleteer, and they began the pamphlet war that lasted until 1603. The activities of the Essex faction and the arrival of Bancroft in the London see must have been important in starting that war, but once again, an exploration of the politics and culture at the location of a dispossession is vital to an understanding of the case.

3 'SINNFUL, SHAMFULL, LYING AND RIDICULOUS': THE POSSESSION OF WILLIAM SOMMERS

Nottingham (heretofore not so forward) became for a time very zealous (as I heare) in hearing the worde

The Triall of Maist. Dorrell (1599), A3v.

It may seem a facile pun, but the demonic possession of William Sommers was partly a battle for the physical and spiritual possession of the town of Nottingham itself: its corporate body and ecclesiastical soul. Darrell, his friends' dispossession and their joint account of it had found a warm welcome in Burton, where the godly were at home with such ideas and dominated town politics. But Nottingham was different: a much larger and more conservative town ripe for conflict between godliness and established authority. It was just the kind of town Richard Bancroft had had in mind when he spoke of places where the godly might dangerously gain influence, to the detriment of the national church and national peace. From the Pilgrimage of Grace to the Civil War, Nottingham was of vital religious and strategic importance: David Marcombe calls it a 'front-line base'. The author known only as the 'Narrator', who published the first account of the Nottingham dispossession, celebrated the fact that 'God hath lighted a candle, not in a corner, but hath advanced it as it were on a candlestick in the heart, or center of our land'. And there was a further, textual, level of meaning of 'possession', in that what was being contested during and after the dispossession at Nottingham was the possession of the meaning of events surrounding Sommers – the control of the narrative (both verbal and then in print) and its interpretation, which now came to be highly controversial as the events surrounding Thomas Darling were not. Nottingham's civic divisions, mirroring those between the godly and the ecclesiastical authorities so effectively, contributed a decisive intensity to a battle over cultural ownership which Darrell's reading of dispossession and its embodiments in text could not be allowed to survive.

'Owar Towne': The Corporation and its Critics

In 1597 Nottingham was a town waiting for a symbolic confrontation. In fact, it got two – one worldly, one spiritual. The first occasion for conflict was the expiry of a lease, that which granted the right to the tithe of hay in the fields around the town. The tithe had been the property of Lenton Priory before the Dissolution and the rent paid for its cutting and sale now went to the Free Grammar School, founded in 1513. Cut from 1,265 acres, the tithe hay was worth a large sum.[1] The lease was part of the School Estate, which was managed by the Mayor and Corporation of Nottingham. They yearly chose two schoolwardens to administer it. A major part of their work was the granting of such leases, and their stated aim was to maximize yield from these for the school. However, some among the 'common burgesses' – those not part of the inner circle of the Council and aldermen – suspected that another use was being made of the schoolwardens' power. Their suspicions extended also to the other town properties, the Bridge and Chamber Estates. The Bridge Estate – property given to the town to help pay for the upkeep of the Trent bridge – was involved in the issue of the tithe hay, as some of its revenues were shared with the School Estate. From the burgesses' suspicions came the first confrontation.

It is possible to see in the estates' rentals why some of the townspeople were unhappy. The tithe hay had been leased to Edward Jowett, a councillor perceived as an insider with the Mayor and aldermen. Jowett had served the Corporation as Chamberlain of the Chamber Estate and Under-Sheriff of the town in the early 1590s. He was thus one of 'the Clothing', former sheriffs entitled to wear a robe, take part in decision-making and process with the Mayor on public occasions. And in 1598, he was to become one of the schoolwardens, with Thomas Wallis, the brother-in-law of John Darrell.[2] Like many other members of the Corporation circle, Jowett leased land from the Corporation estates. What some of the common burgesses suspected was that these lands were being leased out at less than their proper value, to oblige cronies of the Mayor and aldermen – and indeed often to allow them to profit directly from the town's assets themselves. They wanted to know who would take up Jowett's recently-expired lease, believing that it would be one of the town's oligarchs, and they were right.

Who were these men – who appear so frequently in the pages of the pro- and anti-Darrell pamphlets – and were they justly accused of cheating the town? Nottingham was a county in its own right, by Charter of Henry VI, and its government consisted of seven aldermen, one of whom was chosen annually to be Mayor. The Mayor in 1597–8, Peter Clark, was an elderly man in his final mayoralty of three. He was a barber, had held town offices since the 1550s, and he was to die in 1601. As events in the Darrell case and the tithe hay revolt were to prove, Clark was no longer a commanding leader, but a man swept along by popular feeling, trying to please the unruly factions in his town. Of the six other aldermen in 1597 one was Humphrey Bonner, Darrell's host in Nottingham for much of his time there. He lived on High Pavement, next to the huge St Mary's Church.[3] It was the best address in Nottingham, where people like Sir John Byron, the Stanhopes and Lady Zouche lived when in town, and St Mary's was the Corporation Church, to which the Corporation, Clothing and other dignitaries processed annually and in whose vestry the new Mayor was chosen every August. Assize sermons were preached there and archiepiscopal visitations held. Bonner was at the heart of the town establishment, and a cut above some of his fellows. In the assessments for the subsidy of September 1598, Bonner stood alone of the aldermen in the highest 'tax bracket'.

The other aldermen were also wealthy, however. Robert Alvey, a former Mayor and barber also from St Mary's parish, rented an expensive property in Chapel Bar or the Long Row, the streets fronting the Saturday Market.[4] Richard Morey or Morehage lived on High Pavement near Bonner. He too had been Mayor and was an older man. Morey was a glover, one of Nottingham's most powerful interest groups. Richard Hurte, mercer, was a former Mayor, active in town offices since the early 1580s. He came, however, from St Peter's parish, the mercantile centre of the town. Clark was also a St Peter's man, as were the rest of the aldermen. William Freeman, a draper, was less experienced than most of the others. He had not begun serving in town offices until the late 1580s, and had fewer holdings from the town's property than some of his brethren. The final alderman was Anchor Jackson, a mercer, who was also younger than Clark, Morey and Alvey, but had been holding town offices since the early 1580s. He was omnipresent in the financial transactions of the town by the 1590s.[5] These men's complete dominance of town offices can be seen in their ability to play pass-the-parcel with the office of Mayor. Hurte was Mayor in 1595, 1602 and 1609; Morey in 1596, 1603 and 1610; Jackson in 1598, 1605, 1612 and 1619; Freeman in 1599, 1606 and 1613. Clearly the mayoral elections were based on the notion of 'Buggins' turn'.

The financial and spatial dominance of the aldermen is also clear: and it was their ability to accumulate leases of valuable town properties, taken out in their private capacity from themselves in their public capacity, that raised questions about their probity. From the Chamber Estate in 1598, Clark leased a garden in Bugholes, a holm at Leenside, a building on the town's ground in Back Lane and a barn elsewhere. Morey leased two limepits, and property at Hollowstone and Eastcroft, in the southern meadows. Freeman leased property in the outlying East Steynor and Westcroft, Bonner a tenement and land at Westcroft. Bonner was also charged rent for fencing standing in the street. Hurte was charged for easement of water (the right to take water over or from the Corporation's land), and property in the Eastcroft, and Jackson for the Westcroft. Freeman also rented a draper's stall in the market. From the Bridge Estate Clark leased another garden, on which had been built a house, some assorted 'landes', and a close in St John's near the Bridewell. Hurte leased a close in Porter Bar, land near the 'todeholes' and a barn. Morey rented a barn in Barkergate and land at Goldswong, Freeman land at St Michael's Close, in the Clay Field to the north and near the sheepcote. Jackson rented land near the dovecote and windmill (Derrymount), to the west, and Bonner land at the Sandfield. The complete rental for the School Estate is lost, but Jackson leased part of the Free School Close in 1596. Others renting lands from the estates included the well-connected, like Edward Jowett and the surgeon William Langford, and wealthy men like Thomas Wallis. Wallis leased land near the Hethbeth (Trent) bridge, a close called No Man's Part bordered by the River Leen, the Chainy Bridges and the Nottingham–London road, land in the Pool Yard and at Eastcroft.[6] These holdings amounted to a huge slice of the town's assets.

It is no surprise, then, that others trying to rent prime sites with secure income or opportunities for development were angry about leases like that of the tithe hay. One of the most revealing transactions is between the Mayor and burgesses and the partnership of Alderman Hurte and Lewis Oxley, tallow-chandler. In 1606, Hurte and Oxley took a lease on a parcel of land fifty-five yards by seventeen, for an initial rent of one penny for the first year, and there-after six pounds, thirteen shillings and four pence annually. The land was on Timber Hill, the south side of the Saturday Market, now Nottingham's Old Market Place. It was the section of the market where timber was sold, but Hurte and Oxley were to build sheep pens there. Not only was this some of Nottingham's most valuable land; the lease also bound the Mayor and burgesses not to allow anyone else to erect sheep pens in any other part of the town, on wasteground, streets or in the market places. These pens, and these alone, the lease continues, will be the common and usual sheep market. Finally, Hurte and Oxley were told that they could have as much extra land as they needed on Timber Hill, for more pens, the only proviso being that these were not sited so as to hinder the market from trading, or block the pavements.[7] It seems, then, that there might justifiably be complaint about the amount of town ground leased to the aldermen and their associates, and also their attempt to create situations of dominance and monopoly where profit might be made.

And complaint there was, of a kind that would be damagingly echoed by John Darrell and his party. In 1588, for example, the Mickletorn Jury had presented Jackson for building a shop or stall on the town's ground, arguing that he was morally and legally obliged to pay rent for it. The Mickletorn Jury was an anachronism: the jury of the old manorial court, which was supposed to perambulate the town (in a great or mickle turn) noting public nuisances. It made presentments to the Mayor twice yearly, and several aldermen sat with him to hear these. A typical presentment was that 'the Rowill [runnel] at Mr Wallis dore wants railings', or a request for the removal of a 'noyfull' midden by St Mary's Church wall. But the Jury had extended its remit, and often the presentment would be more pointed: 'we present Mr Alderman Clarke for settinge his bancke and hedge uppon the heyway [highway]' (a presentment which was both rejected and crossed out by its hearers, as was another at the same Sessions – Nottingham held its own Quarter Sessions). Other presentments attacked the aldermen for lewd behaviour, missing official occasions, failing to inspect their wards and failing to act after repeated presentments. In 1593, Clark was accused of converting his barns into houses and renting them to people who were 'a gret decaye' to the town. He was also building 'a sort of pawltre howses wyche hathe downe gret hurt to owar towne'. In essence, the Jury thought Clark was encroaching on town land with his private property, raising the value of his lands by jerry-building and renting out his speculative developments to undesirables. Quite often, this meant 'foreigners' – those who were not burgesses from Nottingham, whose trade allegedly undercut burgesses' businesses. Jackson was presented for the same kind of property development by the same complainants.

This was troublesome enough, but because of these economic grievances the Mickletorn Jury also concerned itself with the inclusiveness of town governance. The phrase 'owar towne' is a suggestive one. The issue of whose town Nottingham was to be was an ongoing battle and contributed decisively to the downfall of John Darrell. In the Middle Ages, all the town's burgesses had had a right to full involvement in decisions, at meetings of Common Hall. Gradually, from the mid-fifteenth century, this right to 'call a hall' had been eroded. Instead, the aldermen and a small Common Council chosen from the body of burgesses began taking decisions in private. They consulted the Clothing, but no-one else. In particular, the 'Gild Merchants', general meetings of the burgesses held to settle questions such as the granting of leases, declined. The aldermen and councillors formed a self-perpetuating oligarchy, with aldermen elected from the ranks of councillors, and councillors elected from the Clothing. A split therefore opened up between the common burgesses and those burgesses who were councillors or aldermen. Burgesses who were members of the Clothing, and also had some influence on the Council, had to take sides, and were often perceived as having sided against the 'commonalty'. Matters such as building on town ground, and renting to 'foreigners' began in such circumstances to be seen as an attack by the town's oligarchs on their disenfranchised commonalty. The common burgesses began to demand more rights.

In 1512 the Recorder advised the Mayor and aldermen that any claim by the commonalty to elect the aldermen and town officers should be resisted as 'contrare to alle good and politike order and rule'. The oligarchy had decided to fight for its privileges, believing that any return to an older form of government would lead to anarchy and 'ye distruccion of the towne'. So began three centuries of strife over Nottingham's government, ended only by the Municipal Corporations Act of 1835. In 1577, the common burgesses had campaigned for and achieved a reorganization of the Council. This had consisted previously of the Mayor and the six other aldermen, with six common councillors. It was easy to suspect a built-in majority. So in 1577 the Common Council members were increased from six to twelve. But by 1579, it was obvious that this latest reinvention had not enfranchised the wider community. The Mickletorn Jury bluntly demanded a further reorganization, 'to confer in aney matters for the towne, as there is in othar place wher ther corporations are bettar govarned then this is'.[8] This was still the situation when Darrell arrived in 1597: commonalty pitted against oligarchy.

The Tithe Hay Revolt

In Lent of that year, during Morey's mayoralty, came the issue of the tithe hay. It is known only from examinations of those involved, who were led by the glover Percival Millington and his associate William Cooke, and a lease and minute in the Mayor's Book recording the resolution of the affair. But what does remain is dramatic. There was a revolt against the modern structures of town governance, in which the common burgesses revived their right of Common Hall, assembling without authority to debate town business. They held a protest meeting in the Spice Chambers, under the Town Hall. The burgesses were dangerously accompanied by constables from the aldermen's wards, and the constables were asked to summon any other burgesses that they could, to meet them the next day at the Hall. When examined, the constable Edward Garland said that he had gone through Bonner's ward summoning burgesses 'to gyve there voyces about the townes leases'. The revolutionary mood can be judged from Garland's statement that he would willingly die for the cause. Hugh Swift and William James, constables in Freeman's ward, had both attended the meeting and summoned others. Swift said that the cause was:

> to take order with Maister Maior about the Tythe Haye that the tenantes thereof might have their owne and that the rest might be to the benefytt of the towne and that the Burgesses might have the sayd Tythe Hay att v s. [five shillings] a loade amongst them.

James had collected money proffered to him to begin a suit against the Corporation, with some burgesses giving up to twenty shillings. William Mather said that he had heard from Jowett that the lease was forfeit and had joined in proceedings so that the estate should be used 'for the good of the common burgesses'. None of this was comfortable for the aldermen to hear: order had broken down and at least some of their own constables had turned against them.

Most disturbing was the evidence of the tanner William Sherwyn. He said that his fellow-burgess Cooke persuaded him to come to the meeting by offering him a load of hay if the protest was successful. He had told Cooke that he wished 'we lived togeather and not divyde asunder' and had pointed to the example of Chesterfield 'which ys overthrown'. Cooke swore, and said that he 'would yt were so'. He meant that he would like Nottingham to follow Chesterfield's example, remaking its governance to suit its burgesses. Chesterfield's burgesses had been fighting a battle over the town's status since the fifteenth century. Was it the Earl of Shrewsbury's manor, as he claimed, which should be ruled by a bailiff without the election of any officers? Or was it to be governed by an incorporated, elected body, as a borough? In April 1598 the Earl lost the battle, after a period of turbulence: fighting between officers, intimidation and attacks on property by vigilantes on both sides, lawsuits and open confrontation between the Earl and townspeople. A lawyer had been imprisoned for supporting burgess rights. The burgesses had appealed directly to the Crown, which eventually granted them a charter of incorporation without the Earl's agreement. Cooke wished that a similar overthrow of the powers-that-be might happen in Nottingham. But ironically, what Chesterfield had just gained was what Nottingham already had – a corporate body led by a mayor.[9] What Cooke was saying, therefore, was that he wanted simply overthrow, not a particular system of government of which Chesterfield was an ideal. The burgesses wanted revolution for its own sake, feeling that nothing could be worse.

Their leaders, Millington and Cooke, were examined about these ambitions. It is hard to identify Cooke, because there were several men of the same name: he may have been the man who persistently neglected to pay rent for his drapery stall. But Millington is more traceable. He was not notably poor, renting from the School Estate a messuage and garden in Long Row in 1583, and renewing the lease in 1600. He also rented a lime pit from the Chamber Estate in at least 1596–9. Millington was assessed for the subsidy of 1598 along with other well-off subjects. But Lucy Hutchinson, who knew Millington's descendants, calls them a 'mean family' – and they had a petty stake in the town compared with the magnates. After his marriage to Ellen Sugar in St Mary's in 1576, Millington lived in Hurte's ward, but continued to attend St Mary's, where his children were baptized. He thus sat on the sidelines of the town's governance, watching with obvious fury as others carved up its sweets amongst themselves.

Although he could not write, or even sign his own name, he had other ways to make his voice heard. His attitude to aldermen can be judged from the shocked note in the margin of his examination, added by the note-taker – the new Mayor's Clerk William Gregory. Gregory recorded that when questioned by Hurte, Millington retorted: 'Yow are but a Burges as I, and therefore I will answere the Maior and not yow'. He stood mute when asked about persuading constables to summon burgesses, and the collection money for a lawsuit. He said that he had not wished 'that this Corporation might be overthrowen and become a bailywyck' (the reverse of Chesterfield's transformation). But when asked why the assembly had met, he said that the tithe hay lease was 'a thinge of much better valew than the rent ys'. He asked that the lease might be 'taken and held' for the benefit of 'the wholl Burgesses'.[10] Gregory ended his notes of the examinations with the pious exclamation 'God Save the Queen!'. For this tidy-minded man, who during his period of office as Town Clerk (1597–1617) revolutionized the keeping of the records, persons disturbing good order were anathema, and he would later turn his suppressive energies on Darrell and William Sommers.

Millington and Cooke were imprisoned, and by October 1599 the Mickletorn Jury were pleading with the Corporation not to launch an 'unlaw-full' lawsuit against the burgesses. Meanwhile in the crucial year 1597/8, on 25 February and now in Clark's mayoralty, the lease of the tithe hay, which had only just been granted (as predicted by the burgesses) to Alderman Hurte and the wealthy tradesmen William Greaves and John Hartley, was transferred back to the five other aldermen. This curious little transaction, to which we will return, clawed back the town's property so that a compromise could be reached with the burgesses. On the same day, a minute in the Mayor's Book records an order by Clark and the Corporation that three quarters of the tithe hay should be bestowed on the burgesses. Each person claiming a load would pay six shillings and eight pence to the Free School. The words 'assente', 'comfort', 'good lykinge' and 'increase of love' are prominent in the minute. The burgesses had won this battle, gaining access – at a price – to the tithe hay. Millington's was the first name on the list of those claiming a load, followed by that of Cooke, and many of the constables and others who had protested at the Spice Chambers followed them. But the appearance of amity did not last, and Millington, Cooke and others lost interest in the tithe hay. They did not claim any loads in subsequent years, demonstrating clearly that for them the issue was a symbolic one. Eventually, the inability of the town peacefully to organize its own government led to an attempt by the Mayor to surrender the town's charters and dissolve its corporation. This would have meant the town forfeit-ing its privileges and the loss of the rights of burgesses. Three to four hundred burgesses took counsel and objected formally; the matter was referred to the Privy Council and so to the Assize judges in 1606. The Council was again redesigned, but within eight months the Mickletorn Jury had recommenced its complaints about Nottingham's government.[11]

Mr Darrell goes to Nottingham

It was into these smouldering, unresolvable tensions that John Darrell rode in 1597. He began by associating with the commonalty: as we know, he was met by the baker's wife Joan Pie. He did not refuse her welcome, and he discussed the case with her as he had with the servant Hugh Wilson, who had summoned him. Joan Pie then took Darrell straight to the little house where the demoniac William Sommers lodged with the weaver Thomas Porter, and afterwards he went to stay with a so far untraced couple called the Webbs – not to his ultimate host Alderman Bonner's High Pavement mansion. Darrell's egalitarianism was testified to by his friends: he had 'not been knowne to disdaine the company of any honest man, though never so base'. His apparent ignorance of the political context in Nottingham combined with an unconcern for social standing suggests that he did not see Joan in the way that others might have done – as a representative of the commonalty – but rather as simply a godly sister. However, the Pies probably looked different to the town authorities. Joan's husband Robert had been a burgess since 1579, the same year that he married Joan Briggs. He lived in Listergate and rented premises on Smith's Row, the market street on the north side of the Town Hall. It was only yards from the Spice Chambers. There is no evidence that he did or did not attend the rebellious meeting earlier that year, but he was at the heart of the common burgess community. At the sessions of 1599–1600 he was presented for selling severely underweight bread, which suggests that business was not thriving.[12] So Darrell began his sojourn in Nottingham by associating with some of town's poorer commonalty, an association that continued when they attended his dispossession and supported his fasts.

The question of whether godliness and rebellion went together, or combined with poverty to make revolutionaries, has been discussed repeatedly since Christopher Hill and his fellow Marxists began to wonder aloud if the Civil War was actually 'a class war'. Clearly it was not so simple, but the idea has been refined and revisited since. Donna B. Hamilton and Susan Brigden have both suggested that godliness could become equated with 'oppositionism' of various kinds: to authority, oligarchy or constraint *per se*.[13] The example of the Nottingham commonalty suggests that they are right. But the commonalty's politicized spokespeople on the Mickletorn Jury only intermittently presented themselves as puritanical, and with varying intensity. In 1588 the Jury petitioned the Mayor and aldermen, urging them to consider 'the sarvisse of Almyghty god most carfully before all worldlye matters'. The Jury pointed out that they already had in place 'a most godlye exercise of preachinge, on the ffrydaye once a weake' – organized, the wording suggests, by persons outside the Corporation bodies and dating, in fact, back to the 1570s. What troubled them was that the chief persons of the town were not attending, and they asked that the Mayor, aldermen, Council and Clothing should be there. Moreover, they demanded that a special order be set down to enforce attendance. Had they succeeded in this aim, Nottingham would have begun to resemble godly Northampton, the 'English Geneva'.[14] A godly discipline would have been written into the town's instruments of governance. But the Nottingham oligarchs could not well have been more opposed to such a suggestion.

The Jury also intermittently commented on issues of personal morality. In 1577 they presented the former Mayor Alderman Newton as not worthy of public office because he not only (they stated) opposed burgesses' interests but had been 'abussyng him sellfe wit a nowghte quene'. They attempted to limit the number of ale- and tippling-houses, and ensure that their keepers 'be bound for the good behavyour of their house, and that all such p[e]rsons as shall resort to their housses take their rest in dew tyme at the nyght uppon a payne'. Again in 1593: 'we request you mr meare that all the alhousess of the back syd of the town may be loukte tow'. In 1601 they presented the schoolmaster for not ensuring that two of his scholars came to church. There is no evidence of a sustained puritan agenda, but there are repeated flickers of godly empathy – as Paul Seaver suggested, Nottingham contained 'a zealous minority' working against an ungodly grain. However, it is notable that godly concerns appear only when they could be used as a stick in the Jury's wider purpose, that of beating the oligarchs. Similarly, some of the participants in the tithe hay revolt had godly connections, but seem to have identified with godliness only when it suited them. The Millingtons, for example, were prominent in the government of Nottingham under Parliament. Gilbert Millington, probably Percival Millington's nephew and just as vexatious to authority as Percival in his day, was Nottingham's MP and subsequently a regicide. But Lucy Hutchinson regarded him as an enemy of true godliness, describing with disgust how, despite being 'a man of sixty professing religion', he quickly forgot his 'religious, matronly' wife and after her death married an alehouse wench, 'a flirtish girl of sixteen'. He also, she alleged, took up with royalists at the first opportunity.[15]

Some of the burgesses did behave in ways that suggested a more sustained dislike of the established Church and State. In 1595 Joan Pie's husband Robert was presented to the Archdeacon's court with some of his neighbours for 'refusing' to pay two pence towards the purchase of communion wine and bread. The glover and burgess Edmund Garland, one of the chief supporters of Darrell, may well be the rebellious constable Edward Garland, since the names are used interchangeably. A descendant of William Cooke served as

John Hutchinson's quartermaster as he held Nottingham for Parliament. The common ground between godliness and the rebellious commonalty reinforces the point made in the last chapter: that godliness could easily appear to be a revolutionary force given the right interpreters and circumstances, and could in some repressive circumstances actually become one. Whilst some of the 'godly party' in Nottingham clearly believed deeply in their creed, others seem to have adopted their politics because for them godliness was associated with opposition to an *ancien régime*. And, as Christopher Durston and Jacqueline Eales sum up, 'puritanism won converts from right across the social spectrum, including within its ranks aristocrats, gentlemen, clothworkers and cobblers'.[16] Despite the arguments of R. H. Tawney and Christopher Hill that the godly were proto-Marxist revolutionaries, what united the Nottingham godly was not class in itself, but a shared sense of dissatisfaction with the town's condition that was partly religious but mostly economic. Together, godliness and economic woes began to look like a coherent oppositionism.

Nottingham's Corporation seem to have been genuinely conservative in religion, apt to suspect that the godly were plotting sedition. 'Anchor' Jackson sounds a godly name – not as extreme as Praise-God or Comfort, but perhaps referring to the anchor of faith.[17] Peter Clark's initial interest in Sommers suggests an openness to godly argument. But as an official body, the Corporation acted conservatively. They offered ceremonially-charged gifts to St Mary's, out of keeping with godly emphasis: Robert Alvey, for example, presented a silver communion chalice in his capacity as Mayor in 1595. They clung to their peculiar rite of the burial of the mace in rosemary and bayleaves and its rebirth at the hand of the new Mayor – which must have struck observers as so far beyond popish as to be heathen. There were ties to Catholicism: Alderman Morey's wife was presented for recusancy in 1587 and referred to the Assizes as obstinate. A pro-Darrell pamphlet of 1599 stated flatly: 'M[aster] Morrey ... is generally reported to be a Papist, and either for his owne or his wyves popery hath ben before the high Commission at Yorke'. The immediate ancestors of the present oligarchs, Nicholas Bonner and Alderman John Gregory, had resisted the Protestant assault on St Mary's, asking the bellman to continue prayers for the dead, and hoarding vestments and furniture. Bonner had been presented to the Archiepiscopal Court as 'a seditious man'. William Freeman and William Gregory were similarly accused of 'affecting witchery [and] ... Popery' by the author of *The Triall of Maist. Dorrell*, it was frequently asserted that Gregory had not received communion for eleven years, and Darrell called him 'a popish mate'. During William Sommers's possession 'one Palin' of Tamworth, a recusant, came to Sommers bringing an *agnus dei* and relics, and the godly had him committed to the sheriff's house. But 'after a fewe dayes the matter was so ordered, that the papist went quietli [*sic*] home again'.[18] By the 1590s, it was Elizabeth and Whitgift's conservative settlement that was orthodox, and it appears that Nottingham's oligarchs either toed that proto-Anglican line, or were on the Catholic side of it.

The aldermen who would end Darrell's career as an exorcist displayed little initial interest in him, or William Sommers. Darrell had been invited by Mayor Clark by letter and later stayed with Alderman Bonner. Clark visited him on Sunday 6 November, accompanying him to Sommers's bedside. But although Darrell met a cross-section of local society there is no report of conversation with the other aldermen. Bonner does not appear to have visited Sommers. Instead, when he arrived at Porter's house on Saturday 5 November, Darrell found, among many others, Porter and his wife Anne, Edmund Garland, Elizabeth Milward, probably a relative of the Porters', Nicholas Shepherd, a fletcher and one of the keepers at the town's Bridewell, William Sommers's stepfather Robert Cowper and sister Mary, Thomas Wallis, the mercer who was Joan Darrell's sister's husband, and John Wiggen, another neighbour, who later tested Sommers's Latin. Also visiting on 5 November – either at Porter's or Bonner's house – were John Atkinson, Clerk of the Kitchen to the Willoughby family, Robert Evington, rector of Normanton-upon-Soar, Dr Barnaby Evans, Thomas Porter's neighbour and the curate of St Mary's, Thomas Hayes, incumbent of Kirkby-in-Ashfield who was in town attending on Sir Charles Cavendish, William Hinde, tailor and burgess, and John Sherrart, clerk of St Mary's. There were no reports of aldermen or their representatives being present that evening: instead there were family members, obscure friends, clergy, and, interestingly, two men who served the nobility. Nor did Darrell apparently meet the vicar of St Mary's, Robert Aldridge, who had also written to invite him, until the next day.[19] There is a strong impression that the exorcism was being treated as an orderly, everyday event by the Corporation and the vicar of their church: they were not about to drop everything to attend on Sommers. Why then did they invite a puritan exorcist like Darrell to their already divided town, if they were themselves lacking in godly enthusiasm?

Darrell's relationship with Thomas Wallis was one factor. Mrs Wallis, with a group of townswomen including Mrs Gray and Lady Zouche, certainly sent a letter to her brother-in-law on 2 November to invite him to Nottingham. A second factor was print itself: Mrs Gray had read *The most wonderfull and true storie*, and tracked down Darrell through Mrs Beresford, of the same family involved in the Katherine Wright case, so that he might come to Sommers. But it seems very likely that pressure from below and outside the upper levels of town society was also important. The number of lower clergy from St Mary's and beneficed men from other parishes present from day one of the exorcism process is interesting. Robert Evington was a well-known nonconformist, who had been before the Archdeaconry Court as long ago as 1583 for 'unreverent behavyour of himselfe in wordes in the church and for rayling agaynst M[aster] Archdeacon in open court', and had been suspended. Evans, Aldridge's curate, was more learned than his vicar, and stood in uneasily presbyterian-like relation to him, as doctor to pastor. It was he who had first suggested that William Sommers might be possessed, on about 21 October. He had called in John Sherrart, a clerk of St Mary's, to confirm his suspicions. Like Mrs Gray, Sherrart had been reading pamphlets, and owned a copy of *The Most strange and admirable discoverie of the three Witches of Warboys* (London, 1593), which detailed the symptoms of those obsessed or possessed by the agency of witches. The book had been written and published by members of the Pickering family of Northamptonshire and their associates, who were godly to the point of presbyterianism, and Sherrart's ownership of their expensive book suggests common interests. Darrell also mentions the involvement of the godly John Ireton of Kegworth in his decision to come to Nottingham – when he at first demurred, Ireton wrote to him to urge him to go. Finally, the Mayor was advised to send for Darrell by one of the household of the Earl of Huntingdon.[20]

These were men like Darrell – not powerful within Nottingham itself, but keen to influence events there. In contrast, Robert Aldridge, vicar of St Mary's, was asked several times to visit Sommers, but refused. Aldridge was not godly. He was a pluralist who was believed by at least some of his parishioners to be neglecting his duties at St Mary's in favour of his church at Wollaton, where his patrons the Willoughbys lived. In 1595, just after the communion wine issue involving Robert Pie, Aldridge was presented to the Archdeacon's Court for non-residency, and the presentment alleged that he did not give a fortieth part of his living to the poor either. His vicarage was in disrepair, which it had been since at least 1592. The Mickletorn Jury also pursued Aldridge with repeated pleas for the revival of their ancient right to be provided with a common boar by the vicar for the use of their sows.[21] It seems for them to have become a totemic example of the town's neglect of their needs. Aldridge, like the Mayor and aldermen, was thus under huge pressure to demonstrate godliness, probity and charity to the less well off. Inviting John Darrell may have seemed a sensible, concessionary response. From *The most wonderfull and true storie* it was, apparently, clear that he was a respectable minister: the book had been authorized and there had been no fuss about it in Burton. What could possibly go wrong?

Aldridge would have been under additional pressure to act because Robert Cowper, Sommers's stepfather, was one of St Mary's clerks. St Mary's records reveal that he and Sommers's mother actually lived in the churchyard, only thirty yards from the church door. Cowper had married Elizabeth Sommers, the widow of Henry Sommers, in St Mary's in 1593 and the family were doubly connected when his son (also Robert) married her daughter Mary in 1595.[22] Their home was rented from St Mary's and Robert had lived there for a decade at least. He was paid eight pence every half year for keeping the clock and his multifarious activities brought him into contact with Aldridge, other ecclesiastical officials and the Archbishop on his visitations. His plight must therefore have been impossible to ignore. The involvement of Evans and Sherrart in diagnosing Sommers's possession in late October suggests that he involved the curate and his fellow clerk early on, and actively sought help for his wife's son. But despite its intimate connections with the church, his was not a particularly respectable household by the standards of its time. Mary, William's sister, had been abandoned by her husband, Robert Cowper junior, 'long before' she came to the attention of the authorities in 1598. She too lived with his father and her mother.[23] Sommers himself had been apprenticed to Thomas Porter in 1594. Like Mary, he should have been settled. Instead, he ran away several times, blaming Porter's inability to teach him, 'having no skill at all in musicke'. Porter was a weaver who had turned to music as a sideline.[24] Sommers's stepfather had tried to free him from the apprenticeship to begin again, but Porter would not release him. The Cowper household was embarrassed and embarrassing in more than one way, and the clerk must have had an undeniable claim on the attention of his employer when he told his story.

A Tale of Robin Hood

Whose story is the tale of William Sommers's possession? Was it the hard-pressed clerk's invention? Opponents said he gained financially from it and this seems quite likely, though Darrell denied it.[25] Despite room for doubt, the evidence suggests he was not complicit in the deception. Cowper seemed genuinely moved by Sommers's dispossession, to the extent that he confessed one hundred and fifty sins to the assembled company and later was called to London for reciting an inflammatory psalm in St Mary's in defence of the truth of Sommers's claims. Sommers never accused his stepfather, instead speaking of their difficult relationship and with some pride in his own inventiveness. He took an easier way eventually in blaming Darrell, the outsider, for his inspiration. Yet it does not seem credible that Darrell was involved in the fraud (as we saw in the previous chapters), although he and the godly party had much to gain from a successful dispossession. The town was ripe for an attack on ungodliness. As Peter Lake and Michael Questier point out,

> at such moments of high crisis and anxiety, ordinary Christians, who habitually, as the preachers were only too aware, tuned out the godly, came back within the ambit of perfect protestant preaching.[26]

Did the Nottingham godly, then, conspire to bring Darrell to their troubled town with the bait of a fake demoniac? There is no evidence that they did. It is hard to read through Samuel Harsnett's single-minded attempt to bespatter Darrell with blame, but if anything Harsnett is more critical of conservative leaders like Aldridge and Clark than he is of godly Nottingham citizens. It seems most likely that William Sommers, alone, was the author of this 'tale of Robin Hood', as Darrell called it: a tale, proverbially, for fools, which Darrell himself thought the Mayor, aldermen and Harsnett had concocted between them.

Before he began to accuse Darrell of teaching him to fake possession, this was Sommers's story. He said that on 20 March 1596 he was sent by Porter to his wife's sister, Mary Millwood, who was living in the household of Sir William and Lady Isabel Bowes at Walton. Isabel Bowes was formerly Isabel Foljambe and, as we know, Isabel and Darrell had a connection dating back to the Wright affair. Perhaps Sommers was told the story of Wright there, especially as the Boy of Burton was about to be dispossessed. Something prompted him to resume the fits he had practised at Brackenbury's in the early 1590s. He said that on the road back to Nottingham he had met an old woman who told him she was a neighbour of Wright's. The woman asked for money and then forced him to eat some apparently bewitched bread and butter. After this, Sommers returned to Porter's house and began to exhibit symptoms of possession. Visitors from 'the towne and countrie' began to pray for him. But Sommers also told *another* story of a witch, saying that the spirit had been sent into him by a woman from Worcestershire, now dead, because he had refused to give her his hatband. Samuel Harsnett says cryptically that 'there falling out a matter contrary to his expectation', he changed his story, and alleged that this was to cover up Darrell's instruction of him by backdating the bewitchment to before Sommers supposedly met Darrell in Ashby.

It was helpful to Sommers in his contradictions that it was hotly debated whether he spoke always in the devil's voice, or sometimes in his own. Sommers had two voices, and two stories, and was in effect calling for someone to interpret his speeches, organize his narrative and decide on a definitive version which would give holy meaning to his words. Since he knew of the pamphlet about the Warboys witches and *The most wonderfull and true storie*, he may even have hoped for a printed account to result from his activities. Such a text would bring him godly fame and possibly deliver him from the misery of his apprenticeship. As a first step in creating that account, quite unknown to them, Robert Aldridge and Peter Clark wrote separately to John Darrell, asking him to come to see Sommers. Sommers eagerly predicted Darrell's arrival and began to tailor his story into one perfect for puritan sententiousness. Speaking in the persona of the devil, he said: 'Dorrell comes, Dorrell comes, he wil have me out, but I wil come agayne for Nottingham and Lenton are jollie townes for me'. Lenton was the site of the old Martinmas fair, beginning every year on 11 November.[27] Sommers timed his possession perfectly, for at fair time the Nottingham area swarmed with merchants from London and the Midlands, and clergy came to stock up for the winter. So Sommers had a ready market for his tale. His story settled rapidly into a form saleable by the godly: God's providential warning against sin.

Darrell believed he would find Sommers possessed, and at their first meeting decided that he was. Harsnett used this as evidence that Darrell had prior knowledge of Sommers. But in fact it simply suggests the successful implantation in Sommers's story of the right motifs. Darrell's instant identification of providential messages in Sommers's words and actions was hardly surprising. But there was bitter argument about whether he had affirmed publicly on the first night that Nottingham's sins were the cause of the possession, and Darrell admitted that he had. This was crucial. Previous demoniacs, like John Starkie, had described the sins of the nation, but Sommers was being very specific: he had made his possession an overtly political statement during his first evening with Darrell, and it was evident that Darrell embraced the opportunity, along with others. Criticism of the town's morals and polity from an apprentice was nothing. But to have a minister endorse his claims, especially if they came not from the boy but the devil himself, was potentially troublesome. Samuel Harsnett sneered that the possession was 'a pure play, containing two principall parts, of a vice and a devill … a pageant of Puppittes'.[28] Harsnett was only partly right, however. His aim was to make Darrell sound popish, and degrade him by likening his activities to the theatre. Sommers certainly used the platform that possession gave him to act out the sins of Nottingham in dumbshow: these included brawling, quarrelling, fighting, swearing, highway robbery, picking and cutting purses, burglary, whoredom, male and female pride, hypocrisy, sluggishness in hearing the Word, drunkenness, gluttony, dancing, dicing and the playing of cards, killing and stealing. To Harsnett this was popish stageplaying. But to the godly, it was the Word made flesh: what it needed now was interpretation – hermeneutic marginalia like the Geneva Bible, exegesis, commentary – to make it a fully godly text. Who wrote that text? And how did these interpretations impact on the wider political situation at Nottingham?

The first author is a man previously unknown: probably John Atkinson, observing on behalf of Aldridge's patrons the Willoughbys on the night of 5 November. Atkinson, 'Clerk of the Kitchen', was by the late 1590s effectively the Willoughbys' steward and agent in Nottingham. He managed their property, family and household affairs in town, conveying news to them at London and Wollaton Hall, in 'very friendly letters' written to his lord. Atkinson was also trusted by the family with medical affairs, to such an extent that an eighteenth-century observer concluded that he must be 'the family physitian'. His profile thus matches perfectly the 'Mr. Atkinson', present at Porter's house, who was called to Sommers as early as All Saint's Day because of his experience in advising melancholics. Atkinson almost certainly wrote the text now in the Willoughbys' papers, and it concentrates exclusively on the acting of sins.

Atkinson's description of Sommers's rendition of excessive interest in dressing long and facial hair is typical:

> Was shewed the abuse of longe heare lyinge upon their shoulders, and the pryde and glorie they tooke in wearinge of yt, and the abuse of barbars, with their trickes in clappinge and showinge and tryminge up the heare of the upper lippe, and twyrlinge the little pycke under the lippe, and strokinge the longe and broade bearde ... and the annointinge of the eyebrees with the sweete balle, and the lookinge in the glasse to amende the loose and straglinge hears with pickinge of the hears oute of the nose, and dressinge the eares ...'[29]

This was clearly based on observation, on the part of both Sommers and Atkinson. The question was: which sinful persons were they observing so critically?

Atkinson's language betrays his reading of Sommers's representation as an attack on ungodly hate-figures – here, long-haired cavalier types and their effeminate flunkeys. Interestingly, both Mayor Clark and Alderman Alvey were barbers. No doubt they were long past cutting hair themselves, but they still used their trade as their descriptive 'addition'. Fornications of the type attributed to Alderman Newton might have been another target, and other concerns of the Mickletorn Jury such as excessive drinking in the town and the hypocritical dealings of merchants and officials. Those with long memories might even recall the fall from grace of Aldridge's predecessor in the Corporation church, William Underne, whose absenteeism, combined with womanizing and gaming (other sins acted by Sommers), had drawn the attention of, successively, his patron, the ecclesiastical courts and the criminal justice system.[30] But, crucially, Atkinson does not name any names: he simply attributes many of the sins he describes by using the word 'their'. So we read of 'their sterched ruffes' and 'their quaffing'. Only one sin was identified by Atkinson and his fellow observers as belonging to themselves: when Sommers acted out the 'sluggeshnes' of resort to church, the pretence of studying the prayer book and sleeping during the service, Atkinson spoke of 'we'. Apparently the godly held themselves to be as guilty of this sin as any others. Otherwise, Atkinson's text instinctively interpreted Sommers's possession as a reprimand primarily to people unlike himself – among whom might be numbered the town's oligarchs and its people. Because of what we know of their lives and the way they were perceived, they stand implicitly indicted among the cutpurses and whoremongers (also referred to as 'they'). But the identification is only implicit.

In a locality dominated by binary 'us' and 'them' thinking, then, the first text about Sommers delineates two parties but leaves their identities creatively ambiguous, up for appropriation. It is both diplomatic and politically revealing, because of course it presupposes that the reader knows who 'we' and 'they' are. Why would such an account, accusing no-one yet inviting identifications, be written? It seems far too acute to be merely a private memo. Its place in the Willoughby papers suggests that it was sent to Wollaton, for consumption by the family themselves. Firstly, then, it could be read by anyone and no matter how obvious might be their similarities to 'them', they could peruse it from the safe position of 'us'. Notable in Sommers's acts are some of the favourite sins of the Willoughbys – fighting, wearing cork-heeled shoes – which are traceable in their letters and household accounts. But as 'us' they need not acknowledge these faults openly, and a private penitence might result in public reformation, just as desired. Secondly, Atkinson, from his position in the Willoughbys' Nottingham town house, might expect that his employers would know enough about the town's sins to identify its people, and especially its powerful people, as 'them'. Was it not time they set the oligarchs a true godly example? And thirdly, the Willoughbys were patrons of the living of St Mary's. An increased commitment to godliness on their part and that of their vicar as a result of the Sommers affair would also help advance the godly cause in the town. Robert Aldridge's embrace of Sommers's message, despite his previous uninterest in godliness, seems to suggest that the godly party met initially with success in this aim.

Finally, Atkinson must have known that he was writing at a crucial time, for the Willoughbys, though powerful, were weakened by recent events. There was a real chance that a godly reading of their troubles as the result of sinful living might prevail and force reform, but only if it was not too obviously aggressive. As Lake and Questier note, it was not enough that merely 'formal Christians' identify sins in their own communities, but that as a result of godly interventions they 'see clearly ... the usurer, whore or papist within' themselves.[31] The trick was to encourage that identification without alienating the powerful potential convert. At Wollaton, this was Percival Willoughby. The death of Francis Willoughby in 1596 had left the family in deep debt and litigious turmoil, as the estate was contested between his widow and his son-in-law, Percival. Percival referred to the former countess openly as a 'whore', accusing her of attempting to substitute a male child for her newly-born daughter, since a male heir would have entitled her to keep her husband's estate. Both sides mounted lawsuits and petitions, and the control of the estate, with its vast territories, coalmines, ironworks and patronages hung in the balance for months before Percival's victory. The account of Sommers's sin-acting seems designed to intervene in this family feud by encouraging the rightful heir to associate himself with virtue and propriety through patronizing the godly in Nottingham.

Beyond the immediate religious context, the Willoughbys were also important in the map of allegiances in the Midlands, for despite their luxurious lifestyle they professed a moderate godliness. They had done so since the involvement of Francis with the attempt by his guardian the Duke of Suffolk to place Lady

Jane Grey on the throne, forty years earlier. It cannot be an accident that an attempt was being made in 1597 to secure the continued loyalty of the family to the reformist agenda – strengthening its now weakened intensity. There also seems to have been an attempt to interest another family in supporting it. The presence of both Atkinson and Charles Cavendish's chaplain Thomas Hayes ensured that both powerful camps were informed of Sommers's activities. The godly party had good reason to try to secure the backing of the nobility in their cause at Nottingham. At Ashby, from which Darrell had just come, the loss of a puritan patron, the Earl of Huntingdon, had already begun the process of transformation that would turn Ashby from a godly mini-commonwealth to its opposite. Within ten years of Hildersham's death, Huntingdon's powerbase would be a Royalist stronghold, later besieged and slighted by Parliament. So Atkinson's report on Sommers, like all the texts in the Darrell affair, has a significance out of all proportion to its apparent referents. One day Willoughbys would fight Cavendishes, Parliamentarian against Royalist, and texts like Atkinson's were interventions of key importance in the cultural battle to be fought before, and perhaps instead of, the war.

So it was the surviving textual, non-dramatic elements of the dispossession that were actually the most important. Harsnett noted as much, although to say so damaged one strand of his anti-puritan rhetoric, the slur of theatricality. But focusing on the subsequent writings – manuscript accounts, printed accounts and sermons – allowed him another sneer about puritan fetishizing of the ministers' Word. Whilst Darrell might say that God's physical signs of possession and dispossession, and the physical acts of prayer and fasting, were central, Harsnett suggested that a closer reading would produce the impression that 'preaching bare away the bell'. If Sommers acted out a play, therefore, Darrell was culpable for its critical exegesis. He stood over Sommers reading each gesture: 'see you not how he doth thus, and thus? These thinges signifie that such and such sinnes doe raigne in this towne.' The godly laity offered their own critical readings: 'oh, he doth so for this sinne, and so for that sinne' they echoed. Sommers became tired of this scrutiny: 'I could doe nothing in any of my fittes ... but some would still make an interpretation of it', he fumed later. It was noticeable that some of his sins were explicitly musical – playing viols, dancing – and he made an attempt to suggest that he was possessed because his apprenticeship forced him to sing filthy songs.[32] Darrell might have interpreted this solely as meaning that Sommers was practising a sinful trade and must be freed from his indenture. But he did not, and it was the local political interpretation that he took from Sommers that mattered. But Darrell was certainly not alone in reading Sommers's possession as he did: a sign of a sinful locality urgently needing reform. He denied initiating this widely-accepted interpretation, and it was eagerly carried forward by others, as the Willoughby manuscript shows. Eventually, however, it became too pointed to be assimilated into the cycle of rebellion and containment that characterized Nottingham's politics.

Possessing and Repossessing the Narrative

When Atkinson wrote, however, all this was still in the future. On 6 November, Aldridge visited and Darrell invited him and the godly William Aldred, rector of Colwick, and Nicholas Hallam, rector of Trowell, to assist him in dispossessing Sommers the next day. It became clear that public interest was such, and Darrell's desire to offer an inclusive prayer-meeting so great, that Sommers would have to be moved to a bigger room. George Small's house in Clark's ward was chosen, and Small's later defence of Darrell suggests that he shared his godly views. There was clearly debate about the correct location for the dispossession, however, which was itself highly politicized, given the town's contested geography. Darrell did not want popish church theatre and refused to dispossess Sommers in St Mary's precisely because it was a holy place and any dispossession might be attributed to its sacredness – as Ralph Shute, the vicar of St Peter's, Hallam and Anne Porter all disapprovingly swore later. He would have preferred a meeting in a field with no sacred associations, where 'all people might behold it'. Darrell was prevented from this – Harsnett speaks cryptically of 'better advice' prevailing – and settled for 'a narrow, low roome'.[33] At least it was an ordinary room in a house rather than a church, which gave it godly significance in reminding participants of the accessible commonness of the divine. But ironically it was also physically inaccessible. Not everyone could get into the room, which was probably intended by the town authorities to minimize the danger of gadding. Yet however small the space, the impact was enormous.

Because of its location, apart from any religious content, the dispossession was bound to seem threatening to the Corporation, and ultimately to the vicar. Like other godly cultural events – exercises or inter-parochial gadding – it shifted the centre of cultural gravity away from the church and town hall. And beyond the physical was the verbal danger: emerging speech that could not be controlled. It must have reminded some observers of the Spice Chambers meeting earlier that year. On top of that, it was religiously threatening, taking a form like that of the prophesyings put down by the Queen twenty years earlier. Like a prophesying, the dispossession lasted all day, from seven in the morning. It began with exposition in three sermons – unlike an exercise, which tried to minimize theological controversy by having only one. Aldridge preached on Hosea 4:1–2, which exhorted his congregation to hear the Word of the Lord. Like everyone else, he had responded to Sommers's acting out of sins, for the verses went on to state that God was angry with the inhabitants of his land, because there was no truth, mercy or knowledge of Him there. Instead, the people swore, lied, killed, stole and committed adultery. Later Aldridge was to reject Darrell's insistence that Nottingham was a particularly sinful town, but on 7 November he was quite content to use Sommers for his own instructive purposes. Darrell then preached on Mark 9:14–30, a favourite passage that described in detail Christ's dispossession of a boy by prayer and fasting. Aldred preached too, and weepingly confessed his own sins. This was impressive stuff, and John Pare said that 'the preasse was so great that he could not come to the sight of the boye till about … 3 of the Clock' – eight hours after the prayer and fasting had begun. By the moment of apparent exit by Satan, the massive audience was weeping and trembling and cried out: 'Lord have mercy upon us, Lord have mercy upon us'. 'And so did M[aster] Darrell with his hands lift up as high as he could', the pamphlet tells us: for Darrell it was a moment of supreme satisfaction, for the first part of his work on God's behalf was done. It was now time for the follow-up sermons, and for people to choose their reaction, to decide who – in Atkinson's terms – 'us' and 'them' might be.

A battle began for control of the message of the dispossession. On either the Sunday before or after the dispossession, Aldridge repeated from his pulpit the claim that Darrell had first made on 5 November: that Sommers was troubled for 'the sins of the people, or of the inhabitants of Nottingham'. But Aldridge gave the message a particular conservative spin:

> affirming that forasmuch as they in Nottingham, notwithstanding the admonitions of many godly Preachers did still continue in their sinnes: God had sent the Devill to reprove them, and to make them ashamed of their former obstinacie.[34]

The vicar was responding to events by asserting his control over the situation: I, your preacher and the preachers in your Corporation's church, told you that you were sinful, but you would not listen. He was asserting both that he was a preaching minister, and that claims that he neglected his town congregation were untrue. Darrell alleged that previously Aldridge's 'people of Nott.[ingham] have hearde his voyce oft times but once in a monneth, sometimes sildome', but Aldridge was arguing that his people had been rightly instructed all along. It was not his fault that sins still occurred in the town. However, other interpretations were also being acted upon. People were coming to Darrell, not Aldridge, confessing their sins and 'craving mine advice', as Darrell put it. And then, as Darrell said:

> after I had publikely used some words of exhortation unto them (which was a weeke after the said worke [the dispossession]) they made choice of mee for their preacher.

Aldridge must have assented to this choice but Darrell's words suggest an almost presbyterian election of him by the laity, which Harsnett confirms: he was chosen as preacher without proper authority by those with 'Presbyteriall conceits' and 'favourers of the overworne Consistorian faction'. Having got their man into St Mary's, these people 'flocked to the house of God, made hast, and were swift to heare the word. And so the worde of God grew mightily in Nottingham, and prevailed.' But it was Darrell's version of God's word, not Aldridge's, that was prevailing. As Paul Seaver suggests, loyalty could quickly transfer from the parish minister to his star lecturer.[35] The story of the dispossession was becoming a glorification of Darrell and his godly beliefs, and an attack on the incumbent at the corporation's church.

If Sommers had not taken Darrell's unconscious hints and become 'repossessed', then matters might have gone no further. Although Darrell claimed that he had given up two better offers (from someone at Nottingham and from 'a Gentelman off great worth') for the St Mary's post, which he said was 'no such great benefite', he had a foothold in Nottingham: a post in a key church in a key city. Aldridge was still on the godly's side, the Mayor and aldermen were quiet, and it was unclear how godliness might benefit further from Sommers's activities. However, possession stories almost always contain a threat of repossession – and the ones with which Sommers was most familiar, Wright's and Darling's, certainly did. Darrell had taken steps to keep the devil out: he bought Sommers out of his contaminating musical apprenticeship, using money collected by public subscription and administered by the still-helpful Corporation. He issued instructions to Robert Cowper, to whose house Sommers had gone, that the young man should not be left alone, lest he be repossessed or harm himself. But he talked frequently about the threat of repossession, and soon Sommers began to appear to be under demonic attack. His sister Mary Cowper joined in. A new element was also introduced: Mrs Wallis, Darrell's sister-in-law, stood talking with others in Sommers's and Cowper's bedrooms about witches as the possible cause of their illness.

After about 25 November, Sommers and Mary Cowper accordingly began to accuse witches. Darrell sent for the suspects, had them tested by bringing them to the demoniacs to see how they reacted, and accompanied those who failed the test to prison. He could not do this alone: once the accusers had provided names, magistrates (the Mayor and aldermen) would have had to hear and record their informations and the examinations of the accused, and commit them for trial. Now Darrell was reliant on the co-operation of the town authorities and the criminal courts for sustaining the propagation of his message, and he was fully embroiled in the town's politics. The interpretation of the godly was now incorporated into official texts, examinations and informations whose reception at the Assizes would test the religious and political credibility of the Corporation. The Mayor in particular nailed his colours to the mast: he told Robert Cowper that at Darrell's request he had asked around the town whether anyone else wanted to charge the accused with any witchcrafts.[36] The more the Mayor invested in the narrative, the more success the godly seemed to be enjoying, but the higher the stakes became. And then Mary Cowper and Sommers made a fatal choice of one of the accused: Alice Freeman, a cousin of Alderman William Freeman. Sommers first named Freeman and then Mary said that she had bewitched her and had caused the death of her only child. Suddenly, as with the developing situation at St Mary's, and the sidelined tithe hay revolt, the story of the possession became a direct instead of an implied threat to the Corporation.

The accusation of witchcraft was not only personally threatening, it was also politically so. Witches were associated with Catholics (even the theologically-suspect Harsnett describes the Pope 'bewitching by his counterfeyte miracles'), atheists, the rebellious and traitorous. Magistrates who failed to take action against them, never mind being related to them, were regarded by the godly as negligent in their duty to the Queen's subjects, and poor protectors of their commonweals.[37] If Sommers was now, as Darrell suggested, claiming the ability to 'discover all the witches in England', he was already close to suggesting that the magistrates of Nottingham were negligent. Maybe they were even popish, wicked and ungodly. So when Sommers began to utter cryptic sayings such as 'the saide stone is softe and the bolder, and flint is hard', Darrell dangerously interpreted this to be a description of Nottingham's magistrates. Some, he said, had soft hearts and believed God's mighty works. Others were hardhearted unbelievers. This kind of critique chimed so closely with the views of the Mickletorn Jury and others that it was unlikely to be allowed to stand. Now Sommers and Mary Cowper were saying that one of the aldermen harboured a child-killing witch in his own family. Later Sommers said that he had chosen suspects' names because each already had a reputation for witchcraft, so Alice Freeman may already have been under attack. One of his other candidates, Thomas Groves, was mentioned in a presentment at the Sessions in 1604/5 as a well-known 'wiseman', whilst Darrell said that widow Higget was thought to have killed a child and Millicent Horsley had admitted offering healing.[38]

But the accusation of Freeman, whom Harsnett says already quietly disliked Darrell's activities, galvanized opposition to the hitherto authorized narrative. The aldermen were no longer willing to go along with it, and instead began to deconstruct it, drawing out all its dangerous potential. Darrell attributed his own and Sommers's disgrace directly to:

> the mallice of M[aster] Freeman Alderman, because his kinswoman Allice Freeman was by So.[mmers] detected for a witch … he hoping … to recover the good name of his kinswoman, and partly to disgrace and so consequently to be

revenged of me, whome ... he hated extreamely, so as at the length he could not indure to come to the church, when I exercised my ministery.

According to Darrell, Freeman and the 'popish' Gregory were quickly joined by the 'unsound and popish' Morey, and 'these three did draw with them M[aster] Hart [Hurte] Alderman and M[aster] Clarke then Maior a man very easy because of his simplicity to be misled'. Jackson later joined with attempts to persuade Sommers to confess, offering him inducements which he later described as 'pollicye, to drawe the boye on'.[39] A majority of the oligarchs were now working against Darrell and the godly.

Aldridge was now also rapidly converted to scepticism, along with Hallam. Hallam was moderately radical himself: as curate of West Bridgford he had been presented for not wearing the surplice in 1587, and in 1591 a repeated offence at Trowell had led to temporary excommunication. But he did not believe Darrell's claims that Sommers was repossessed. Attempts began to discredit Sommers and Darrell, by tricking the boy into failing to react to one of the accused when disguised. Widow Boote, whom Sommers's pattern of fits and recoveries had identified as a witch when she was brought openly to his bedside, was smuggled in secretly again under a cloak and Sommers failed to reproduce his reaction. Widow Else, another suspect, was led away by Aldridge, and then returned to Sommers's room hidden behind him. Again Sommers failed to react. Darrell says that Hallam and Freeman then together 'gave it out that So.[mmers] was a counterfeit'. 'They that used this devise', Sommers confirmed, 'did presently publish the same, and thereby affirmed, that out of all question I was but a dissembler'.[40] By 7 December, he was being openly accused of counterfeiting his possession. Now there were two stories in public circulation. One came from the cony-catching genre: the version portraying Sommers as a reprobate con artist that Darrell dubbed the 'tale of Robin Hood'. The other came from the signs-and-wonders genre: the story of a godly work of providence.

Darrell 'flew to the pulpit' to defend his reading of events. He preached, by his own account, six or seven sermons on Matthew 12:43–5, which affirmed the existence of repossession, and ended with a reference to a 'wicked generation' of doubters, of which he made ample use. He also preached at another fast, which drew attendance from the surrounding countryside. He had support from other ministers: Evington and Aldridge were joined by Arthur Hildersham in believing Sommers to have been repossessed. But other local people were now ready to argue with Darrell: the brief dominance of the godly was over. Some, said Harsnett, 'blamed him for [his sermon] to his face'. Aldridge said that:

the people were cloyed with his often repeating of one thing, and much offended, in that as they said, they could heare of nothing in his sermons, but of the Devill.

Darrell denied this, but said that 'two or three of the cheif frendes to counterfeiting, naturall men, not favoring of the spirit, shewed some dislike to my
preaching, and advised me to preach of love and charity, sayinge that they were
ever in charity before I came'. Aldridge, however, pursued his claim that the
feeling became general that Darrell was attacking the town:

> I was especially moved with his often repeating of these words: even so shall it bee
> with this wicked generation, applying them still to the people of Nottingham,
> where I have beene a preacher these twentie yeares: the people there being but as
> other such congregations are, and as willing to heare the word of God preached,
> as any other in mine opinion.

Samuel Harsnett, ever on the alert for human frailty, noted acidly that
'M[aster] Aldridge was then a great companion of M[aster] Darrels ... how-
beit, when he thought his freehold touched, he was moved with it'. Harsnett
was right. Aldridge had been impressed, but he was not going to be criticized
in sermons preached in his own church for allowing his congregation to remain
unreformed. He was now not of the opinion that Nottingham was a particularly sinful place, and many supported his view.[41] Existing tensions produced a
backlash against Darrell. Slanderous political intention was read into the possession story and it was linked with other attacks on the vicar, as well as on
Freeman and the Corporation.

Revelations and Revolutions

The pressure for resolution became irresistible after Christmas 1597. There are
indications that Freeman and Gregory were already seeking external help to
break the deadlock in Nottingham. They went together to London, on unspecified business. But when they returned they were presented with a perfect
opportunity to bring matters to a head. William Sommers was accused of witchcraft himself. In early January, the widow of one Sherland or Sterland (accounts
differ), who had died accusing Sommers of bewitching him, went to Freeman's
house with her concerns. Afterwards, she and her neighbours offered informations against Sommers to the Mayor in the Town Hall. Sommers, responding
in the only way he could by further entrenching his position as the victim of
witches, reiterated that he had been repossessed, and demanded another exorcism. But he was now a felony suspect, and was imprisoned. He was bailed by
his uncle Randolph Milner, but his fear of being hanged brought about the
desired result for the anti-Darrell aldermen. Before them, Sommers offered
a full confession, not of witchcraft but of counterfeiting. On 24 February he
was sent by the Mayor to stay at the town's Bridewell, St John's. And here he
produced the first publicized text of the affair. He wrote Darrell a long letter

confessing in writing, and asking him to let the matter go, 'for the more you meddle in it, the more discredite it will bee for you'. Copies were clearly made and later deployed against Darrell. There were hints in the letter of what was to come, as Sommers blamed Darrell for inspiring his tricks with his 'speeches' – but only since his arrival, and apparently not wittingly.[42]

Events now came full circle, back to the tithe hay revolt. On the day after Sommers had confessed counterfeiting and been safely shut up in the Bridewell, the Mayor and aldermen signed the new lease of the tithe hay – which they had bought back from its controversial lessees – and gave the town's burgesses what they wanted. Now Millington and Cooke had their victory over the oligarchs, and could claim the tithe hay for the burgesses. There was no need for them to continue fighting the Corporation. So it is hard not to see a connection between the two consecutive events: Sommers's committal and the ending of the tithe hay protests. The signing of the new lease separated the godly from the rest of the commonalty in one neat stroke. If the hard-line godly wanted to continue to make a fuss about Sommers, so be it. He was in the unsympathetic hands of the town's employees at St John's, John Cooper and Nicholas Fletcher, who threatened him with whipping and with pincers if he should recommence his 'fits'. Meanwhile the rest of the commonalty could go back to business as usual. All the indications are that the oligarchy bought peace in the tithe hay battle with the Mickletorn Jury, Millington, Cooke and the disaffected constables and burgesses, so that they could finish off Sommers and Darrell in peace.

A convoluted endgame was now played out at Nottingham. The Archdeacon of Derby, John Walton, had been told of the trouble there and had attended a conference with the Darrellites about it. He wrote to Whitgift, alerting Bancroft and Harsnett to the matter as he did so. The anti-godly leapt into action to ensure that their version of events would prevail. An investigative commission was procured from the Archbishop of York. But the Archbishop, Matthew Hutton, was relatively sympathetic to godly interests and a majority of those appointed to the commission were friends to Darrell's cause. Accordingly, there were objections to the commission and it was reformed. The second group of commissioners were: John Thorold (High Sheriff of the County), Sir John Byron (of Newstead Abbey, former antagonist of Henry Darrell), John Stanhope (of Shelford), Robert Markham (a relation of the Catholic Markhams at Ollerton, and father of the dramatist Gervase Markham), Richard Parkins (Recorder of Nottingham), Mayor Clark, Walton himself, Miles Leigh (official of the Archdeaconry Court of Nottingham), and the ministers John Ireton, John Brown of Loughborough, Robert Evington, and Thomas Bolton, who was Byron's chaplain.[43] The commission met in Nottingham and the Mayor and the Bridewell keepers Cooper and Shepherd prepared with Sommers a strategy for ending the affair conclusively. Sommers would fake a fit in front

of the commissioners and during it Clark would call him. At once, Sommers
would get up and everyone would see that his fit had been dissembled. It was
a good plan, discussed and agreed with Freeman (who had the most personal
interest in the outcome) at least a week before the commission met.

But it relied on the fortitude of the Mayor. On the day, 20 March 1597/8,
Sommers fell into a fit and waited to be called. There was, however, silence
from Clark. Sommers:

> began to suspect, that either Mayster Maiors opinion was altered, who was fully
> perswaded before (as I thought) that I had altogether dissembled: or els that he
> durst not speak his mind therin, and call me, seeing the rest of the Commissioners,
> and many others so confident in deed, that I was repossessed.

This was in fact the case. In an astonishing upset, the commissioners had been
convinced by the evidence they had heard and by Sommers's fit. Clark lost
his courage when faced with a hall full of clamorous godly and a supportive
commission. Harsnett impatiently noted that Shepherd even prompted him
to call, but Clark was 'terrified, by reason of the hard speeches of the Justices,
given out against those that had said the boy was a dissembler'. The hall was
filled with emotion, and a dog that was seen at the chamber door was identified as the devil. Sommers cried out that Satan was tempting him by offering a
bag of gold, and the commission concluded that Sommers had been possessed
and dispossessed as Darrell claimed. It was a great victory, but it could not be
allowed to be the last word. Conservative Nottingham could not be left in the
hands of the triumphant godly, and the national church could not be seen to
endorse Darrell's claims. Townspeople railed at one another in the streets as the
Darrell faction burst from the commission hearing to 'runne abroad into the
towne, telling their friends with great joy, that Somers was now found to have
been no dissembler'. Some were 'rated at exceedingly', said Nicholas Shepherd,
and 'some violence was offered'. 'The pulpets also rang of nothing but Divels
and witches', and it was clear that earlier 'disquiet' had become the even more
dangerous 'stirres', which might in turn become 'quarrels and mutinies, or ...
some greater inconvenience'. This beautifully understated apocalypse is, of
course, Samuel Harsnett's vision, and he was particularly disturbed that (as he
alleged) in Nottingham in this period a servant could no longer 'go into his
maysters cellar about his business without company'. As always, the lower sort
and their relationship with the godly and the town's business were pressing
concerns.[44]

The application of external authority by the anti-godly was now vital, and
the Lord Chief Justice of the Common Pleas was petitioned to intervene before
the Assizes (which were to take place in the week of 27 March). This was
Edmund Anderson, scourge of the godly and a well-chosen investigator. It is
not clear who involved him, but he liaised with Whitgift, and instructed the

Mayor to call Sommers before him. Strengthened by two of the sturdiest anti-Darrellites, Hurte and Freeman, on 31 March Clark obtained the renewed confession of counterfeiting that was needed. Sommers was removed from Edmund Garland's house, where he had been placed ten days before on his release from St John's. He was then questioned by Anderson, who came to Nottingham as Assize judge. Then he was sent to London. At the Assizes, Alice Freeman was acquitted, possibly after the empanelling of successive juries until one would acquit, and probably also by the direction of Anderson, whom Harsnett says stepped in after Freeman's indictment had been approved by the grand jury. He 'discerned somewhat, and rectified their [the petty jury's?] courses to a due issue'. Darrell seems to have been called to York, where under pressure from Whitgift, Matthew Hutton deprived him of his licence to preach on 20 April. Sometime around this date, the Mayor and four others served a warrant (courtesy of Archbishop Whitgift) on Darrell to appear before the High Commission at Lambeth.[45]

These men had formed a second commission, so quiet and hasty that its dating is not even clear. They were Clark, Morey and Freeman, William Gregory and Samuel Mason, all of them Darrell's enemies. Mason was a conservative gentleman from St Peter's, with property in the Long Row. His descendant would be, according to Lucy Hutchinson, 'a great Cavalier'. Gregory was both member and notetaker. These commissioners, Darrell's supporters would later allege, made journeys to and from York and London and wrote letters mobilizing others against Darrell. They prevented pro-Darrell sermons at St Mary's and even threatened to bind over anyone who spoke in his favour. When Robert Cowper sang Psalm 94 – which exhorts God to destroy the triumphant workers of iniquity and asked 'who will rise up for me against the evildoers?' – he was sent to London. Gregory went so far as to tell Darrell that he would be hanged. The second commission questioned Alice Freeman's main accuser, Mary Cowper, and together with other later commissions it interrogated many of the witnesses questioned by the first commission.[46] Sommers was already on his way to Lambeth, and Harsnett was waiting to talk to him at greater leisure, after he himself had visited Nottingham.

How had it all gone so badly wrong for the godly project? Harsnett and Darrell both said that Darrell's accusation of Alice Freeman had ended his career. Others argued that he had threatened the judgments of God on negligent pastors, and so Aldridge and others had moved against him. This account has shown for the first time the truth of both these insights, but has also demonstrated exactly why the attacks on Alderman Freeman and his colleagues and on Robert Aldridge were so deadly to Darrell's aims. Not only were they part of an intensely unstable wider political situation both nationally and at Nottingham, but they were particularly inopportune given the ongoing tithe hay revolt. The common burgesses and the godly were by no means a single political unit but they were both unquiet elements in Nottingham's polity, and their common enemy became the Corporation.[47] Darrell's activities, and especially Sommers's acting of sins and the sermons that offered readings of it, brought together these threats. To the embattled conservative Corporation, just as to Bancroft and Harsnett, there appeared to be a deliberate two-pronged attack on the patterns of spatial and cultural dominance in the town, that could not ultimately be absorbed by the fragile municipal authority.

The battle to control the story of the possession became one of competing public voices and texts. The first, John Atkinson's, set out the case for Sommers's truthfulness and the godly implications if he was believed. Although it disappeared into the Willoughbys' archives, its content lived on in the writings and statements of the others who had been present on the night of 5 November. The second, Sommers's letter to Darrell, sowed the seeds of the accusation that would be made against Darrell: that he was complicit in counterfeiting as part of a godly plot. It would reappear in the writings of Samuel Harsnett, and then be repeated *ad nauseam* elsewhere. In response to this slur, the godly were forced onto the defensive as the affair moved to the High Commission court at Lambeth and stagnated there. Now the only way forward for them was print, and with no possibility of getting their books authorized this would have to mean illegal publication. Darrell himself would have to begin writing and publishing in his own defence. The apparent godly revolt at Nottingham therefore became an actual godly revolt in print.

But it was the forces of conservatism who were responsible for this. It does not seem to me that there was any godly conspiracy to foment rebellion in Nottingham in order to seize a preaching post in the town, as Harsnett and others alleged. As this account has shown, Nottingham had its own existing tensions which burst into such rebellion every few decades with or without godly help. Nor, as we discussed in Chapters 1 and 2, was there a wider conspiracy involving everyone from William Sommers to the Earl of Essex and justifying Darrell and More's imprisonment and deprivations. The godly had made a lot of noise in Nottingham, and would now pour their words into unauthorized texts. But they would not have done this if the second commission at Nottingham (and beyond them the High Commission) had acted less unjustly. Repression bred revolt, not the other way around. And in fact, it was not godly speech and writing but a key silence, the inability of Nottingham's Mayor to call Sommers's name at the first commission and so seize control of the narrative, that began the spiral into open conflict. Because the Corporation was widely perceived as corrupt and could not speak authoritatively for their divided community, the possession of Sommers exploded onto the national scene.

4 'PARE THY NAILS, DAD': AUTHORITY AND SUBVERSION IN POSSESSION NARRATIVES

For your children. Make it your chiefest work to make them, 1. Godly. 2. Useful …
Robert Harris to his family, quoted in Samuel Clarke,
A General Martyrologie (1677).

Had I a sonne to serve mee so, I would conjure a divell out of him
Thomas Heywood and Richard Brome,
The Late Lancashire Witches (1634).

As the complex histories of the first texts on John Darrell's work in Burton and Nottingham suggest, what was going on at a literary level at the dispossessions of Darrell and his friends was just as important as their political or otherwise factual context. How and why the events were written about and how and why they were responded to in print are as important as the historical facts of the case, because the battle was one of representation and perception, fought through mutual stereotyping. It is difficult enough to establish the circumstances of the texts' production – the basic story of what happened when – because each fragmentary account has its own cultural limitations and biases. But what can be said about how those accounts construct something beyond the factual – not just establishing that Darrell used Rogers's prayers, or Harsnett investigated Darrell's financial affairs, but taking part in a literary and cultural battle where imagery, genre and *topos* mattered as much as the disputed facts?

Chapter 2 established that the habitual discourses of social status and education, as well as constructions of godly culture as likely to be particularly sociable, were important ways in which contemporaries thought and wrote about the affair. It seems to me equally important to consider two other recurrent rhetorics, those of youth and brotherhood, because early modern people habitually thought about government and rebellion in familial terms. Images of the rebellious youth and the schismatic sibling pepper the texts about Darrell and More and their trial, and both take the debate about godly sociability further, because they suggest that the godly perceived themselves and were perceived by others as a family unit in their own right, as well as being part of a wider family, that of the Protestant church. Before moving on to explore what happened at Darrell and More's trial and afterwards, it is important to examine the languages in which contemporaries talked and wrote about these events, and to try to understand how the emotive weight behind images of a dysfunctional family drove forward the pamphlet war. I am not arguing that the Darrell affair was really 'about' family or sociability, but simply that this theme, which was already important in political and religious controversy, insistently attached itself to the texts on the case in the minds of their authors.

Thus, one of the most insulting invectives used against the godly writers who supported Darrell was that of youth: as Harsnett put it, that they were just 'children'. It was also one of Whitgift's favourite slurs on godly ministers in general: 'I will allow no protestation … neither shall you rule, but obey' he told one group who came before him for nonconformity. He added that:

> Younge men and unlearned have done more harm in translateinge then ever they will do good …
>   You are unlearned, and but boyes in comparison of us, who have studied divinity before you for the most were borne.[1]

In a similar vein, the preacher John Wilson was called 'asse … dolt' and 'beardles boy' by ecclesiastical commissioners, and told he had acted 'a lewd yonge mans part', whilst Archbishop Sandys of York told the Bishop of Chester (and former Queens' College President) William Chaderton in 1581 that 'the young ministers of these our times run mad'. Ministers who were also exorcists were further accused of making tools of the enthusiastic or impressionable young layperson. Harsnett wrote that they would 'finde any youth, boy or girle, that is not well at ease' on which to practice their temptation. Children between fourteen and eighteen were best and those 'of the poorer sort, either the children, or servants of such persons, as the Exorcistes doe well know, to be of their owne stampe'. The attraction offered by the would-be exorcists to their accomplices was that pretending possession would allow the children, 'having thereby libertie, to doe and say what they list, and in a sorte to worke won-ders'.[2] Of course, these were exactly the 'liberties' that the exorcists themselves desired, so that the threats of the rebellious young and the godly overlapped most completely in the image of the youthful and independent-minded dis-possessor such as John Darrell.

This rhetoric of age against youth was perhaps not surprising coming from Whitgift, Sandys and Bancroft, who were genuinely older than the ministers who displeased them. But it was surprising coming from Harsnett, who was no older than Darrell when he wrote. The word 'children' clearly implied more than mere physical youth in his case. Paul Griffiths has argued persuasively that childhood and youth were seen as quite distinct stages of life in the early modern period, but when used insultingly such terms were often conflated. M. M. Knappen revealingly compares the imprecise, pejorative use of such terms to the accusations of youthful ignorance made by Catholics against early Protestants.[3] Yet it was not true that the Darrellite godly were uniformly younger than their accusers – which, if it were so, might have been read as a sign that Protestantism was hotting up as each generation produced more radicals than the last. So was a scattershot rhetoric of youth and disobedience being constructed by those who wanted to portray themselves as not merely older, but wiser? It seems to me that something rather more specific was hap-pening. Among the many rebellions that we have begun to see in demonic possession and dispossession, a rebellion of the young was sometimes seen to be in progress, when children defied their parents or refused to behave at school. It seems to me that anti-godly pamphleteers built their imagery of wilful young ministers around the challenge to authority posed by teenage demoniacs, conflating the two and re-imagining them in terms of a revolt of boyish godly ministers against the prelates. The metaphor of unfilial sons worked on many levels: Sir Thomas Overbury, in his character of 'A Puritane', wrote metaphorically that 'whose child he is, is yet unknowne; for willingly his faith allowes no father'. Godliness was, in his view, hostile to all author-ity that might be construed as paternalistic.[4] Inherent in this language of old and young were assertions of the naturalness of gerontocracy, the necessity of mastery and instruction, and the danger of ignorance, inexperience and enthusiasm, some of which arguments we have already seen deployed against the tradesmen-authors of Burton and the burgesses of Nottingham.

Of course, there was a way of reversing this rhetoric in favour of the young. Griffiths, in his history of early modern youth, stresses the creativity and positive contribution of young people in the period, and some of their con-temporaries agreed with him. The godly sometimes portrayed youth as 'the dangerous season', as Arthur Hildersham's mentor Richard Greenham called it. But conversely they sometimes wrote with pride that their followers were likely to be idealistic young people, brought up under a Protestant regime and untainted by the failures (as they saw them) of the past. If these people wanted change, then it was likely to be the right course, based on a purer wisdom than that of their forefathers. Patrick Collinson once called the Reformation 'a revolution of youth', and the godly preacher Henry Smith, whose nephew would one day become a demoniac and an accuser of witches, said that:

> If it be so, as they say, that none but young men do hear our doctrine, then this text is well chosen for the auditory, to teach young men that which if they learn, they may say with David 'I have more understanding than the ancient' … God hath chosen the young things to do his works.[5]

In the early Elizabethan period, reformation was often associated with younger people because the existing church post-holders were linked with Catholicism – most obviously, and sometimes unfairly, due to their age. Because Catholicism was equated with ignorance and superstition, young people were easily able to be portrayed as better informed than their elders. 'Young persons' could 'overthrowe them' in debate, complained one preacher. But there was less justification for this stance as the reign went on. And as part of this construction of popish ignorance, the godly also turned the accusation of youth on their opponents, which demonstrates nicely the gap between the reality of the situation and the language in which it was being imagined and disseminated. Godly ministers complained that that due to favouritism and the evils of ecclesiastical hierarchy, 'boyes' had prebendaries when they, who were better qualified, had no livings.[6]

The wider debate about the relationship between authority and age in the Church was played out on a number of actual and metaphorical levels in the controversy over the dispossessions of Darrell and his friends. Most striking, as we have seen, were the analogies between rebellion within the church and rebellion within the family. As Peter Lake and Michael Questier state, 'the little church and commonwealth of the household' was 'a microcosm … of the godly commonwealth'. Disorder in one might well reflect or symbolize disorder in the other.[7] Just as the struggle over godly dispossessions was between a group portrayed as naughty children and the 'Reverend Fathers in God' Bishop Bancroft or Archbishop Whitgift, so stories of possession frequently involved challenges by children and young adults to parental authority. Here the rhetoric of youthful rebellion was embodied; and it was given much-debated demonological ambiguity by the supposed involvement of the devil who was speaking for, but was also the internal adversary of, the young demoniac. The existing cultural tension, common in most societies, about the behaviour of youth was thus amplified and greatly complicated; and the godly pamphlets of the Darrell affair participate in this process both by telling stories of families in crisis and by themselves becoming the focus of anti-juvenile rhetoric.

The first question to be asked in exploring this knot of notions about youth and its place in society is a simple one with complex answers: what was at stake in possession cases involving young people? Firstly, many such cases seem to be revolving around a battle for authority between filial and parental figures. And, secondly, given the degree of cultural significance being imputed to youthful rebelliousness, it is no surprise that agents from outside the home (exorcists, physicians, magistrates and magical healers) were given great power to intervene in family life to bring about a resolution. Thus the discourses of theology, medicine, the law and so on were applied to try to solve problems in individual families, giving the once obscure and private household enormous significance. The outcome of each case thus came to matter to a wide range of people for different professional reasons. And despite (and, in fact, because of) all this external attention designed to restore order, in cases of possession sons and daughters were often assaulting their parents and other adults in ways that suggest savage resentments and fears being worked out in the space created by supernatural possibilities. Pamphlets on possession thus opened up to literary scrutiny a murky area of private family life that was usually closed to public view: whilst conflicts over inheritance, parental consent to marriage and other more public and practical matters were often dramatized, fictive literature and theatre steered clear of many central concerns of childhood. Children's lives within the private patriarchal sphere, and especially their inner lives, were of little interest to fiction until they reached marriagable age – despite the fact that they clearly had stories to tell. So unless children became the victims of sensational crime, details of their individual lives were quite unlikely to appear in writing or, especially, in print. Pamphlets on possession (and obsession and witchcraft attack, other supernatural afflictions) are one of the few places therefore where we can read about the inner workings of early modern family life with a focus on the younger members of the family. And the issues that are important there are just the ones that were important to the godly: hierarchy, autonomy and the balance between obedience to worldly and divine forces.

This does not seem to me to be a coincidence. Pretending to be possessed, or experiencing something that could sincerely be experienced as demonic possession, created many opportunities for children and young adults. But it also created opportunities for godly authors and the two came together in a moment of cultural serendipity that reflects interestingly on both parties. Lawrence Stone's classic picture of 'many children' growing up 'with a fear and even hatred of their parents' who had beaten and ranted at them may be related to his challenged argument that parent-child bonds were weak in the early-modern period, but the 'extreme deference to parents' expected of children seems to have been general, in public, at least.[8] When both the family and the wider political world were so regulated by hierarchies enforceable by violence, then recourse to the supernatural world offered an opportunity to challenge, invert, mock and subvert those hierarchies, as well as eventually reaffirming them, sometimes on better terms.[9] When this challenge occurred in a godly possession, traditional socio-political and religious power structures came into direct conflict with radical godly ones, in which babes and sucklings were empowered to speak the truth. Whilst this was occurring, there was also an opportunity for godly ministers to aspire to reform their own authority figures, the bishops and archbishops who kept them in a position of subjection and silence, sometimes literally. The same opportunity for self-assertion was undoubtedly also given by young demoniacs to Catholic exorcists. But the cultural dynamic would work very differently for those who were members of a rival church, that of Rome. Within the Protestant church, where everyone was supposed to be part of the same family, there were very strong synergies between young unfilial demoniacs and marginalized ministers, and this chapter explores these with specific reference to three cases which seem to illustrate them particularly well.

Tensions in the Family

That the young should be particularly receptive to attack and temptation by witches or by Satan directly was an obvious extension of the view that youth was 'a metaphorical battleground between good and evil'.[10] Childhood and adolescence or 'youth', the last of which stretched from the age of puberty to the late twenties, were periods of intense surveillance, instruction and correction, particularly for anyone whose parents had even the slightest pretensions to respectable gentility or godly life. And as J. A. Sharpe demonstrates, where statistics can be obtained it can be seen that children and adolescents were very frequently cited as the supposed victims of witchcraft attack, possession or demonic obsession. Possession was almost exclusively a malady of the young, not the old, as the ages of Darrell's patients (from the very early teens to the early thirties) confirm. It did not seem to matter here whether one was a child or a youth: Satan was an ever-present threat and until the mid-thirties – Darrell's age at the time of his final exorcism, in fact – the young offered little resistance to his temptations. However, once they had 'fallen', they were often in a better position in many respects than they had been before. If accounts are to be believed, the young victims asserted that they were supernaturally afflicted even in the face of considerable adult scepticism, and their activities suggest that claiming this special status was empowering, despite its discomforts. Superficially, and no doubt satisfyingly, it allowed all kinds of behaviour normally punished with severity. Sharpe lists undesirable behaviour in the young as 'sensuality, disobedience, levity, wantonness, idleness, excess, envy, ambition, and mocking of elders and authority'. Possession, he notes 'not only made these adolescents the centre of attraction: it also gave them a licence for bad behaviour'.[11]

There are many good examples in the possession cases associated with Darrell and his friends of what Sharpe means, but the Lancashire case is perhaps the best. The children of Nicholas and Anne Starkie physically attacked not only the visiting ministers but also their own parents. They 'fleed from all the familye and neighbours ... calling them devils with hornes'. Darrell argued that they were certainly possessed, because in their right minds:

> they would never have spoken so malapertly in theire fits as usually they did to those that were then present, especially to Maister Starchy (whome commonly they called good fellowe, all their speaches also in a manner suting with that tytle) and Mistres Starchye whose owne childe called her whoore.

John spoke, praying and singing psalms, for over two hours, and although one of his prayers was 'for those that have Authoritie, for his parents', when his father 'wished him to lie stil, and to speak no more' he would not obey. He also bit his mother. The five children in the Starkie household collectively made up what seem to be games (collecting and arranging leaves from the garden) and also did things that children love to do, but which are not decorous or godly, such as hopping like frogs, hiding under beds and dancing.

Claiming a possession freed the mind as well as the body. Thirteen-year-old Margaret Hardman, in supposedly attacking by words and actions the pride of modern women, appears to have actually been fantasizing very specifically about being given a present of a silk petticoat, a French bodice and farthingale, a satin gown with wired sleeves, a cap with a feather, cork shoes and other fine gifts by the devil, whom she referred to as 'my lad'. One of the demoniacs, despite her virginity, spoke 'filthie uncleannes' during a sermon. Most overtly demonstrating that possession could be rewarding, the children had fantasies of complete empowerment. Identifying themselves with the devil, and speaking in 'his' voice, some even blasphemously claimed to be God himself. Normally such behaviour would be unthinkable: the possession victims could only do these things, said Darrell, 'because they knew not what they said and did'. Insensibility was a very good excuse, or a very useful symptom, depending on how one looks at it.[12] And whilst the young demoniac consciously or unconsciously expressed frustration about his or her disempowerment, the godly exorcist was doing something very similar himself. When the matter reached written and printed form, a set of issues thus came before the public – and especially the godly public – that were only usually discussed, if at all, in very limited terms.

Ironically, in such a prescriptive society, many adults had little more autonomy than their children. The godly, subjected to the hated church courts, to an unsympathetic parish structure and liturgy, and to demands for subscription enforced by suspensions and deprivations, felt this particularly deeply, and their fascination with a phenomenon that broke all the rules is thus the more interesting. It is very suggestive that supposedly repressive and repressed godly people published and read pamphlets about children who shouted down and physically assaulted the authority figures in their world. I am not arguing here for the sympathetic 'discovery of childhood' by the godly which was suggested by C. John Sommerville, but rather for a more covert and problematic identification in certain circumstances and rhetorics between the stereotypically rebellious godly and the rebellious young.[13] Looked at this way, demonic possession was (to risk a undoubtedly troublesome analogy) the early modern punk: it not only allowed its young participants to flout social norms, but to the wider community it pointed up the repressive and arbitrary nature of the controls on persons supposedly of an age to govern themselves, controls which they were expected to enforce upon others. It expressed the frustration of a subjected society. And it also focused attention on the frequent hypocrisies inherent in authority, which the godly saw only too clearly in everyday life, and which – like Sommers's sin-acting at Nottingham – were an important focus of godly dispossessions and the preaching and writing about them.

An episode of possession (or obsession or witch attack) also offered an irresistible invitation to plural authorities to enter the battle for social and familial control: other adults who could overrule parents, God who was above mere bishops, multiple ecclesiastical commissions, appeals to different doctors and cunning-men, sees and courts. The historian Robert Muchembled, writing on children's accusation of their mothers and other 'peasant women' as witches in early modern France and the Netherlands, found a challenging and fragmenting of authority in these witchcraft accusations. He suggests that the women accused of witchcraft:

> are the exact equivalent, in their own culture, of demonologists and judges in theirs. They bring up children, but in a very different way from that in which theologians and magistrates seek to educate the people.[14]

In accusing witches, therefore, children were at some level inviting outside authorities to enter their homes and, having assessed their parents and carers, to find them wanting, as had the devil within. For Muchembled, it is the very identity between the macrocosm and microcosm of family (in the state and the private household) that made this a likely outcome. Family and state should be identical in their aims, but find that they are not. A jealousy springs up in those in public authority that those in private authority – parents, the wider family, women who educate and socialize children – are doing so wrongly, and are undermining the fatherly acculturative role of the state in doing so. So the state must step in and encourage the removal of these false leaders. By extension, this must be done at the expense of inverting usual hierarchies and allowing, even requiring, the child to control both parent and magistrate or churchman by directing inquisition and prosecution.

Although this is rather a crude model, tending for example to construct 'the state' as unified and tyrannical, it is useful in pointing to the multi-layered conflicts over control in possession and witchcraft events – and I think that the violence of debate over possession and exorcism in pamphlets like those about the Darrell dispossessions can be partly explained by the horrors of this anarchy.[15] As Lana Condie has noted, just as the demoniac could offer a challenge to the apparently unassailable authorities in his or her world and bring them crashing down, so 'the exorcist could pose a threat to the hierarchy within the clergy'.[16] In the ideal pejorative image created by Harsnett in response to this threat, the young rebellious demoniac invited in a young rebellious exorcist, and together they promoted verbally and in print the accusation of elders: innocent 'witches' and pious bishops. The world was thus turned upside down, in precisely the way that early modern people had been taught to fear. It is an extraordinary world-view, but no more extraordinary than Richard Bancroft's practice of likening godly ministers (instead of bishops) to witches. And as Alexandra Walsham has shown in her work on the godly artisan William Hacket, who planned an uprising in London in support of Cartwright in 1591, charismatic churchmen and religious enthusiasts had in fact many similarities with cunning men and mystics.[17] Sometimes an apparently extreme metaphor or simile can give a unique insight. In the case of godly dispossession, the metaphor of the family offers just this: Darrell and More found themselves slapped down as naughty children (and also, *pace* Walsham, demonized like witches). And this was because they were actually behaving quite like naughty children, revelling in the vicarious experience of their own conflict with the devil by another young godly person, and extrapolating from this a duty to engage in various kinds of criticism of authority. They saw this as legitimate, but the paternal authorities of church and state did not.

It was the playing out of this multiple power-grab – first by the young demoniac, second by his or her dispossessor, and third by the reactive ecclesiastical authorities – that led to the publication of the pamphlets about Darrell and his friends' dispossessions. The final irony was that in publishing such stories to the wider public, the godly were repeating the pattern of inviting a challenge to established authorities. Once again, they appeared as rebellious, appealing to the reader as an authority beyond the immediate circumstance of ecclesiastical court or prison. In comparing the Lord Chief Justice to Pontius Pilate or calling Bishop Bancroft a favourer of atheists, the godly paralleled themselves with Sommers acting out the sins of Nottingham's worthies, and they did so in defiance of the Queen and her ministers by publishing their tracts illegally, because they had to.[18]

From Print into Practice: The Throckmortons and Darling

Once such stories were in print, they tended to replicate themselves in new cases of 'possession' involving those who had read the tracts. One of the narratives referred to most often in pamphlets about the Darrell exorcisms as a model for fraudulent young demoniacs is *The Most strange and admirable discoverie of the three Witches of Warboys* (London, 1593). It is also one of the best examples of the *topos* of the dysfunctional family, and its association with and healing by godliness. Ironically, no-one at Warboys, in Huntingdonshire, ever claimed to be, or was diagnosed as being, possessed until John Darrell said that he took it that they were. The five daughters of Robert and Elizabeth Throckmorton represented themselves as being bewitched, and obsessed by demons outside their bodies rather than possessed by devils inside, as were seven servants in the family home. But whilst it does not give precise instructions for feigning possession, *The Most strange and admirable discoverie* does offer a model to readers like William Sommers of the kind of challenge to adult authority that can be successfully mounted by claiming supernatural affliction. Right from the outset of the case, the Throckmorton children's parents are doomed to lose the battle for control, and their children are seen to be in an unassailable position, if one is a cynical enough reader. A young man trapped in an apprenticeship, for example, might see many advantages in copying their behaviour. It could work so well because as soon as the parents, guardians or masters of the supposed victim accepted that they could not solve the problem and called in outside aid, the demoniac had already transformed their world and its prospects. In the case of the Throckmortons, the parents' first mistake was to call in medical expertise, perfectly reasonably yet fatally abdicating their own authority over their unruly ten-year-old daughter Jane. This led them into the opening skirmishes of a battle that would last for an astonishing three years.

On or around 13 November 1589, Jane had casually identified her neighbour Alice Samuel as 'the old witch', as part of the little girl's 'strange kind of sicknes and distemperature of body'. But her parents resisted formal accusation of Alice and her family until 1592 – when finally they accepted that their children must be obsessed through the agency of witches and took the matter to the Bishop of Lincoln on 26 December. Three days later magistrates became involved.[19] In the intervening years, the position of Robert and Elizabeth Throckmorton is represented as being weakened step by step until eventually they are almost written out of the story of their daughters' lives. They are open to almost any suggestion about the cause of their children's illness, resistant only to the belief of the young 'victims' that witches were responsible: and, paradoxically, this refusal to scapegoat witches facilitates their own disempowerment. Elizabeth Throckmorton was in fact 'very angrie' with her daughter Jane for calling Alice Samuel a witch in November 1589, 'and rebuked her for saying so'. But two days later the first explanation was sought from authority outside the family: Jane's urine was sent to Dr Philip Barrow, renowned Cambridge author of *The Method of Physicke* (1590) and, as the pamphlet is careful to tell the reader, 'a man well knowne to be excellent skilfull in Phisicke'. Barrow said that he could not identify any distemperature, but 'thought she might be troubled with wormes'.[20] His medicine was given to Jane but had no effect, and two days later, he was asked for a further opinion and given a fuller description of Jane's symptoms. Again, he replied that the urine contained no clue, and this time rejected her parents' specific suggestion that her disease was the epileptic 'falling sicknes'. The Throckmortons had begun the long process of having their judgment over-ruled by an external authority that supported the subversive claims of their own child.

However, they were determined people, and they continued to follow Barrow's prescriptions whilst reporting back to him their lack of efficacy, 'as his desire was to understand how his Phisicke wrought'. Dr Barrow then, the pamphlet details methodically, re-examined Jane's urine and her body, and finally asked whether witchcraft was suspected. But instead of taking his cue, the Throckmortons replied that it was not (despite Jane's assertion in November) and with Barrow's encouragement sought a second opinion, probably from William Butler, an early experimenter with the theories of Paracelsus and thus probably expected to be of rather different opinions than Barrow. In fact, Butler made the same diagnosis (possibly worms) but again commented 'if it were the wormes … it was a very strange kind of griefe to be caused by them in that sort'. Barrow's last word on the case was that Robert Throckmorton should save his time and money and abandon the search for medical remedy: Barrow 'had some experience of the malice of some witches, and he verily thought that there was some kind of sorcerie and witchcraft wrought towards his childe'. Throckmorton, however, saw an authority beyond doctors and 'resolved himselfe to rest upon Gods pleasure'. 'Both himselfe and his wife' notes the pamphleteer 'were free of any such conceit of witchcraft'.[21] The pamphlet places the reader (who knows from the title onwards what the pamphlet is about) in a privileged interpretive position, alongside the ultimately vindicated child, and sets them up for a satisfyingly long wait before the parents realize that their view cannot prevail. In the meantime, like their imitator William Sommers (and Thomas Darling, Katherine Wright and the Lancashire seven), the Throckmorton children took control of their home and could get away with almost anything. Interested by this anarchy, various godly people began to take notes on their behaviour and the girls' lives began to become part of the text which would one day result in the pamphlet *The Most strange and admirable discoverie*.

When a month after Jane's Throckmorton's first symptoms two more of the family's daughters 'fell into the same like extremities' and began to accuse Alice Samuel openly ('it is she (sayd they) that hath bewitched us, and she will kill us if you doe not take her away'), Robert and Elizabeth Throckmorton did begin to suspect that witchcraft might be involved. They were, as was conventional with godly people, opposed to trying counter-magic such as scratching the woman their children and servants had named as a witch. Says the pamphlet, 'both the parents and ... M[aster] Pickering had taken advise of good Divines of the unlawfulnes thereof'.[22] Yet the Throckmortons' proactive and even more godly relative Gilbert Pickering, Elizabeth's brother and a magistrate (who by 1612 would be happily swimming witches), went beyond this advice on 13 February.[23] Jane, lying on a bed in convulsive fits, stretched out her hand and began to claw the coverlet saying 'Oh that I had her'. Pickering, although he 'was of that opinion, that scratching was meerley unlawful', offered his own hand as a test, but Jane would not scratch it. However, when Pickering (believing, the account justifies, that 'the occasion [was] thus offered by the childe, or rather by the spirit in the child, to disclose some secret, whereby the Witches might be ... made manifest and knowen') brought Alice Samuel to Jane, the child scratched her hand so hard that her nails broke.[24] This was also tried with another woman, Cicely Burder. Despite the many attempts made to justify this 'experiment' (as the writer referred to it), both Robert Throckmorton and the rector of Warboys Francis Dorington, husband of Robert's sister Mary, put a stop to it as soon as they discovered Pickering's activities – nor is any further action against Cicely Burder reported. Robert had had his authority questioned by one brother-in-law and found an ally in another – but the logic of the narrative in *The Most strange and admirable discoverie* is simple. Eventually both he and Dorington, and Elizabeth Throckmorton, would bow to the judgment expressed by Barrow, Pickering, Pickering's brother Henry (a Cambridge scholar and grandfather of John Dryden), and, firstly and consistently, by Jane and all her sisters, that they were bewitched.

The relationship between accusations of witchcraft and the loss of parental authority is further complicated by the insight that in many ways those accused of witchcraft – in this case the Samuel family – function as a substitute for the accusers' family. The pain and shame the Throckmorton children inflicted on 'Father Samuel' and 'Mother Samuel' parallels the indignity, disruption and reversal of judgment that they forced upon their own parents. Most obviously, the afflicted children inverted the usual parent-child relationship of educative lecturing and punishment. Their parents were forced to listen to hours of their children's opinions and imaginations, which read like parodies of their own, and inattentiveness was rewarded with behaviour calculated to re-engage attention. The 'witches', however, were especially targeted with this. The Throckmortons' eldest daughter Joan, reporting a supposed vision of Alice

Samuel, began a trend of criticizing her demeanour and character by noting that 'mother Samuel is very loude', and later all the girls joined in 'heavenly and divine speeches' to her: 'they rehearsed … unto her, her naughty manner of living, her usuall cursing and banning of all that displeased her … her negligent comming to Church, and slacknesse in Gods service'.[25] Her husband John was subjected to similar sermonizing, Elizabeth Throckmorton junior telling him 'he was a naughtie man, and a Witch … exhorting him to prayers'. When he interrupted the twelve- or thirteen-year-old child, she continued to talk over him, for one and a half hours.[26] The girls' attitude to Agnes Samuel, the daughter of Alice and John, sums up the tensions in their own position: they repeat 'thou art a wicked child … thou wicked child', and offer criticism of her relationship with her mother, whom they say allows Agnes 'to be her dame, both in controuling of her, and beating of her'.[27] As Barbara Rosen noted, 'it is almost as if they were punishing themselves in this other disobedient and uncontrollable daughter'.[28] In fact, all the failings that they remark so disrespectfully in their elders are those they themselves act out: loudness, immodesty, irreligious speech and activity, and refusal to be corrected.

The witches are avatars of the girls and their parents too. This observation becomes more pointed when Gilbert Pickering advises Alice Samuel 'to keepe the womans vertue, and be more silent', something that Joan repeats in her account of their meeting.[29] As a fifteen-year-old girl, her very ability to make this lengthy statement depends on her being 'bewitched' and presenting her desire to speak and be heard by adults as a report of a vision. Likewise, her and her sisters' pious sermonizing trances reiterate their interpellation into the ideology of absolute love of and submission to their parents, at the very moment when they are in deepest revolt against that position. It was not until they had been utterly vindicated against parental scepticism by a five-hour trial at the Assizes ending in the agreement of the Judge and twenty-four grand and petty jurors that they would submit to their parents: a movement begun by Jane when she 'came out of her fit: and then seeing her father, kneeled downe, and asked him blessing'.[30] The moment of submission to her father is in fact the moment of conquest by his own child, facilitated by a story of devils and witches, published and crushingly endorsed by the law and its ministers, and by various godly outsiders. No wonder the story of such dramatic battles over authority was thought to be attractive to Sommers, a problematic stepson and a run-away apprentice. When Harsnett identified it as the source of Sommers's inspiration, his account gained in plausibility. But Darrell remained unmoved, and challenged Harsnett to examine the Throckmorton case as closely as he had done that of Sommers. Why, he asked sharply, had Harsnett not said flatly that the five girls were counterfeiting their symptoms, and why was the case not followed up? Could it be 'because they were the children of an Esquier'? He believed that if investigations had been carried out, it would have been discovered that the girls were indeed obsessed by the devil and that their godly relations had been right to persist in convincing their parents of this truth. He had, he said, considerable sympathy with these 'gentlewomen', whose reputation had been done such an injury by Harsnett.[31] In this sympathy, we can see the homology between youth and godliness at work.

Just as it was easy to imagine that the godly were wicked and seditious simply because they were nonconforming, so it is easy to construct an argument that supposedly possessed children and young adults in the early modern period told and had published their stories of demonic attack because they were naughty or bored. It is sometimes impossible to suppress the kind of response that Rosen recorded after her reading of *The Examination and Confession of certaine Wytches*, the 1566 pamphlet describing the apparent demonic obsession of twelve-year-old Agnes Browne. Rosen calls her narration 'breathless' and 'glib', responding angrily to 'one of those pious, polite little girls whose hysterical spiritual dramas land her centre stage with a halo every time'.[32] Since men and women were executed as witches because of the accusations of such children and young people, this is a quite justifiable response. But clearly there were also more complex religious and cultural imperatives at work for demoniacs, different in each case, just as there were for godly ministers. In one of the cases associated with Darrell and his group, we now know exactly how a demoniac accounted for his counterfeiting of fits. A recently-discovered document gives Thomas Darling's reasons, as given to his examiners at Lambeth.

Darling had faked his possession, he said, 'partlie for his owne praise, and partlie for that he thought therby the worde of god would be better reverenced'. In addition he had told his examiners that he imagined that:

> he might lawfullie have counterfeited suche fitts, because he did them with some good intent and thought that therby god should be glorified and his worde the better thought of by those w[hi]ch sawe him in his supposed fitts.[33]

Darling, therefore, presented himself in exactly the same way that Darrell did: as a godly person seeking to advance God's Word by unusual but not unlawful means. These means were extraordinary precisely because godly religious commitment was extraordinary, with its tendency to license the faithful to follow their consciences and their own interpretations of scripture without tarrying for the magistrate, as the godly put it. Darling was like Darrell too in that he even wanted to 'be a preacher to thunder out the threatenings of Gods word, against sinne and all abhominations'.[34] Again the identification between minister and youth is apparent: without recourse to accusations of insincerity, theatricality or psychological anachronism, both can be seen to be telling the same story of themselves.

Darling's godly representation of himself is especially interesting because it is part of exactly the same generic story of childish rebellion as that told in *The Most strange and admirable discoverie*, which he had read. There are striking similarities, again stressing the gradual disempowerment of the adults who were Darling's guardians. In *The most wonderfull and true storie*, the account of Darling's possession, a very similar tale to that of Robert and Elizabeth Throckmorton and their children is told. The people whose authority was most obviously at stake in Burton were Robert and Elizabeth Toone, Darling's aunt and uncle, with whom he lived. As we have seen, the Toones were wealthy and respectable people, leaders of town society, and Darling must have been placed with them – as the Hardman sisters and Ellen Holland were sent to Nicholas Starkie – because it was thought that they could offer their nephew advancement. Both the boy's parents are mentioned in the account of his possession, so we know that he was not housed with his relatives because he was, for instance, an orphan. He was, however, in a position of dependence and expected gratitude, and his apparent rebellion is thus the more pointed.

Like Robert and Elizabeth Throckmorton, Darling's aunt and uncle initially, and quite determinedly, refused to accept that he was supernaturally afflicted. Eventually, they were forced to accept his special and holy status as the site of a work of God, but it was a long process, as *The most wonderfull and true storie* details. At first, Elizabeth Toone was convinced that his sickness was merely physical. She 'went to a Phisition with his urine', who, like Dr Barrow, 'saw no signes of anie natural disease … unles it were the wormes', and she went again when the prescribed medicine failed to work. Like the Throckmortons, she was then advised by her physician that the boy might be bewitched, but 'holding [it] incredible', she chose to ignore his opinion and keep it secret. Like the Throckmortons, too, she believed the problem might be epilepsy.[35] But as her house filled with those who came to see Darling, Jesse Bee, who had come to take notes on his condition and read the Bible to him, also offered the opinion that he was bewitched. Once again Elizabeth Toone refused to credit his assertion, although she did now reveal what the doctor had said. Darling then produced his story of having fallen out with Alice Gooderidge. Events began to move towards a witchcraft accusation, despite Darling's aunt's misgivings.

Mistress Toone's judgment was further questioned by the boy's grandmother Mistress Walkeden, but she too was cautious, 'making conscience to accuse her [the suspect Alice Gooderidge] till it appeared upon sure proofe'.[36] She sent for Gooderidge and, in conjunction with Oliver Rampaine, the boy's schoolmaster and his uncle Robert Toone, questioned her in the town hall of Burton, away from the Toone household. Robert was now open to the conviction that his nephew was bewitched, but others were keen to push him further. 'Some of the standers by' persuaded Darling to scratch Alice

Gooderidge, and although the pamphlet – in a section probably written by the minister John Denison – argues strongly that scratching is 'to be receaved amongst the witchcrafts … to the great dishonor of God', an opinion that the Toones shared, subsequent questioning elicited from the suspect that she had been in the wood where Darling said he had met her, that she did not attend Communion and could not say all of the Lord's Prayer or Creed. After that, Robert Toone began to believe his nephew, and reported Gooderidge to the magistrate Thomas Gresley.

Once this capitulation to magisterial intervention had occurred, Gooderidge and her mother Elizabeth Wright were questioned and submitted to further tests by Gresley and Sir Humphrey Ferrers. Both women were searched for witches' teats by a team of matronly women and examined by a surgeon, and Gooderidge was then committed to jail on 14 April by the magistrates.[37] This plethora of outside authorities, together with longer and longer reports of Darling's speeches to the devil, effectively remove the once central Elizabeth Toone from the narrative, and Robert too is soon sidelined, replaced with figures familiar from the Warboys case of a few years before: the zealous experimenter with counter-magic, the authoritative relative, the magistrate, medical man and minister, and, ultimately and suggestively, the penitent witch. Alice Gooderidge died in jail serving her sentence for bewitching Darling.[38] Meanwhile, the boy, the godly and their ministers Darrell, More and Hildersham all emerged victorious from the events at Burton in 1596, at the expense of those who were previously authoritative in Darling's life. Possession stories and their publication were thus seen in yet another godly pamphlet to be effective in changing the balance of power in favour of the young and the godly.

Darling went on to do what he had wanted: make a difference for the godly in public life. It is not clear whether or not he became a minister, but in 1602, as a student at Oxford, he was tried in the Star Chamber and sentenced to be whipped and to have his ears cropped, because he had criticized the Vice-Chancellor and his old adversary the Bishop of London for promoting papistry.[39] Even before this, Harsnett described Darling in disgust as an 'apte scholler of M[aster] Darrel', because he had dared to write to Bancroft repudiating his confession of counterfeiting, which he said he had made under duress, in no uncertain terms. Darling said that 'he had beene drawne on by subtilties to make the said confession' and added 'what is all this to the purpose? If I of frailtie should say, that all was dissembling, was it therefore? If I say that this paper is blacke, is it so therefore?' 'A more proude and desperate forsworne boy, hath not lightly fallen into any mans examination' said Harsnett, using once again the generationally-loaded language of men and boys.[40] A boy who could stand up to a bishop, and do so in writing, was indeed an astounding creature in early modern England, and Darling must have been seen as a (dis)credit to his mentors. As his example summarizes, two kinds of self-assertion came together in polemical accounts of dispossessions by prayer and fasting, which could be read as parallel rebellions of the godly and of the young. Culturally, they fitted perfectly.

Confrontation in Context: The Daughters of Edward Fairfax

That cultural match also extends into what we can sometimes see of the relationships between older and younger participants in a possession or obsession, in the period before it began. Sometimes we are given vignettes of the family's past during the course of an account. One especially interesting example, because the victims' parent took unusual pains to describe carefully in his own words his domestic and public relationships, is the case of Edward Fairfax and his daughters Hellen and Elizabeth, of Fewstone in Yorkshire. In October 1621, Hellen, aged twenty-one, began to exhibit symptoms of trance and experience visions and in January 1622 her seven-year-old sister Elizabeth joined her. Their father presents a spectacle of frustration and puzzlement as he details in an unpublished manuscript account the symptoms that debilitated his daughters and, most surprisingly, describes the refusal of physicians, divines and magistrates to identify these as anything other than natural or pretended. Like many of the recorded cases, the exact nature of the victims' affliction is fluid: witches were accused but there seems to have been no question of exorcism (Fairfax denied that he was either 'a fantastick Puritan, nor superstitious Papist' – the types of people who might be supposed to run to exorcists). However, the victims' symptoms were those which in other eyes would have been of a possession or obsession, and Fairfax came to believe that his daughters were so bewitched.

Hellen in particular was tormented by pious visions including apparent ghosts of her dead siblings, the devil offering temptations, and a sermon by Alexander Cooke. Cooke was the godly vicar of Leeds and an acquaintance of Arthur Hildersham, who was deprived with him and John Brinsley in 1604–5 after a lengthy battle with the Bishop of Lincoln.[41] Cooke later appeared spectrally to Hellen to banish the devil (surely a plea for dispossession?) and to drive away would-be invasive creatures such as the cat that she said breathed poison into her mouth. But instead of flocking supportively to the Fairfax house at Fewston, Fairfax's neighbours and spiritual advisor doubted his judgment, as Fairfax reports:

> I sent for Henry Graver & for Mr. Smithson ye Vicar of Fuystone, to whome, (as my good neighbours) I reported ye strangeness of ye case, and of ym expected advice & comfort, as soe great a perturbation needfully required. But I found my selfe deceived in yt expectation.

Instead, the men urged Fairfax to be very cautious in pursuing witches on the basis of his evidence. To the reader of accounts of possession, which tend (as we have seen) to be rhetorically framed so that any resistance to belief is represented as being subsequently overcome by experience and eventually helps confirm the diagnosis of demonic attack, the blunt report of their scepticism comes as a surprise. Here the parent is credulous, the external authority sceptical. However, the outcome was curiously similar: a loss of parental authority. Worse was to come for Fairfax: when he proceeded to accuse six witches, and have them committed for trial (twice, in fact), he faced continued and vehement opposition from the very first examination onwards. Later, at the second Assize hearing, he was told there had even been a petition from his neighbours to the judge stressing the good character of the accused. Ultimately the trial was stopped, on the grounds that the victims were not physically consumed, as the statute demanded, and the accused were freed. We are presented with an account that reverses the usual generic expectations of possession stories, but which offers us a fascinating insight into the sympathy between the godly and the young demoniac, both at the expense of paternal authority.

The case could have collapsed for a wide variety of reasons: the fact that the suspected witches really were of unimpeachable character, local politics and family feuding, the unreliability of the Fairfax girls' fellow-witness Maud Jeffray, a pattern of judicial scepticism. But Fairfax himself suggests otherwise in his comments on the painful chain of events. He humiliatingly records his neighbours and the authorities' suspicions about his family's psychological state, and especially his competence as a father:

> upon my selfe was put an aspersion not of dishonesty, but of simplicity & it was given out yt Jeffray & his family devised ye practice, to w[hi]ch they drew my eldest daughter and she ye younger, and yt I (like a good Innocent) beleeved all w[hi]ch I heard or saw to be true and not feigned; they add an end my children should aim at in ys, Vid[elicet] to be ye more cherished.

Self-accusingly, Fairfax presents his children as neglected and therefore disobedient, even as he denies that this is a correct perception. Siding with the indignant father, J. A. Sharpe says that Fairfax 'shows himself to have been a very caring and loving parent'.[42] But although this may well have been true, Fairfax records the opposite representation as having been promoted by his neighbours, and presented by them to the authorities whom he invited to judge his children and himself. Once again a possession narrative is seen to be empowering a young person at the expense of her parent, and the account elaborates on Fairfax's paternal faults even as he strives to justify himself.

To begin with, Fairfax distinguishes hierarchically between his daughters, in the longest passage on the family's internal dynamics:

ye Elder Hellen Fairfax [was] a maid of 21 years, of person healthfull, of com-
plexion sanguine: free from melancholy, of capacitie not apprehensive of much,
but rather hard to learn things fit, slow of speech, patient of reproofe, of behaviour wthout offence, educated only in my own house, and therefore not knowing
much. Elizabeth my younger Daughter an Infant of scarce 7 years, of a pleasant
aspect, quick witt, active spirit able to receive any instruction, and willing to
undergoe pains.

Hellen, although the elder, is also represented as the less favoured. She appears
simple and worthy: not worth much education, good, but dull. This is despite
the fact that her father and teacher was the learned translator of Tasso and a
poet himself, and that he stresses his patriarchal-tutorial role at the account's
opening: 'I live a faithful Christian and obedient subject, and so teach my
family'. Later he describes teaching Elizabeth to read. Yet he makes it clear that
he feels he has not been able to teach Hellen in the same style, and that she is
distressingly unfit in various ways. Elizabeth, however, though 'scarce' seven, is
seen as intelligent and lively, learning well and pleasing her father.

It is also striking that Hellen, although twenty-one, is not spoken of as mar-
riageable, nor is her marriage recorded until 1636, the year after her father's
death, when she would have been thirty-six. Elizabeth, though fourteen years
younger, was married the year before, 1635. Hellen's visions, however, suggest
fantasies of being wooed, and resentment of her father – perhaps symbolizing
her imaginings of a lack of parental provision for her. Her fits are reminiscent
of those of Margaret Hardman, and like Margaret, Katherine Wright and Mary
Cowper, she engages in a gendered as well as a generational rebellion in expressing sexual feelings and female disobedience in defiance of her father.[43] She saw,
she said, a young man, handsome and fashionably dressed, who told her that
he was a prince and came as a suitor to her. When she challenged him, telling
him that he was the devil, his real wife appeared and they urged Hellen to kill
herself. The young man added that her father was 'naught'. Hellen also had a
vision of a malignant child sucking at her breast.[44] It is interesting that the girls'
mother is hardly mentioned at all, although Hellen's visions in October and
December of dead siblings and the suckling child suggest what is known from
parish registers: that her mother had given birth to another child, Ann, in June
1621 and Ann had died in October.[45]

Hellen's demonic world, then, is full of weakened mothers, ghostly children
and flawed fathers who are, she says, 'naught' – both naughty and nothing.
The imagery of a dysfunctional family unit fills Fairfax's narration of her experiences, and once again we are pushed back to the parallel metaphor of the
church family and its internal strife. It should be stressed that there is no way
of knowing the actual circumstances and tensions within the Fairfax family,
just as with other families discussed here: but the written record of their vicis-
situdes powerfully pushes a particular reading, which we know was echoed in

the rhetoric of polemical writings about possession. That Hellen began her visions by appearing dead, then imagined joyful attendance at a sermon, followed by the appearance of supernatural abilities in conversation with ghosts, devils and angelic preachers suggests a powerful desire to compete with both living and dead siblings for love, to be the centre of attention and, above all, to appear godly. She presents herself, therefore, as the worthier child, just as the godly ministers like Cooke tried to convince the Church of England that their version of Christianity was the better one: the practice of the apostles in the primitive church. Yet Hellen is in fact the less cherished child, and if we look at the other demoniacs dispossessed by Darrell and his friends we can see a similar pattern in a majority of their cases.

Katherine Wright is represented as the victim of her stepfather's abuse; three of the Lancashire demoniacs were in a similar position to Thomas Darling, committed (with their all-important portions, to a wealthy guardian), whilst one was a servant and the other a dependent and unmarried kinswoman; William Sommers is repeatedly portrayed by his accusers as a graceless stepson in an unhappy and impoverished household, whilst his sister Mary is an abandoned bride forced back to the parental home. All these children and young people, just like the godly within the Elizabethan church, present themselves or are represented by others implicitly or explicitly as being uncherished. Despite their virtues, and their powerful capacity for self-assertion, they are ignored, or abused, or eclipsed by others. In the case of both the young and the godly the shape of the story is the same, and in a society where 'magistrates became fathers and fathers became magistrates', with 'the parent-child relationship ... proposed as a pattern for imitation, thereby casting all social relations in a paternal hue', this should come as no surprise. As Muchembled suggested, the family – as the basic unit of society, religion and economy – was the image that early modern people used when they thought and wrote about macrocosmic government and revolt.[46] In the Darrell case, pushing for attention in words and text worked for each of the uncherished junior parties involved. Hellen Fairfax certainly displaced her sister Elizabeth in her father's text – for Elizabeth's affliction is barely mentioned, whilst Hellen's mood, activities and words are detailed at length. Meanwhile, the godly brought themselves to national attention in writing about cases just like hers.

Staging Inter-Generational Conflict: *The Late Lancashire Witches*

As so often, the stage was the place where the power-struggles implicit in documentary accounts of 'real' events were played out in their most stripped-down and evident form – although in the case of the demonic empowerment of children this was not until the matter was becoming more obviously one of jest and satire than of real conflict. In the famous 'possession' scene from *Twelfth Night* further discussed in the final chapter, Shakespeare's jester Feste sketches an unfilial 'lad' who 'cries "Aha!" to the devil', adding 'Pare thy nails, dad?'. There is a taunting conflation of the medieval Vice figure, offering his dagger as nail-cutter, with the disrespectful child who regards his father as devilish (and in metaphorical need of having his claws clipped), or the devil as fatherly.[47] But, more fulsomely, a play of 1634 lays bare and sums up precisely the complex of issues of parental and church authority visible in popular literature on witch-craft, possession and obsession events. In 1633 a cluster of witchcraft accusations was made in Lancashire, close to the scene of the 1612 Pendle witchcraft events and not far from Cleworth, by a ten- or eleven-year-old boy named Edmund Robinson. His father endorsed his accusations, but magistrates were unsure how to proceed. The exact sequence of events remains unclear, but there was sufficient doubt over the verity of alleged victims of demonic possession (and the episcopal and royal perception of those who believed them) for the persons accused to be brought first to Chester and then to London, to be examined by the Bishop of Chester and then by Charles I and several physicians. As a result, the case became notorious and Robinson confessed that he had fabricated the accusations, blaming his father for inciting him to counterfeit.[48] Meanwhile in a dramatization of the case, *The Late Lancashire Witches*, playwrights Thomas Heywood and Richard Brome had created another dysfunctional family whose bewitchment represented in thumbnail form all the issues of inter-generational conflict in the Robinson case and those discussed above.

In their play, the Seely family (the name implies innocence or foolishness) is one in which everything is 'turn'd topsie turvy' by witchcraft, which has given the devil control of the actions of the members of the household.[49] Most nota-bly, as well as servants compelling obedience from their employers and women ruling men, the two children of the family domineer over their parents, exact-ing from them exactly the submission usually expected in reverse:

> The good man,
> In all obedience kneeles unto his son,
> Hee with an austere brow commands his father.
> The wife presumes not in the daughters sight
> Without a prepared courtesie. The girle, shee
> Expects it as a dutie; chides her mother
> Who quakes and trembles at each word she speaks …[50]

As Alison Findlay says, this is a rebellion 'against the gerontocratic order' in which the family have become completely naturalized.[51] And although the inversion and disarray seems intended to provoke amusement in the audience – 'in some as it breeds pitty, and in others wonder, so in the most part laughter' – the reaction of the other characters is one of horror.[52]

The topsy-turvy situation suggests the shame of a skimmington (such as occurs later in the play) and Master Arthur, nephew of the afflicted Master Seely, notes that he was once 'respected ... as master of a govern'd family', now fallen into 'rare disorder'. Master Doughty, meanwhile, responds vigorously to the disrespect shown by Gregory Seely to his father:

> they say oldmen become children againe, but before I would become my childes childe, and make my foot my head, I would stand upon my head, and kick my heels at the skies ...
> Blesse me what lookes the devilish young rascall,
> Frights the poore man withall! ...

Eventually, he upbraids Gregory: 'you forget yourselfe ... in this foule unnaturall strife wherein you trample on your father'. Yet at the same time he comments on the bad parenting displayed by implying that he would be a less indulgent father: 'had I a sonne to serve mee so, I would conjure a divell out of him'.[53] The uneasily metaphorical dialogue, with its imagery of witch and devil, demonstrates perfectly the paradoxical connections early modern culture made between disorder, inter-generational strife and Satan. The boy Gregory is both devilish and possessed, seely/innocent and unnatural/wicked. His behaviour is both a commentary on misbehaving youth and an indictment of the evil that the devil could inflict on innocents (contraries which united in cases of demonic possession). His father is both a victim of his son's wrath, and culpable for allowing it to prevail.

But, as Findlay's account of *The Late Lancashire Witches* persuasively suggests, this generational disorder is in part an anti-puritan satire, based on the idea that the godly were inherently rebellious and iconoclastic, and giving the Seelys several 'puritanical' attributes to allow the audience to mock them. They are referred to as a 'family of love' and there is a teasing reference to godly New England.[54] The connection made with exorcism is clear in the lines above: the world of witches and exorcists is a perfect arena for the play's depiction of rebellious youth. That the portrayal is intended to be amusing adds another dimension. Like their friend Ben Jonson's works, discussed in Chapter 6, Brome and Heywood's play offers an equivocal and satiric account of the relationship between godliness and trickery, possession and religious deviance. Are the audience intended to feel amused scepticism about possession and obsession, and by extension godliness? Do they expect a godly dispossession, a Catholic exorcism, or a confession of fraudulence? Or are they intended merely to respond to the play's entertainment value as saturnalian and grotesque, inherently ungodly attributes?[55] The play has its cake and eats it too: the witches are wicked but their victims' sufferings are fun to watch; the older, supposedly wiser generation are humiliated and detected in magical (popish?) wickedness, but the young are reproved for their insubordination; and the situations played out seem also to be a comment on lying, naughty children as false accusers who would be believed only by the schismatical godly. It may have been politic not to be too precise about the deeper demonological and confessional alternatives offered by the play, and the anti-godliness is perhaps the strongest aspect of an essentially opportunistic piece of theatre. But the rhetoric of youth and that of godliness once again meld together here, just as those of godliness and of rebellion do.

'Sonnes of God, or the Children of the Divill'?

We began with Harsnett's assertion that Darrell and his supporters were child-ish in their attempts to promote his cause. This chapter has suggested that this was not just a throwaway insult, but part of a wider pattern of portraying the godly as the rebellious children of the church, which – as one of its implica-tions – linked them with their young demoniacs in a mutually beneficial way. And Darrell's response to Harsnett helps confirm how seriously such imagery was taken. He read into Harsnett's jibe a reference to the children of the devil, distinguished by their 'bitter envying and strife' (James 3:14–15), speaking against the truth out of merely devilish wisdom. In a typical response, which we have seen already in the attack on the boy prebendaries of the ecclesiastical hierarchy, Darrell turned this imagery back onto Harsnett, claiming that *his* work was a 'childe-ish tale', written as if he 'had never gone to schoole', and that 'this Discoverer and such as he, are the children of this earthly, sensuall and divelish wisdome'. Oozing filial humility, Darrell then embraces the imagery of childhood, but he adds that we must know 'whose children we are, whether we be the sonnes of God, or the children of the divill … the spirituall childe followeth and can not but followe the disposition of the spirituall father'. In his 1617 *Treatise of the Church* he was still referring to himself as a child of the church.[56] But in claiming God as his father, he posits the devil as Harsnett's.

Overbury was wrong to imagine, then, that godliness was inherently opposed to images of paternalism and gerontocracy, just as Whitgift and his colleagues were unwise in rebuking godly ministers as unfilial boys and Heylyn was wrong to see the godly as revolutionaries. As Darrell's reply to Harsnett shows, there was actually a profound reverence in puritan thought for images of fatherhood and authority, but only when that patriarchal figure could be seen to be genuinely beneficent and godly, ideally to be God himself. But the wider attraction to the notion of good fatherliness can be seen, for example, in the account given by the young divinity student John Swan of the dispos-session of Mary Glover in London in 1602. The Glovers were a godly family living in Thames Street, who numbered among them martyrs to both Marian persecution and Whitgift's drive to imprison troublesome precisians, as well as Alderman William Glover. Mary Glover was fourteen years old when she began to believe that she had been bewitched by her neighbour Elizabeth Jackson, and to have convulsive fits as a result. She was dispossessed by a team of ministers working together. But what is striking about Swan's report of her affliction is his emphasis not only on the complementary, sociable teamwork of the ministers involved, but on their respective ages: 'the good ould preacher', 'a gratious yonge gen[t]leman', an 'old experienced souldier'. By the end of the account, he is expressing himself in loving familial language ('the old fatherly preacher') at the same time as likening Mary to 'an old grandmother of hers Mary Magdalene'. The ministers and the Glovers work together in familial harmony, with the result that Mary is successfully dispossessed, uttering as she is delivered the same words that her paternal grandfather had done when he was burned at the stake. This acknowledgment of the familial solidarity of the godly Glovers and their ministers, with faith descending from one generation of godly laity and ministers to another since Apostolic times, shapes Swan's whole account.[57] The godly were not simply or reductively anti-paternal or anti-authoritarian, but rather rightly selective in their choice of good 'fathers in God'.

The problem with such imagery is, of course, that language strains constantly in likenesses and analogies, and a single word like 'child' may have multiple, flexible associations – especially for those raised on the Bible, which is rich in self-contradictory imagery. And as if to demonstrate the slipperiness and indeterminacy of such figurative language, Darrell is finally caught in his own metaphor in the passage in his *Detection*. One of the characteristics of the devil's children, which he enumerates apparently without considering its implications for himself, is that they 'speake evill of them which are in aucthority'. This is precisely what Darrell is doing. As his trial dragged on at Lambeth, he had begun to perceive that it was his godly duty to speak evil of the authorities of the national church, or at least of certain errant churchmen. So in his argument with Harsnett we can see him torn by what John F. H. New has called the 'tug-of-war' within godliness. As Peter Lake and Michael Questier note, the godly wanted both to suppress youth and lower social groups, in their pursuit of order, and to reform and increase their power in society, in their pursuit of radical change.[58] In the texts studied here, we can see this tension drawn out and then dramatized. It exposes the fact that the godly dispossessed for both conservative and liberal reasons. They encouraged rebellion but, paradoxically, also sought to restore social order by engaging with notions of the world turned upside down and righted again: the church family taken apart only to be rebuilt as a smaller but more godly family of the truly elect. In this world-view, rebellion was a painful duty, but it was imposed only when authority refused to listen to the reasonable requests of the good children of the national church.

Darrell was one of the more obviously independent-minded godly ministers of his time, which was what drove him to the rebellious side of the move-ment, and finally into the open rebellion of illegal print. In the next chapter we shall examine that process – the creation of a godly author by persecution, and his 'self-fashioning' through the imagery of both explosive filial rebellion and decorous brotherly correction.

5 DIALOGICALL DISCOURSES AND SUMMARIE ANSWERES

He that is not with me, is against me

> Matthew 12:30, chosen by Darrell as the epigraph to
> *A True Narration* (1600).

If we dissent from one another in these things … it must be without bitterness, in brotherly love

> Arthur Hildersham,
> *Lectures upon the Fourth of John* (1629), lecture 65.

As Darrell moved towards open confrontation with the ecclesiastical authorities, he was doing what they expected him to do, as a young and turbulent lecturer. But it has been argued that he was also taking up a position which the authorities wanted him to choose. With characteristic insightfulness, Peter Lake has suggested that the end of the threat from presbyterianism in the mid-1590s was actually a bigger problem for Whitgift, Bancroft and Harsnett than it was for the godly. 'The whole logic behind the careers of such men was threatened' and

> the disappearance of presbyterianism … removed the central point around which all existing anti-puritan ideology had been organised and laid to rest an extremely useful shibboleth with which at least the most radical spirits could be flushed out.

When John Darrell emerged from obscurity in the Midlands in 1596–7, Lake suggests, the trio of godly-bashers fell upon him joyfully as 'an alternative focus for anti-puritan polemic'.[1] Lake's analysis suggests that the impulse behind the controversy over John Darrell's activities was something rather like contention for its own sake. Whilst there were many valid theological and political reasons for worrying about godly agitators – and this book has added more with its exploration of the local political contexts of dispossessions – a continued binary opposition between the church authorities and the godly had become essential to the self-definition of the Church of England. The godly must continue to be 'the other' whilst Whitgift and Bancroft were in charge of it. They must continue to be represented as having all the classic characteristics of an 'other' – rebelliousness, hypocrisy, vice, excess and so on – and demonized accordingly.

In response, the godly often had recourse to another familial strand of imagery, that of brotherhood. This time the dispute was about who was and was not acting in a brotherly fashion to fellow churchmen. The rhetoric of brotherhood allowed a certain claiming of parity between those in different parts of the church which was not possible in the imagery of father and son, which – as we have seen – pushed participants into extreme positions of rebellion and repression. Brotherhood was also a key concept with the sociable godly, and they were sometimes mocked for calling each other 'brother' (and 'sister') when no familial links existed. Bancroft, who had intercepted many godly communications, sneered at these forms of address, quoting from his haul:

> Salute the brethren. Salute the reverend brethren … Salute our most reverent brother … the brethren with us here are in health … Let him be accounted among the brethren … I trust you are so linked together by the bond of brotherly love … that nothing may sunder you.[2]

He parodied the speech of the godly too: 'God be thanked good Brother: the lord blesse you and contynew his graces towardes you'. Among many examples from Darrell's group of friends, Darrell called George More his 'beloved brother' and urged other godly people to comment on his opinions in 'brotherlie love'.

He and the godly often referred also to the letters of the Apostle Paul, where there were frequent injunctions to treat all men as fathers and brethren, women as mothers and sisters, and examples of the Apostle addressing his colleagues and congregations as 'brethren'.[3] To behave in an unbrotherly way was thus to indulge in the controversies that Paul had feared would destroy his fragile new churches, and the godly felt the same about their own communities. But paradoxically, the extreme expression of brotherliness was the separatist way – a shared covenant, binding together all church members. Yet the separatists were by definition those who had disunited themselves from former congregations, and they were also known for their vicious infighting, and repeated separations from each other.[4] Darrell knew many separatists during his life and would devote his final work to attempting to answer and reclaim them. It was a revealing choice: whilst Darrell was passionately committed to the ideal of brotherhood, he is, like the separatists, rightly remembered as the cause of great disunity in the Church of England. To chart the progress of this warring family through rhetorics of unity and separation, and see how Darrell moved from attacking the church authorities in paternal and filial terms, to arguing with them about brotherly parity, and finally to sparring bitterly with actual godly 'brethren' who were not much unlike him, we must first complete the story of his trial and the publications that came out of it.[5]

Hearings and Writings

We resume the story in Nottingham, for upon hearing from Lord Chief Justice Anderson of the trouble there sometime in early 1598, Bancroft moved quickly to begin collecting evidence against Darrell. According to Darrell's support-ers, after Sommers had confessed before the Nottingham aldermen, he was taken to London, kept in the Bishop's house – apparently under an assumed name – and questioned. Inquiries were made about *The most wonderfull and true storie*, which was recalled, the unpublished 'History' of the Lancashire seven was examined, and the Katherine Wright case was discovered, presum-ably because Sommers knew of it. Investigative commissions were dispatched to Derbyshire, Leicestershire and Nottinghamshire, although *not* Lancashire. This process is not well documented, but Harsnett and his colleague the secre-tary William Piggott travelled to Derbyshire, apparently with William Gregory of Nottingham, to question Katherine Wright and others, working with the new Mayor of Chesterfield, Ralph Clarke – ironically, the beneficiary of the 'overthrow' there so much admired by William Cooke.[6] Harsnett also went to Nottingham, where the second commission that considered the Sommers case was followed by other enquiries: Darrell mentions three or four commissions in Nottinghamshire in this period. Every effort was made to gather evidence, and witnesses from Joan Pie to Thomas Wallis were forced into qualifying or repudiating their previous statements in support of Darrell. This evidence was written up and Harsnett deploys some of it, especially the witnesses' retrac-tions of their evidence, in the *Discovery*. It must have become clear during this process that the most effective line of attack that could be pursued against Darrell was not simply to assert that he was wrong, but to claim that he was a fraud.

Before the second commission met at Nottingham, Darrell had also been sent to London and was now in the Gatehouse prison at Westminster. After he had been in prison for a month, he says that he heard that the charge on which he had been arrested – heresy – had been replaced by a charge of fraudulence. The heresy charge would have been politically and theologically difficult to press, but the new charge was one of dishonesty, petty and damaging. And, conveniently, Sommers had now changed his initial story of having fooled Darrell, accusing the minister of teaching him to counterfeit.[7] On Midsummer Eve 1598, Darrell was accordingly examined by Bancroft on some one hundred and eighty to two hundred interrogatories under *ex officio* oath, so that he was not told what the charge or questions would be before he was presented with them. He was accused of meeting Sommers in Ashby, as we have already seen, and plotting with him to fake a possession and dispossession. Afterwards, he was sent back to prison, and at Michaelmas (late September) he was recalled, and examined by Lord Chief Justice Popham and 'some other of her Majestyes most honorable privy counsell' on the same charge. The author and editor of the *Triall*, who give the fullest account of the High Commission's proceedings, imply that there were three or four hearings before Whitsun (early June) 1599 – when the commissioners agreed 'in pollicy' to side with Bancroft and not Darrell – with Darrell and More being suspended from their ministry (which was effectively the outcome of the trial and part of their punishment) some-time in winter 1599.[8] There was not one single trial date, as so many accounts wrongly assume, but a series of hotly-contested hearings ending in a kind of political stalemate.

The hearings were very thorough, from the prosecution's point of view. Our old friends Thomas Darling, his uncle Robert Toone, Katherine Wright, Mary Cowper and Robert Cowper senior were all brought to London. But none of the former demoniacs were called to give evidence in public, which infuriated the defendants. They believed that examination of these witnesses would in fact produce evidence of their innocence and of Harsnett's bullying and manipula-tion. Darling did try to intervene in the proceedings, as Darrell's supporters tell us, because he wanted to argue that his statement had been tampered with. But Toone, who had stood bail for him, silenced him. Darling's claim was one of several allegations of abusive treatment. Harsnett was said to have threat-ened to burn Wright's feet if she would not confess counterfeiting. Darling was quartered with Sommers in the Bishop of London's own home, where Sommers was alleged to have joined in attempts to get him to confess, and then he was put in the Counter prison.[9] It was even alleged that Bancroft had forged letters from Darrell instructing Darling to confess, and that Harsnett, having threatened Darling with branding and death and forced him to watch a public execution, had made him sign a page containing only a few statements, to which more were later added above his signature. How much of this is true is unknown.[10] But as soon as Darling was released from custody, he withdrew his confession in person and in writing, and it does not appear that he ever implicated Darrell in teaching him. He also tried to damage Sommers, by questioning him about his allegation that Darrell had sent him to Burton to see Darling's fits, so as to perfect his own simulations. Sommers's answers to

Darling's questions – about his uncle's house, and whether Burton's famous bridge was long or short – revealed that he had never been there. Darling was no use as a witness against Darrell, and he in particular might even speak up for him or attack the testimony of others. So he and the other demoniacs were not permitted to speak during the hearings. Sommers was not permitted to demonstrate his counterfeiting either, for fear that it might be taken seriously as at the first Nottingham commission hearing. Many people were called, in other words, but from Darrell and More's point of view they were not the right people.

As we have seen, the 'Lancashire seven' were not even visited by examiners, and although Nicholas Starkie was capable of coming to London (as he showed by visiting More in prison) he was not asked to do so by Harsnett and his team. Starkie continued to believe in the honesty of the ministers who had 'cured' his children and in the efficacy of their method and would have been a very useful witness for them. He may even have come to London at the request of Darrell and More's defenders, but if so he was not allowed to give evidence. Both sides might call witnesses, but Darrell and others protested that many of their proposed witnesses, in addition to the demoniacs themselves, were not heard. This was because the court was not compelled to hear evidence of the defendants' good character, and it chose not to do so. Therefore, no evidence at all from Lancashire was presented. And because Sommers was the prosecution's most important accuser – as the most recent and eloquent – the trial focused closely on events at Nottingham. Occasionally a deviation from this focus can be seen to catch the defence out. Darrell and More had brought written statements from witnesses at Nottingham – which they also complained were not able to be used as they had wished – but, as Darrell's fumbling answer to questions about his lying upon Katherine Wright suggests, they were not prepared for the examination of all the minutiae dredged up by Harsnett elsewhere. And when Joan Darrell requested a copy of all this evidence, including material from the second commission at Nottingham, she was threatened with being sent to Bridewell.[11]

The accused were thus facing a very determined group of prosecutors, bent on convicting them. The demands made by those who wanted more rights for the defendants were ignored, because they could be, quite lawfully. Yet Darrell said that he did not believe that Bancroft or Harsnett really thought him guilty. We are not used to associating England's leading clergymen with aggression and sophistry, but in Darrell's writings at least it would be difficult to find three tougher men than Whitgift, Bancroft and Harsnett. Undoubtedly they truly believed that godliness was a political threat and theologically misguided, and so whilst there was no question now of torture or execution, every repressive measure short of that was considered to be an option. We have already seen Whitgift's capacity for forcing church affairs in the direction that he wanted, by bullying, deprivations and imprisonment. Bancroft, as the new Bishop of London, was no less bruising. He actively liked annihilating dissent and Thomas Fuller, in his *Worthies*, describes him chillingly as 'the soul of the high commission'.[12] Harsnett, his chaplain, was – as we have also seen – a man who relished a scrap, and he was willing to exaggerate, bend evidence, and deploy innuendo and sarcasm to secure victory. He was a man of ambition and charisma who would himself become both Bishop and Archbishop, and he held strongly proto-Arminian views. These organizers of the prosecution case were backed by a range of talented graduates, masters and doctors, who were in their posts because of their intelligence and ambition: men like Barlowe, who would become the Queen's chaplain, and Bishop of Rochester, then Lincoln. Even the court officials were eminent men. Evidence would have been produced and read out in court by Abraham Hartwell, the registrar, an MP, translator and a member of the Society of Antiquaries.[13] Darrell and More stood no chance of receiving what we would now consider to be a fair hearing, much less of acquittal. But by the standards of their time, their position was not unusual.

Part of our impression of the trial as a travesty of justice comes from lawyers from the other judicial systems that ran alongside the ecclesiastical courts. Civil lawyers practised in church courts, whilst common lawyers could not. The latter, as we have seen, tended to favour the godly, and often offered help in defending them. We can probably see Darrell's unofficial team of common lawyers at work in some of the pamphlets, but they wrote because they were unable to help Darrell and More in the court itself. They attended hearings to observe, and then commenced battle outside the walls of Lambeth Palace, presenting arguments and petitions and writing letters and pamphlets. Some of their objections, drawn from both common and civil law, no doubt appear in Darrell's writing, reflecting also his own short career as a common lawyer: was it lawful for the defendant to be denied the right to submit written questions (interrogatories) to prosecution witnesses? Was it lawful to convict on the evidence of a witness who had himself admitted perjury? Was it lawful to deny the defendants bail?

It was also argued that fraudulence was not an ecclesiastical offence, but a temporal one – so why was it being tried by the High Commission? This was correct and there may have been, as there were in other cases, attempts to get the trial moved to another jurisdiction. Darrell and More were further disadvantaged, the lawyers argued, by the conduct of the hearings. They were assigned no proctor or advocate to plead or defend their cause, although the prosecution's advocate was the distinguished lawyer Dr Thomas Crompton, prompted in court by Bancroft (it was alleged), and they were not given enough notice of hearings to allow them to prepare their cases. Finally, after the trial was over, and the court had supposedly agreed a verdict, it was not given in open court or made public and no sentence was officially passed, although Darrell and More were suspended from their ministry and re-imprisoned to await further punishment. All of this seemed to lawyers who usually practised in the Queen's Bench or Common Pleas courts to be unjust, but in church courts it was all quite lawful. The question was whether the matter should have been tried by the High Commission at all, as well as how. It should not have been. But once the trial had commenced, it seems to have proceeded as a regular High Commission hearing: harsh, but normal practice.[14]

Yet even if the court's basic practice was lawful, the tone of the proceedings can be seen in a number of different accounts. William Bradshaw, who was well acquainted with Darrell's trial, wrote of the ecclesiastical courts that when they had a defendant before them they:

> scorn, deride, taunt and revile him, with odious and contumelious speeches, eye him with big and stern looks, procure proctors to make Personal invectives against him, make him dance attendance from Court day to Court day, and from term to term, frowning at him in presence, and laughing at him behind his back.[15]

According to the author and editor of the *Triall* the defendants and witnesses in Darrell's and More's cases were interrupted by commissioners, especially Whitgift and Bancroft, and shouted down in exactly this manner, so much so that Darrell was only allowed to speak once and was then cut off. In an exchange that has exactly the same flavour as the abuse that the godly reported Whitgift lavishing upon them, Harsnett was said to have shouted at Darrell that he 'durst as well eat a toads head as name particulars' of an allegation that he had made about the conduct of his examiners. In an impressive verbal beating, Darrell was told that he was 'the most impudent varlet ... asse, a heretick, a Devil, one that had seven Devils' and that 'he should be the Devils m[a]rthyr, and either recant, at Pauls Crosse, or be burnt at Smithfeild'.[16] This was no way, said Bradshaw, to treat a minister, when the court ought to 'use him brotherly'. It was a word used with increasing confidence as the godly perceived that behind such abuse lay fear that the anti-precisians could not win in a fair fight. Injustice strengthened their feeling of parity with, and even moral superiority over, those churchmen who opposed them.

Harsnett rejected the claims of Darrell and others that the trial was unjust. But his responses, together with his practice in using evidence in his *Discovery*, do suggest that its conduct was heavily loaded against defendants – in ways that would not be visible in court records and were not illegal, but were plainly unfair. The close connection between the compilers of prosecution evidence (Harsnett in particular) and Bancroft and Whitgift, who were among the judges, was questionable. It was wrong to intimidate witnesses by bullying them in court or threatening them with jail, but it clearly happened. It was unfair that anyone who was Darrell's and More's supporter and was allowed to speak was used as a witness against them, presumably by a process of selective and aggressive questioning. It is hard to account by any other means for the surprising statistic produced by Harsnett: of forty-four witnesses against Darrell, thirty-four were his friends. It is an attempt to suggest disunity in the Darrellite circle, and create it by dividing ministers. There was already some dispute about what exactly was unjust about the High Commission's procedure: Darrell's partisan 'G. Co.', who attended at least once, said that among those forbidden from giving evidence in Darrell's favour were Hildersham, More, Brinsley, Ireton, Evington and Browne, but the author of the *Triall*, possibly at a different hearing, said that Garland, the Grays, Small, Porter, Ireton, Browne and Evington had spoken for Darrell. However, their depositions were not discussed, he said, keeping the evidence focused on matters damaging to the defence. Harsnett did not even contest most of the other claims made by Darrellites: that Darrell and More were denied the sight of the evidence against them, for instance. This was quite common.

There was, of course, another recourse open to Darrell's party, and that was in appealing to the great and good outside the ecclesiastical establishment in writing: if their own godly community could not prevail, there were friends in high places who might. The godly's appeal took two forms: private letters and printed dedications. Harsnett confirms that 'great personages' were petitioned on Darrell's behalf by those in Nottingham and London, amongst them Privy Councillors. 'Lordes and Ladyes of Honor' went to court for Darrell and More, although according to the Darrellites there were attempts by his opponents to forestall them. Someone wrote to Bancroft 'threatening him with the authority of great persons, who were said (but falsely) to have taken upon them the defence of M[aster] Darrell'. The *Brief Apologie* was dedicated to Lord Keeper Egerton, Sir William Perriam and Sir John Popham, Lord Chief Justice of the Queen's Bench, all judges of the common law courts who might be expected to take an interest in doing justice to the godly. The *Triall* was more pointed: dedicated to Popham, it asked him bluntly to apply the same standards of justice to his role as a High Commissioner as he did in his common law work.[17] Only two of the 'great persons' who were involved with the trial are named: the Earl of Shrewsbury and the godly courtier Fulke Greville were present at hearings. Shrewsbury (Gilbert Talbot, seventh Earl) was an active disliker of godliness, and must have attended for other reasons. He knew most of the prominent people involved in the dispossessions – Edward Beresford, Anthony Brackenbury, Isabel Foljambe Bowes – and therefore had a personal interest in the trial. Fulke Greville, friend of the Dudleys, Devereux and Sidneys, was a much more promising observer, and Darrell's defenders attributed his presence to the Queen's desire to see that he and More received a fair hearing. Optimistically, Darrell asked God to reward the Queen as the fountain of justice. But if Greville made any attempt to intervene it is unrecorded, and he was not a particularly powerful figure in any case. Although later he became Chancellor of the Exchequer and a peer of the realm, in 1598 he was acting as treasurer for 'the wars' and the navy: a middle-ranking post. His presence emphasizes the absence of any more senior godly figure: the old age and death of Burghley combined with the exile of Essex meant that this was a very thin time for the godly at court.[18]

Other people – godly brethren and the wider community – were also asked to give their written support to Darrell in the form of testimonials to his good behaviour and character, and to the truth of the events which he had described. We have seen that forty people signed such a document in Burton, and the magistrates Gresley and Ferrers sent their own joint statement. Another testimonial was sought in Nottingham by Thomas Wallis and others, a third came from Ashby, a fourth from Bulwell, a fifth from Mansfield. About two hundred names were listed on the last three alone, in a substantial letter of protest. The Ashby testimonial, Darrell said, confirmed that: 'he hath lived among us in very good reporte, behaving himselfe every way as became his profession, and the gospel of Christ'. Abraham Hartwell, the High Commission's registrar to whom such materials would have been submitted as evidence, was sufficiently impressed by Darrell's unspotted character to praise it in his translation of an anti-possession French work. Even as he damaged Darrell's cause he wrote of his 'stoical conversation and holy life'. Darrell's 'beloved brother' George More also sprang to Darrell's defence, as the ministers at the Ashby exercise had charged him back in early 1597. He characterized Darrell in his *True Discourse* as 'as cleare, and was ever as free from counterfeiting as I my selfe am ... such a thought came never once into my minde'. He spoke of Darrell's 'simplici-tie'.[19] But none of this evidence of Darrell's good standing in his community of Midlands godly was considered in the court itself: it was simply ignored. Seeing this, John Ireton tried to involve the scholarly community of godly in Darrell's defence, asking that Oxford and Cambridge Universities hold a debate on the theology of demonic possession. But Ireton's plan produced no recorded result, and Darrell says that because of his support Ireton was him-self examined by Bancroft and kept in London for several days. Writing and gathering support for the accused was a dangerous thing to do, but it became a brotherly duty when Darrell and More were imprisoned for months between hearings, and it appeared that they would stay there indefinitely.[20]

However, the trial did eventually come to an end. Sometime in early December 1599, there was a final hearing, at the end of which Darrell and More were told to stand aside, were suspended from their ministries and sent back to jail to await further news from the court – which never came. Presumably a private discussion followed their dismissal, at which a verdict was reached. But this was never publicly announced and it sounds very much as though it was so controversial that it could not be. It is also quite likely that a decision on sentencing could not be reached, and that some of the commissioners recommended immediate release because the defendants had already been in prison for about eighteen months. Formally, however, Darrell and More remained indefinitely remanded, and Darrell never accepted that a lawful judgment had been reached.[21]

From Preaching to Pamphlets: A Deal and its Consequences

The trials did not, then, prove that dispossession by prayer and fasting was heretical, and the godly network was not shattered but paradoxically strengthened by it. Further, the unclosed nature of the case meant that the contest not settled in court must be continued in print. Darrell said that Bancroft and Harsnett had been unable to proceed against him lawfully – because he was not guilty yet they needed him to be punished – so instead had decided on a sort of trial and punishment by tract: 'what a jest it were to punish treason or rebellion by Booke-writting' he sneered. In opposing this smear campaign, the godly compulsion to write and 'register' their witness became a necessity. As Darrell put it: 'I durst not keep my pen from writing'.[22] Publication, about which Darrell had apparently been so reluctant in 1597, was now a Christian duty and Darrell said that witnesses were bound to 'publish' (and the word can be read in both senses) God's works. They could not speak their truth 'in a corner to some few' since the report of the dispossessions has 'spread it selfe farr and neare, even throughout the whole land'. In addition, Darrell hoped that one specific reader might be moved by his argument, asking that those who had access to the Queen might 'present' his *Apologie* to her.[23] Given Elizabeth's known views, this inflammatory little book was very unlikely to sway her in favour of its author.

The *Apologie* was not the first book on the case to appear, however, and Darrell was not the first to defend his cause. That was the anonymous author of *A Breife Narration*, of which we have already heard because A. Ri., the editor of *The Triall of Maist. Dorrell*, claimed that he knew him, calling him 'the Narrator'. The *Breife Narration* was published in 1598/9, prefaced by an introduction by G. Co. When the *Narration* was written, Darrell was still awaiting further hearings of his case, having been ill-treated at at least one, and the 'Narrator' was putting into print for the first time an account of events at Nottingham. He reproduced the depositions given to the commission which sat there on 20 March 1598 – the evidence of people like Joan Pie and John Pare. We can see that the 'Narrator' had knowledge not only of events in Nottingham, including a detailed description of the first commission hearing found nowhere else, but of Darrell's suspension hearing with Matthew

Hutton, during which the Archbishop apparently told him that personally he believed him to be an honest man. He also knew of more recent developments in Nottingham. That this work should be the first to reach the bookshelves suggests the centrality of the Nottingham dispossession to the thinking of the godly and their opponents: this was to be the main battlefield. It also shows that Darrell and More had the backing of a number of people across the nation who were not afraid to take the initiative in their absence, and write and publish illegally in defence of its validity. The work is another multi-vocal one. Its compiler and G. Co. may well be different people, one in London, one in the Midlands (its author may have been from Nottinghamshire himself, possibly a cleric, Thomas Freeman suggests). But also it reproduces the depositions of seventeen people, all of fairly humble provincial origin.[24] It is a classic example of godly egalitarianism and sociability at work, the community speaking and writing together in defence of their silenced brother.

The *Narration* was followed by two related pamphlets, whose connection is rather like that between Darrell's and More's accounts of the Lancashire seven. First out in mid-1599 was *A Brief Apologie*. It was an edited version of a work by Darrell, which would soon be published as *An Apologie or Defence*.[25] Again a helpful community of godly, although unfortunately anonymous, is revealed. The *Brief Apologie*'s editor took the trouble to condense Darrell's lengthy and highly personalized account, which must have been circulated in manuscript, making it clearer and more systematic. His text was very much shorter, and seemed designed to brief busy men about the case, since it was dedicated to Egerton, Popham and Perriam. In his introduction, the editor explicitly asks them to try to slow down the proceedings of the High Commission before it reaches an unjust judgment. Although he protests that he reverences the High Commission as a lawful body, he wants the common law judges to challenge the probity of some of its individual members. The editor hopes that a delay in the proceedings will give time for a change of direction and possibly personnel, opening up the prospect of Darrell receiving a fair hearing.[26] As well as acting in Darrell's defence in a legal sense, the editor also shielded Darrell as best he could from any consequences of his publication, by claiming that the work was 'published without his knowledge'. Although Freeman argues that the work appeared 'after Darrell's trial' the internal evidence presented above suggests that the *Brief Apologie* actually was written and appeared earlier, during the long process of hearings and before any kind of verdict had been pronounced.[27] It was thus an attempt to change the expected outcome of the trial. This suggests the confidence of Darrell's supporters that printing their arguments would be a forceful intervention in a situation where they were gaining power, support and status with each injustice and delay.

It is thus no wonder that in the rush to get works into print the *Brief Apologie* was followed almost immediately by Darrell's full *Apologie*, with its plea that someone try to present it to the Queen on his behalf. The godly were embracing print warmly, producing a body of work that was very unlike the uninhibited Marprelate tracts, but was their direct descendant. This time, though, the aim was very specific. Darrell gives several reasons for his having written: to defend the work of God seen in Sommers's dispossession; to defend himself, especially in his role as a minister; to give the godly detailed knowledge of the dispossession of Sommers so that they may confute 'gaynsayers'; to attempt to persuade those who do not believe that Sommers was possessed; and to ask for the opinions of readers, and their correction 'in brotherlie love' if they believe Darrell to have erred.[28] The godly community was being appealed to in all its diversity – even if ill-informed or sceptical, they should learn about and speak in favour of this godly work, and if they were unable to accept it then they should contact its author. It was an astonishing thing for a man in prison and then in hiding to say, and it indicates the kind of reach and power that Darrell and his supporters hoped – indeed, almost expected – their printed works to have in the church family. The man who had shunned celebrity now felt in touch with a widespread network and desperately wanted them to hear him by reading his words. Speech and printed word finally fused, and if Darrell later promised not to preach on dispossession, as I think he did, we can see why: his pamphlets became his sermons and his auditory was the national congregation.

The Triall of Maist. Dorrell was also in preparation. As we have seen, it was written in sections by at least two men (author and editor) during 1599, and must have been published at about the time of Darrell's release (although its editor did not know of this, and he said that the author had died by the time of publication). The editor, A. Ri., brought forward material mentioned nowhere else, like the fact that the Mayor of Chesterfield signed the papers of the commission that investigated Katherine Wright's dispossession even though he was not at the hearings. Although Freeman says that A. Ri. was unaware of the *Breife Narration*, the *Brief Apologie* and *Apologie*, in fact he mentions at least two of these.[29] The picture Freeman presents of the pro-Darrell publications thus, I think, underestimates the connectedness and mutual awareness of the pro-Darrell campaign authors. They may not have been members of a defined 'Hildersham circle', as Freeman puts it, or 'in touch with Darrell', but the extent to which the godly who lived in different communities, and even disagreed with each other over some of the issues of doctrine raised by the dispossessions, could still work together is made very clear by the pro-Darrell publications, as we have seen. The Ashby coterie found a range of disparate allies in the wider godly family very easily, in Nottingham and London, in lawyers and fellow clerics. Here we see the reason for Bancroft's nightmare vision of witch-like 'Precisians' who knew always one anothers' opinions and activities 'though they dwell an hundreth myles asunder, and one never saw the other'. Each pro-Darrell work comes from a slightly different angle or section of the godly movement, and each has a specific purpose and readership in mind as well as aiming generally to publicize the dispossession cases and vindicate Darrell. But they are all connected through sociable authorship – as they saw it, the gathering together of 'sundry faithfull and discret brethren'.[30] These brothers felt increasingly able to bandy words with their episcopal siblings.

That they were right about their power to influence events through publication can be seen in the care taken by their opponents to answer these illegal pamphlets. Harsnett's massive *Discovery* – of which we have heard so much in this book – and Hartwell's translation of the French anti-dispossession tract *A True Discourse upon the Matter of Martha Brossier* were both intended, as we shall see, to inflict as much literary damage as possible on the godly before a decisive concession was made to them. The attribution of the *Discovery* only to 'S. H.' may have been intended to make the book look more impartial than it actually was, although this was a forlorn hope: like Hartwell, Harsnett was readily identifiable from his inside knowledge of the Darrell case and relationship with Bancroft and Whitgift. Before the *Discovery* was even published, it had been rumoured that Bancroft was writing a book against Darrell and, whilst the text is clearly Harsnett's, much of its material was shaped by Bancroft's requirements.[31] And Harsnett did his worst at great length against the pro-Darrell pamphlets, because what he was preparing for was Darrell's release. When this occurred a few weeks after the publication of the *Discovery*, it became clear that it was written to order, to get the church's retaliation in first and send the exorcist back into the world a disgraced man. That Darrell's release should be tied so closely to the two publications by the High Commission's supporters suggests strongly that it was also related to the success of the works published by pro-Darrell pamphleteers. It has become slightly easier to understand the movement towards release since the discovery of the only known document surviving from Darrell's trial in the Fairhurst Papers purchased recently by Lambeth Palace Library.

Sometime before winter 1599, this document was sent to Archbishop Whitgift at Lambeth summarizing the state of affairs in Darrell's case. It does not mention George More at all. It is not dated, but its purpose seems to be to brief the Archbishop and perhaps therefore to get from him a decision about the further progress of the proceedings against Darrell. The text covers nine pages and is in the form of an argument which moves towards a conclusion: a judgment of Darrell's guilt. Evidence against him from the three demoniacs who had admitted counterfeiting is summarized, and keyed to another document or documents now lost. Katherine Wright's desire to end the cruelty of her stepfather, and make him value her mother more, is recorded, as is her damaging claim that Darrell lay on her belly as part of his attempt to dispossess her. Thomas Darling's motives are listed, along with his suggestion that he thinketh if the Lord Bishop of London will deale favourablie with Mr Darrell he will of himselfe confesse the trewthe namelie that he never thought this ext [examinate] to be possessed and that he will promise never to enter into anie suche course againe.

There is perhaps some steer here from the document's author: if Darrell could not be brought to confess or to repudiate Darling, then he might at least be persuaded to forswear exorcism ('anie suche course againe'). William Sommers's allegations are then repeated at length – that he had met Darrell at Ashby and planned the whole course of events at Nottingham with him.

Notwithstanding all these arguments that his patients had never been possessed, however, the document (which is curiously catalogued as Darrell's 'confession') records faithfully that 'Mr Darrell with all obstinacie maintainethe that there was noe dissimulation'. Rather even-handedly, his seven principal arguments are also summarized – that, for example, such actions are impossible to counterfeit – and they are answered point by point. The document then concludes that

> Althoughe these seaven arguments pretended by Mr Dorrell if they were trewe would acquite him of guilte and being controlled make onelie this proofe against him, that he was ignorant or simple to be soe deluded, yet there be manie circumstances (either proved or confessed by Mr Darrell) besides manie probabilities to confirme Sommers confession, w[hi]ch doe plainlie convince him to have dealt fraudulentlie, coseninglie and deceitfullie with the worlde in the whole course of this Cause.

These proofs, which are recognizable in Harsnett's *Discovery*, are then given and the document ends abruptly with Darrell's claim that Sommers has been repossessed (and therefore is playing the devil's game in accusing him). The document is the most fair-minded representation of the case that we have, in stark contrast to the public portrayal of Darrell in the *Discovery*, which joyously smirches his reputation in every possible way. This suggests strongly that it is an internal briefing document not intended for public consumption, and that it represents better than any other surviving text the true state of play in late 1599, with the godly mounting a serious challenge. Whitgift endorsed the paper with comments and biblical quotations in Latin, and there is an apparently unfinished musing: 'whie he cawsed Sommers to doe his fitts openlie'. The meaning of this snippet on the reverse of the final page is unclear.[32] It seems likely that this document preceded the driving through of a verdict, with Darrell and More's deposition from the ministry, the publication of the *Discovery* and Darrell's release following shortly afterwards as a package.

So how did the ecclesiastical authorities come to the decision that, though 'guilty', Darrell should be released? Whitgift had said at Whitsun that if Darrell and More were released they would 'infect the commonwealth', but by the end of the year that view had changed, in Darrell's case at least.[33] Why? It was obvious that he would not confess and thus allow a straightforward punishment and rehabilitation. We know that Thomas Darling was released a long time before Darrell, just after the Whitsun hearing, and allowed to visit him. This may have been an early attempt to get Darrell to confess, or admit that he had been deluded. But instead of confessing all over again, Darling told Darrell that his admission had been forced out of him, and he apologized for it. The former demoniac and his dispossessor parted with forgiveness and in some amity, which must have hardened rather than weakened Darrell's resolve. William Sommers, meanwhile, disappeared, apparently into a new apprenticeship to a barber – remember his fascination with the trade in his acting of sins – and then to sea or into oblivion – no-one apparently cared which. Darrell continued to regard him as 'vile and infamous', a man still possessed by Satan.[34] Similarly, we hear no more of Katherine Wright, and Darrell thought her also permanently repossessed. There was thus no possibility that he would confess just because some of his patients had done so. This insistent integrity presented the authorities at Lambeth Palace with a major problem, because, as the printed works show, pressure was mounting for a resolution of the affair.

So, as hinted in the briefing document above, the accused were called to a final hearing, a secretive judgment was forced through without specifiying a further punishment, and then they were offered a deal. Writing in late 1599, More said that the terms offered were these:

> we must be bound to the peace, and must promise neither to publish nor practize these matters: or els remaine prisoners still, with expectation of further punishment, which we are willing to endure, seeing we cannot chuse but speake those thinges, which wee have both hard and seene.[35]

More must have refused to accept this deal, and stayed in jail. Would the pious Darrell have consented to bind himself to a promise not to write, which he would immediately break upon being freed? Freeman suggests that this notion 'may not be surprising' but, as he notes, none of Darrell's opponents accuses him of breaking any commitment, which would be surprising if he had. So, if he gave no such commitment, why was Darrell freed? I think that answer lies unnoticed in his statement in the *Detection* of rather more specific conditions of freedom than those which More describes:

> within 14. dayes after the publishinge of the booke made against me [Harsnett's *Discovery*], they offered me libertie upon condition I would promise not to preach of possession: nor in my publike preaching justifie the possession and dispossessinge of the persons controverted, nor deale any more in the dispossessinge of any.[36]

Darrell may well have been able to promise that without reservation or lie. He had not, after all, promised not to write about his activities, only to refrain from preaching about them – a completely different thing.

He did not dispossess again as far as we know, and if he did not preach on dispossession either then this may have been a price he was willing to pay for his freedom, especially as he had always had doubts about the rightfulness of his status as a celebrity exorcist. Harsnett seems to confirm that neither Darrell nor More took part in any further dispossessions, with his remark in *Egregious Popish Impostures* that both their *wives* were still ready to undertake such work in 1603.[37] This would explain why no-one accused Darrell of breaking his word, or referred again to the matter: he had made the authorities look stupid. Were Darrell and More offered different deals? Perhaps Darrell was offered a further deal after he had refused the original terms? Or did More interpret his offer more strictly than Darrell did? There may have been a difference in treatment because More was barely mentioned in the printed propaganda being pumped out in support of Darrell. Perhaps also, as Freeman suggests, Darrell had important backers who were able to secure his but not More's freedom, by the application of pressure and legal argument.[38] But it is just as likely that Whitgift and Bancroft responded simply to the books on the case, which privileged the Nottingham exorcism and so focused almost exclusively on Darrell. His was the name most frequently in print, and so his continued imprisonment was a political problem in a way that More's was not. Ironically, the publicity that had got him into trouble was also his ticket home: publication was Darrell's salvation because it probably prompted the offering of the deal, and it gave him a way to continue making his case without breaking his word.

There is a problem, however, with the exact chronology of Darrell's release, which has not been noticed before. If he was not offered the deal until two weeks after the *Discovery* was published, and it was published after its entry in the Stationers' Register, then he could not have been free before 29 November 1599, since it was entered in Stationers' Register on 15 November 1599. This is inconsistent with the usual reading of Darrell's statement in his *Detection* that he left Ashby at Michaelmas (the end of September) that year. Freeman thus places his release 'sometime around the summer'.[39] But the editor of the *Triall* weighs in with a further account. Mentioning an event on 4 December 1599, which he implies has just happened, he also says:

> within these few dayes not withstanding Ma[ster] Dorrell, and Ma[ster] Moore were both deposed from the Ministerie, and committed to close prison, there to remayne until order were taken for their further punishment (as S H reporteth) ... Yet for all that, they have offered (by M[aster] Barker the Register, who went of purpose to M[aster] Dorrell in the Gatehouse) libertie upon these conditions, That they should not justifie their cause, nor meddle any more with prayer, and fasting for parties possessed.[40]

The editor of the *Triall* may be speaking of a time before 4 December – since his account is composed of documents written at different times – but it does not seem so because of its late placing in the essentially sequentially-written text. So Freeman's suggestion that Darrell and More were found guilty by the High Commission in May (on which he based his summer release date) seems to me to be wrong. It is also odd that, if A. Ri. was still writing on the case in early December and Darrell had been free since September, he did not know, because (as the quotation above shows) he knew many other details of the case. However there is an easy answer to this problem. Darrell says in the *Detection* that he arrived in Ashby at Michaelmas but left *'about the same time of the yeare* 99' (my emphasis).[41] He could thus easily mean early December rather than more precisely late September, and all three pieces of evidence seem to confirm this as the time of his release. What he remembers, however, is interesting, for it was on Michaelmas Day 1599 that Essex returned to England.[42]

A proportion of the other material preserved in the Fairhurst Papers, in which Darrell's 'confession' belongs, and identifiable as documents crossing Whitgift's desk at this time, concerns Essex, along with trouble from the godly in other ways. Clearly much material is missing, but against the background of this wider and more dangerous agitation in autumn–winter 1599, it may have seemed desirable to the authorities to move towards freeing Darrell. His imprisonment, just upriver from Essex House and across the ferry from Lambeth at Westminster, might have been proving to be a *cause célèbre* for the London godly, and seen in this way Darrell's release so soon after Michaelmas looks very significant. It may well have seemed to Whitgift and his fellow ministers that once Darrell was freed, few people would be interested in him for purely theological reasons. They were keen to show that a substantial number of the godly did not agree with him about post-Apostolic possession, the impossibility of counterfeiting and especially about the veracity of William Sommers. Harsnett had uncovered divisions among prominent godly men even when he examined them in 1597–8, hot from the strife at Nottingham. Ireton, a widely-respected minister who maintained a belief in the possibility of modern demonic possession, was of the opinion that although Darrell himself was innocent, Sommers's repossession at least had been counterfeited. John Brinsley, the Ashby curate, agreed, whilst John Browne of Loughborough did not feel able to affirm it under oath. Richard Bernard, a protégé of Lady Bowes and her sister, had never really believed Sommers was possessed at all. He had visited the young man and 'went away fully resolved of the boyes villanous dissimulations' says Harsnett. These well-known men's scepticism could not have gone unremarked. Darrell himself said in 1600 that 'many of the ministers and brethren in England hav[e] bene offended with me ... many not onely of the irreligious, but of such as professe the feare of god (as in experience I have observed) regard not these workes of god'. Releasing him might fracture the godly brotherhood more effectively than locking him up had done.

Time and controversy had also caused other witnesses to re-examine their beliefs. Even Darrell's actual brother-in-law Thomas Wallis, who had helped organize a testimonial for him, did not trust Sommers: 'although ... I had divers times heard that the boy did things past the naturall power of man: Yet when I saw them, I could not perceive any such strangenes in them' he now said. In addition to divergences among the godly and the growth of doubt and apathy, Harsnett had taken pains to flatter many people involved in Darrell's exorcisms, absolving the commissioners, clergy, witnesses and 'simple people' of blame and so attempting to split them off from Darrell's cause.[43] Many people, therefore, had come away from the hearings and especially the publication of the *Discovery* with a feeling that they had been lucky to escape further inconvenience and punishment, and they were unlikely to flock back to Darrell. Even if he did manage to publish writings that he had worked on in prison, his arguments were not universally accepted. They might be ignored or might usefully distract and divide the godly at a time when their supposed champion Essex was becoming a serious threat. If Darrell went home to Ashby, now no longer under the protection of the third Earl of Huntingdon but his non-godly successor, he would also be reasonably visible. The Lambeth authorities might have concluded, therefore, that he was of more use out of jail than inside. But if this was the thinking, it could have been (and in some ways was) a dreadful miscalculation.

Darrell disappeared into hiding – not something that his former jailers had necessarily predicted. He states that he left Ashby in late 1599, and then 'neither friend nor foe knew where I was'. In fact, his whereabouts were known by several godly who disagreed with him, and who were harbouring a sibling-rivalry just as Bancroft and Harsnett might have hoped. The godly ministers John Deacon and John Walker, writing against Darrell in about 1601, stated that he (or rather their caricature of him, 'Exorcistes') had recently visited 'a poore Boy at Northwich in Cheshire' who was believed to be possessed, 'to take a circumspect view of his fearefull fits'.[44] But, motivated by community loyalty, they did not reveal his whereabouts at the time, and Darrell clearly enjoyed the protection and help of a number of godly 'friends' and 'foes' despite his disclaimer. Many people must have assisted him in publishing illegally, at secret presses in England and in Holland. By this means appeared *A Breife Narration*, *A Brief Apologie* and Darrell's own *Apologie*, *The Triall of Maist. Dorrell*, Darrell's *Detection* of Harsnett's *Discovery* and *A True Narration*, and George More's book. Texts were smuggled to printers, the costs of printing were met, and once printed the books were secretly distributed.[45] Books published without authorization remained 'hot', and their circulation was thus a matter of discreet trading among friends. The network promoting the illegal books had to be committed enough to hold out if detected: texts discovered to be unlicensed were burned (which happened to Darrell's *True Narration*) and imprisonment and even death might await those involved. As we have seen, Oxenbridge, publisher of *The most wonderfull and true storie* and would-be publisher of a history of the Lancashire seven, was imprisoned for his part in publicizing the dispossessions, and the remaining copies of *The most wonderfull and true storie* were confiscated.[46] He was punished for quite innocently publishing a licensed work, but the anonymous and illegal pro-Darrell writers faced accusations of sedition, which was far more dangerous. They had a clear, cynical understanding of the allegations that could be made against their writings. The editor of *A Brief Apologie* said that

> It wilbe (perhaps) objected, that by publishing this Treatise, I goe about to raise mutinies among ye Queenes subjectes, or to discredite the Ecclesiastical State, or hir Majesties commission for ecclesiastical causes …

He spoiled his attempt to plead innocence of all these charges by adding a marginal note: 'a cunning practise to intitle the state to private abuses'.[47]

Darrell's most important illegal work was his answer to the *Discovery*, *A Detection of the Sinnful, Shamful, Lying and Ridiculous Discourse of Samuel Harshnet*. It was his second book, published in 1600. The *Detection* is a more assured work than the rather rambling *Apologie*. There is even a suspicion of a pun in the title: Harsnett was indeed harsh and he had tried to net Darrell in his mesh of interlinked accusations. But most noticeable in the title, of course, is the list of abusive adjectives. Brother was now pitted against brother in just the kind of bitterness that Arthur Hildersham referred to in his sermon on John 4. Darrell had been genuinely hurt by how much he was hated and reviled by those who differed from him in their opinions. 'Some' he said 'are so greatlie displeased, and so hott against mee that I might seeme herein either to have broched some notable heresie or error, or to have committed some grevous and intollerable iniquitie'. He lists the epithets that have been applied to him, using his own name in a way that is striking and to which I will return in Chapter 6:

> John Darrell, a poore prisoner, a base and contemptible man … Darrell is forsooth a cogger, a cousener, a Jugler, an Exorcist, a counterfeite, a devill-flinger, a devill-driver, a Seducer, a deceiver, an Imposter, and I know not what.

But the Bible had a ready rhetorical model for him, as for other godly victims of persecution and misrepresentation – Robert Cowper had made the same use of it at Nottingham. Addressing his jailers, Darrell speaks in the vein of the Psalmist: 'the Lord is on my side, and agaynst you … though I be farr weaker then you, yet he that is with mee is stronger then you all'.[48] Again, there is that curious note of triumph, suggesting that even after a long imprisonment and in hiding, Darrell is not conceding any kind of defeat.

He had, however, no intention of descending to his enemies' level of insult. He presents himself as acting in self-defence, putting forward the argument offered by others on his behalf and endorsed in this book. As Samuel Clarke put it, echoing the editor of the *Triall*, 'Master Darrell thus traduced, was enforced to write and publish something for the defence of himself, and clearing of his guiltlesness herein'. He intended his plain, honest style to be contrasted with Harsnett's 'rhetorike, fyne quipps' and alliterative phrases like 'sly silly shift', which he mocked. Darrell presents himself with appealing directness, as 'an earnest suter unto thee whosoever thou art to suspend thy judgment, and not hastily to passe any sentence against me'. He pleads with readers to take his writing 'in good parte' and not to 'be offended with me': we too are invited to respond in 'brotherlie love'.[49] Darrell's approach certainly won some later friends. The antiquarian James Broughton thought in 1832 that 'although Darrell espoused the weaker side of the question, he argued the matter with far more skill and candour than were displayed by his adversary'.[50] And by 1601, he seemed to have won the war of words. The *Detection* had not been answered, and the world seemed to have moved on from Darrell and his dispossessions. But in 1602, two new combatants appeared, and the whole pamphlet war began again, with an extra viciousness. Just as Bancroft and Harsnett must have hoped, Darrell's new antagonists were not just members of the wider church family, who might be expected to disagree with him: they were his godly brethren themselves.

Friends Disunited: Deacon, Walker and Darrell

These two new writers were John Deacon and John Walker. One of the Johns was definitely the John Deacon who was the curate of Scrooby and also of Bawtry in Nottinghamshire in the 1590s. He mentions Bawtry in the text as 'Eirtwab'. This man may very probably have known Darrell, and he was regarded as one of 'the brethren', as he himself confirms, for these two villages were centres of godliness and later of separatist fervour. Darrell certainly knew John Smyth and John Robinson, who later led separatists from Scrooby and Gainsborough, and whose congregations sailed on the Mayflower to the new world. But Deacon was not a separatist. He was curate of Bawtry from 1594, and he ministered to a large and united godly congregation during his time there. He was an older man than Darrell, ordained in 1568 when Darrell was a small boy, and he had long experience in the ministry as rector of Saxby in Leicestershire from 1577, and preacher in several other towns and villages. He was, however, godly enough to be of interest to the church courts: in 1594 he was presented to the Archdeaconry Court for preaching without a licence and in 1598 was summoned to the High Commission. But he was conformist enough to escape without further consequences on both occasions: in 1594 he simply produced not one but two licenses, from the Bishops of Lincoln and Coventry and Lichfield, showing that he had been licensed all along, and in 1598 there is no further record of the case beyond his payment of a bond. By 1598 he was no longer at Bawtry, but probably at Derby, like the character Orthodoxus who in the text now ministers at 'Eibrad'.[51] Perhaps he was unhappy with the growing radicalism at Bawtry, and happier with the conformist Archdeacon Walton in Derby. John Walker is much more elusive. Like George More he has a name common enough to make the paucity of records about him a real difficulty. Two John Walkers graduated from Oxford in the 1570s and 1580s, one of whom was from Staffordshire and gained an MA in 1587. Another was a non-graduate licensed preacher and curate of Brampton in Derbyshire in 1602–3.[52] Deacon and Walker both identify themselves as godly, however, which makes their attack on Darrell the more unexpected.

They published two books against Darrell in 1601–2 – George More having by this time almost completely disappeared from the argument – *Dialogicall Discourses* and *A Summarie Answere*. Darrell wrote two books back, *A Survey of Certaine Dialogical Discourses* and *The Replie of John Darrell* (both 1602, both illegally published). All these works are very long, and completely different in form and content from the earlier group of warring pamphlets, which are characterized by excited argument about topical events, with eyewitness statements supporting accusation and rebuttal. In the earlier works, the reader is taken on a journey into (supposedly) real events, and left to piece together his or her own version of them, rather like the newspaper and magazine coverage today of a celebrity trial – which is, of course, exactly what the Darrell case was. But the second pamphlet controversy was a theological one, carried on in abstract debate and aimed at a learned and godly readership who would be able to reflect profitably on such issues. If the first group of pamphlets were about 'history' (which had a meaning somewhere between story and record), the second were works of theory. Moreover, the antagonists both had major flaws in their reasoning, and their books could all be challenged as advocating nonconformist positions based on questionable interpretations of scripture. Deacon and Walker in particular seem out of their depth, and their pomposity makes their works unattractive reading. D. P. Walker called them 'prolix and logically weak' but did acknowledge that they are 'very erudite', whilst G. L. Kittredge noted their 'unimaginable ponderosity' and 'pitifully weak' arguments. The most favourable review comes from R. A. Marchant, who praises Deacon as 'staid and serious, not given to violent emotions, and capable of deeper discernment than some of his fellow-puritans'.[53]

But the idea of godly fellowship and brotherhood was extremely problematic in the surprisingly uncharitable dispute between Darrell and his new
antagonists, who were also his supposed friends. They began their attack on
Darrell – for this is what *Dialogicall Discourses* is – by claiming to have written
their text three years ago in 1599 but 'suppressed' it 'from a felow-like feare
of procuring untimely disgrace, and of adding affliction to the principall parties themselves'. Presumably this means Darrell and More. But this 'felow-like'
feeling disappears within a few sentences – these 'principall parties' and 'their
under-hand favorites' have been 'pestering the [church] with … impertinent,
obscure and needlesse paradoxes … in their books', with 'factious courses'
springing from 'a malcontented humour'. Deacon and Walker's fellows have
become 'our Antagonists' – although the reader will remember that Deacon
and Walker attacked Darrell first, and not *vice versa*. It is time that this trouble
should be 'nipt in the head', and the 'streaming courses' of it 'intercepted and
stopped in time for feare of over flowing the young buds of our holy Religion',
Deacon and Walker conclude. The mixed and clotted metaphor – first the
trouble is the bud, then the holy religion – is characteristic of the text's confused identity.

The authors acknowledge a cause for their awkwardness as they end their
preface. Anticipating how their work will be answered, they suggest that the
first tactic of their opponents will be to claim that they, Deacon and Walker:

> are quite falne from the brethren and their cause … they are become Apostates,
> revolters, backsliders, formalistes, and such as fawne on the state: and this onely,
> for that we favour not forsooth, these Cabalisticall conceits and phantasticall
> fooleries. Well, whatsoever they prate, we will undergo it with patience.

Professing care and friendship, they then proceed to heap vicious abuse on
their erstwhile 'brethren' before these have even had a chance to counter-attack
their position. Their rhetoric is flatly self-contradictory: 'we thinke it some part
of brotherly duety, to forwarne all those our calumnious accusers …'. Freeman
notes that their work 'drips of a sense of injury and usurped authority'.[54]
Despite the fact that they tell their dedicatees that they 'did even purposely
resolve with our soules, to banish all partiall and private respects from out of
our brests', their treatise has the unmistakable taint of intense personal dislike
and anxiety about it. Is their claim to a former amity merely a rhetorical device,
referring to a shared theological position that they believe Darrell has betrayed,
or were these two men previously acquaintances of and even collaborators with
Darrell? How has 'brotherly duety' become an imperative to launch a public
attack on a fellow minister?

Darrell, of course, had undergone the same process with his fellow churchmen in Nottingham and then London. What Deacon and Walker say about
themselves helps illuminate the inherent confusions and difficulties of using

images of brotherhood. There were inescapable tensions in the politically-committed position of the godly, where brotherhood did not mean constant amity but rather a duty to correct the erring and to expose or even separate from them if they could not be recalled to correct opinions. Paradoxically, then, a good brother could also be one's most bruising opponent. The two authors Deacon and Walker explain: they are embodiments of the process described on their title page in a quotation from Augustine.

> Whosoever heareth, or readeth, where he is perswaded with me, let him proceede with me: where he is doubtfull, let him inquire with me; where he acknowledgeth his errour, let him returne with me; where he espieth mine, let him recall me. So shall we walk joyntly togither, in the way of charitie.

Yet Deacon, they say, disagreed initially with Walker, and this falling out was the genesis of their book. They are therefore very careful to establish separate argumentative identities for themselves, like but unlike, situating their beliefs on a spectrum just as they do with those of their characters. One has 'seriously held and mayntayned' his view 'for many yeeres past' and says he can call on five hundred witnesses to prove it. The other has 'an experimented knowledge' of possession cases to call upon.

Hearing of the events in Nottingham, one believed Darrell's version of events, the other did not. And so they:

> devoted our selves to the timely support of those our severall opinions ... what one Librarie was unransackt, or learned brother unconferred withall ...? and all this for the more enabling and the better furnishing of us to that our former deter-mined skirmish? What sundrie and often recourses the one to the other? What entercourse of writings? What mutuall conferences? ... we eftsoones departed asunder the one from the other ... till the verie truth it selfe (as we verily beleeve) began (after many debatings and bickerings) to breake foorth ... we eftsoones began to speake both of us but one and the selfesame things.[55]

This very lengthy and detailed recreation attempts to show the reader by exam-ple what it might feel like to be a godly brother conferring with others in the right spirit, which the authors feel Darrell and his friends have broken away from. It ends with what sounds exactly like classic sociable authorship: a unify-ing of voices in one pious aim. But truth has been reached through bickering and departing asunder. The imagery of brotherhood thus contains within it the duty to be, temporarily it is hoped, unbrotherly. Darrell agreed. In his *Replie* to them, he remarked that whilst 'reproofe and hatred be not necessarilie linked together', the Bible said that 'thou shalt not hate thy brother in thy heart, but thou shalt plainly rebuke thy neighbour, and suffer him not to sinne'.[56]

Yet Deacon and Walker's dialogue of reclamation of their erring sibling does not take that form at all. It is a Harsnett-like polemic with a predetermined outcome, dressed up as a conference, and there is real hatred in their assault. Perhaps the two Johns are not who they seem to be. It has been argued both that they wrote independently of Bancroft and Harsnett and that they were 'hired pens' of the former High Commissioner and his chaplain. Darrell accused Deacon of having also been 'A. Walker', in an obscure attack on his identity, which is echoed by a marginal note in a later passage on his reversal of names such as Mahgnitton as 'pedlers french, such as upright men once practised': 'M[aster] Deacon you [k]now what I meane'. He even said that the two men might be Bancroft himself.[57] But beyond some lingering suspicion, there is no evidence of a connection to the High Commission – and indeed the pair speak disrespectfully of its treatment of Darrell at the very end of *Dialogicall Discourses* and say that they believe him to be innocent of fraud, contradicting their earlier assertions. Meanwhile, they pitch into him vigorously themselves. Are they distancing themselves from the ecclesiastical authorities deliberately, in order to establish a position which is politically extremely useful to Bancroft and his associates: both godly and anti-Darrellite? Or is this a genuine reflection of their feeling and theological opinion? It is no longer possible to tell. Whatever their motivation, the two men simply succeeded in reigniting Darrell's authorial urge, and his targets were precisely their claims to offer both dialogic 'dissention' and yet to be 'sworne brethren'.

Darrell is on fine form in his *Survey*. Although he portrays himself as 'like a tired and weather beaten bird', exhausted by controversy, he rises to the occasion magnificently with his most confident performance yet, using more frequent and assured imagery and even wit. Again, prison and concealment have strengthened his self-assertion. Darrell accuses Deacon and Walker of playing Bancroft's crypto-papist game by producing 'a proud swelling volume like a Spanish Armada', but he undercuts immediately any impression that this is a genuine threat by the acute observation that 'this new on set is an open declaration … that … the Bishop with his home forces hath bene to[o] weake'. Deacon and Walker's book is an 'ignis fatuus' (will-o'-the-wisp), they brag like butchers' mastiffs, their words are nothing but rattling wind in aspen leaves. In an extended metaphor drawing on the relative merits of Spanish and English ships, *Dialogicall Discourses* is an unwieldy 'galeasse' which Darrell can defeat with a 'poore fisher boate'.[58] But his *Replie* is somewhat more restrained, addressed to the 'Right Reverend Fathers and Brethren' of the church, and the many metaphors are reduced so that prominence is given once again to the notion of family – and especially the friendly conference of a truly godly brotherhood.

Deacon and Walker, he says, pretend that they have tried to confer with Darrell and More since their release, a claim they make in their *Summarie Answere*. But he must expose their claims as lies: in fact they only contacted More and they did not even keep their appointment with him. Now it is they who are the frauds, not Darrell, and the opposed parties stalely trade *Replies* and *Answeres* to that effect. But Darrell ends his preface to the *Replie* with an indication of the direction that his thought is taking: 'little needes such conflict in these times wherein that antichrist of Rome extremely rageth'. Why should brother fight brother when the devil was 'the accuser of the brethren' and it was vital not to play into the hands of real enemies by emulating his example? Referring to 2 Corinthians 7:5, Darrell deplores the fears within the church that match the fighting without, and smartly reminds Deacon and Walker that the godly are supposed to be on the same side with his signature to the epistle: 'your fellow servant in the worke of the Gospell, John Darrell'.[59]

With this intricate and sometimes flatly self-contradictory imagery of brotherly fellowship, Darrell thus out-argued his second group of antagonists, and for the second time had the last word. In 1603 Samuel Harsnett published his *Declaration of Egregious Popish Impostures*, an attack on Catholic exorcists that was at least partly aimed at Darrell. But Darrell had no desire to defend Catholics and could afford to ignore the few references to himself in its text; also, as we shall see in the next chapter, Harsnett's rhetoric had changed.[60] Darrell – victorious in his own estimation – fell into silence for five years. But with Deacon and Walker's entry into the controversy, Bancroft and Harsnett had apparently succeeded in splitting godly from godly very effectively. Whilst the godly's imagery of family and practice of fellowship was a refuge in times of trouble, when relations soured they did so with striking unpleasantness. Their usual sociability thus broken, as Tom Webster suggested in his *Godly Clergy in Early Stuart England*, the godly were far less sure of themselves and their structures of meeting and conferring could implode into mutual recrimination. The early seventeenth century would be a time of reverses and separations, including among the community known to both Darrell and John Deacon. These were reflected not just in Darrell's last work, but before then in an unlikely place, on the London stage. These theatrical representations of issues arising from the controversy over John Darrell are the subject of the last chapter.

6 THE MADMAN IN THE WILDERNESS

Dispossession as Metaphor? Acting and Ventriloquism

Once upon a time, it was possible to argue that the controversy over god-liness in late Elizabethan England was discussed primarily in the kinds of literature that were of least interest to literary scholars. At the head of this list were fat theological works, with supposedly popular pamphlets coming just behind. Beyond these were obscure collections of documents to be mined purely for the 'facts' they contained, like those collected by John Field to form his registers of the persecution of the godly. For example, the story of the tribulations of the puritan agitator Giles Wigginton was useful from this viewpoint primarily because he happened to mention that the pursuivant who arrested him was the dramatist Anthony Munday. But since the advent of new historicism and cultural materialism, literary scholars have begun to argue successfully that works once perceived as 'background' to dramatic and poetic works now stand with them on an equal footing, as both intertextually important and themselves amenable to reading as representations. The read-ing of pamphlets and sermons in this way soon drew attention to the fact that many of the narratives, characters and imageries deployed there also appeared in canonical literary works – and not just in obvious godly or Catholic stere-otypes like Malvolio, Tribulation Wholesome or Oliver Martext, but also less recognizable figures like Olivia, Doctor Pinch, Falstaff and Pisanio. Scholars began to read the works of Samuel Harsnett and Martin Marprelate in great detail, looking for cultural synergies between them and the works of canoni-cal dramatists.

The best known example is the reading of *King Lear* by Stephen Greenblatt in his essay 'Shakespeare and the Exorcists', which had a number of incarna-tions before its publication in this form in 1988.[1] Scholars had realized since at least 1733 that Shakespeare was indebted to Samuel Harsnett's *A Declaration of Egregious Popish Impostures* (1603) for the names of the devils imagined by Edgar in *King Lear*. These were spoken during the exorcisms at Denham in Buckinghamshire in 1586 by a group of Catholic priests, and Harsnett used them in his attack on both these exorcisms and the dispossessions of the godly, which he saw as equally fraudulent. In the 1950s Kenneth Muir identified over eighty specific echoes of *A Declaration of Egregious Popish Impostures* in the *King Lear*.[2] But along with these details, what else had Shakespeare taken from the source or sources on demonic possession that he had read, and, culturally-speaking, was the borrowing all one way? Greenblatt argued that both kinds of texts, the supposedly documentary 'source' and Shakespeare's self-conscious fiction, were concerned with the energies generated by and swirling around power – the display of potency and legitimacy by those referred to as 'the authorities' – and they were exchanging those energies. 'Power' has come to be a horribly commonplace term among literary scholars and students, but Greenblatt and his colleagues meant something specific (if somewhat indefinable) by it. For them 'power' was a kind of cultural impetus: the momentum and persuasive quality that inhered in a narrative, which created assent among its readers to various ideologies and political positions, subversive or orthodox, without its existence being obvious.

Greenblatt saw in *King Lear*'s debt to Harsnett two conflicting impulses: corroboration of the official position on exorcism – that it was fraudulent – and subversion of that position. By introducing into his play a self-consciously fake demoniac, Edgar, who has assumed this role because he is being persecuted by his illegitimate brother, Shakespeare 'responsibly marked out' exorcism 'as a theatrical fraud'. The same thing was happening when Edgar pretended to see a devil fly away from his father, Gloucester, who had tried to commit suicide. But at the same time, the play suggests that for Edgar and Gloucester the fraud offered a kind of protection and healing. Subjected to horrible injustice by his family, each character found a better reality in his belief in or pretence of the devil's presence: the discourse of possession and exorcism was paradoxically associated with virtuous characters and good motivation. Drawing on the perception that Shakespeare may well have sympathized with the position of English Catholics after the Reformation, Greenblatt saw analogies in Edgar and Gloucester with the position of the Catholic exorcists attacked by Harsnett, and we can extend his insight to include John Darrell and George More. What if Shakespeare's play were actually exposing Harsnett's strategies of bullying and defaming even as it seemed to endorse them by borrowing their terms? Harsnett might be right to assert that exorcism was a fraudulent practice, but his criticism of it was part of a violent repression of faithful and nobly-motivated people, some of them, like the priest Robert Dibdale, personally known to Shakespeare.

Harsnett's bitter satire against the Catholic faith also opened up questions of faith itself and its worth: exposing some beliefs as lies might end up destroying all human credit in the healing power of faith, or even in a beneficent deity. What if there was only fraudulence and theatrical imposture and nothing more? As the editor of the *Triall* (not Darrell, as Greenblatt thought) put it, 'no Divells, no God'. In the theatre, meanwhile, the suspension of disbelief was an essential quality. Shakespeare's works seemed to suggest a strong interest in the idea that acting out redemptive exorcisms of various kinds – working through injustice, loss and so on – could offer healing to broken communities and individuals, as well as providing pleasure through 'spectacular impostures'. Although they were known to be false, they worked, entertained and made money. No wonder Shakespeare's play offered a complex response to Harsnett's sceptical tirade. In Greenblatt's reading, *King Lear* seemed to follow and overtake Harsnett in suggesting that there was an emptiness at the heart of belief itself. As Amy Wolf added, both *King Lear* and *A Declaration of Egregious Popish Impostures* 'describe a world in which superstition is replaced by the cold, sharp reality of human cruelty'. The intolerable bleakness of *King Lear*, which C. L. Barber had gone so far as to describe as 'post-Christian', could thus, Greenblatt concluded, be explained partly by Shakespeare's reaction to the violence and injustice embodied in Harsnett's text and partly by his paradoxical endorsement of Harsnett's assessment of exorcism, among other religious shows, as an empty fraud.[3]

Caught up in this argument is the unanswerable (and to literary scholars often unaskable) question of how Shakespeare might have responded to the plight (or, alternatively, well-deserved fall) of Darrell and More. One reading of Greenblatt's work, especially of 'Invisible Bullets', the companion essay to 'Shakespeare and the Exorcists', is that as part of its disenchantment with 'superstition' Shakespeare's work posits an emptiness at the heart of the church/state complex in political as well as religious terms. The state, plays like the two parts of *Henry IV* seem to suggest, whilst insisting on a monologic truth and unity, actually practised a hypocritical doubleness. It was driven by Machiavellian political necessity, constantly putting on shows of dissent and suppressive power, including those of a repugnant theatre of cruelty: for example, in the hanging, drawing and quartering of Catholic missionaries which is the context of *King Lear*, and the execution of Protestant separatists under the same legislation, which was not designed for such a purpose. As we have seen in the last chapter, the trials of Darrell and More could be made to fit into that world-view, although one has to see them in a certain way for the identification to be complete. It would have to be argued that, rather than Darrell and More, it was Bancroft and Harsnett who were the fraudsters, scapegoating innocent ministers in their lying treatises and show trials because it was politically expedient. This was Darrell's view, as we know, and at least one critic has agreed with him. John L. Murphy, investigating *King Lear* at the same time as Greenblatt experienced 'outrage' on the ministers' behalf, similar to the passionate feelings of pity and terror that *King Lear* itself evoked in him.

But others have differed: as we have seen, as a supposedly anti-theatrical kill-joy puritan, Darrell has been almost uniformly disliked where he has been noticed at all by literary scholars. For F. W. Brownlow, Shakespeare was quite rightly following Harsnett's lead in regarding exorcism, and therefore Darrell, as a fraud. Brownlow argues that Harsnett and his party acted in good faith, and that Darrell and More were not treated 'so very harshly', especially when compared with other religious dissidents such as Catholics. This leads Brownlow into a somewhat contradictory claim that, although Darrell was not a fraud, 'it is hard to be very sympathetic with him' despite the loss of his professional reputation, practice and income, and his eighteen-month imprisonment. It has been a common feeling: although it might be assumed that Darrell was not a charlatan or revolutionary, he somehow deserved his punishment because he was a narrow-minded little puritan. Brownlow's otherwise perfectly reasonable argument, like others of this kind, is thus tainted by an ill-concealed dislike of Darrell – a refusal, for example, to accept that he was actually a minister, which was not questioned by any contemporary.[4] In contrast, the most recent accounts of Shakespeare and the Darrell case, those of Amy Wolf and Hilaire Kallendorf, whilst shying away from attempting to resurrect Shakespeare's authorial intent, have both concluded that in staging exorcism he returns fascinatedly to the possibility of its efficacy, in metaphorical and theatrical terms at least. For Kallendorf, this suggests a commitment to exorcism as catharsis – not just in its technical theatrical sense, but at a deep emotional level. She suggests that Greenblatt and other New Historicists have missed an explanation of the emotional impact of plays like *King Lear* which stage possession and dispossession, because they are 'unwilling to view phenomena such as exorcism as legitimate Christian marvels in the early modern period'. Greenblatt, says Kallendorf, is repeating Harsnett's language of fraudulence and anti-godliness because he is mired in twentieth-century rationalism – but Shakespeare was not.[5]

Darrell must have been aware of the connections made between his own practices and downfall and those of the Catholic exorcists whose words ended up in *King Lear*, even if he rejected them completely. He had read the narrative on which Harsnett's *Declaration* was based, in a version copied out by hand by Robert 'Barens' (Barnes), a recusant imprisoned in the King's Bench, and he gave the devil-names 'Hoberdi-Dance, Lusti-Jolly-Jenkin, Lusti-Dicke' to prove it in his *True Narration*.[6] He would thus have recognized the attack on him in the *Declaration* even though he did not wish or feel able to respond to it. But he was a little more like Harsnett than is suggested by Greenblatt's reading, since he was not averse to using theatrical language himself, and there is no evidence that he joined some of his godly contemporaries in making any explicit attack on the theatre. Brownlow was right when he pointed out that the use of theatrical terms was 'commonplace for the subject', that is, for attacking Catholicism.[7] But it was in this case, and others, also used by the godly against fellow Protestants and vice versa. Richard Bancroft quoted the godly's criticism of the current form of the communion service and its celebrants: the godly alleged that 'they eate not the Lordes Supper but playe a pageant … they have but a shadowe of the bodie and bloud of Christe, or rather a Counterfett … an Idoll …'. Darrell himself – since he was convinced that Bancroft and Harsnett did not believe him to be guilty – accused them of playing parts like masquers 'on the stage'. He also accused Harsnett of writing like an 'Interlude-maker'.[8] Accusations of theatricality and its companion popery cut both ways, and were used as ammunition fairly indiscriminately.

The critical discussion of *King Lear*, a play on which the Darrell affair has (as far as we can tell) only a limited influence, should by now have made it clear that it is extremely difficult to extrapolate from any text about exorcism anything of import that is not immediately, and quite rightly, contradicted by other legitimate readings – fascinating and illuminating as the attempt may be. Exorcism was a subject fraught with contradictions and mysteries, even to its practitioners. Reading becomes even more difficult with the surviving texts that refer to Darrell, either explicitly or implicitly, at length. The most important point about these texts, in my reading, is that they are all fragmentary and polemical, constantly shifting their stance and imagery in relation to one another as argument develops between them, and each of them is conditioned by the limitations of their author(s) and the purpose and history of their composition. This is why I have found it imperative to attempt, as far as this is possible, to reconstruct the circumstances in which each was written, and the world from which it came – which is itself accessible only through other surviving texts. What has emerged is that first, these individual circumstances of production determined fairly precisely when and how a text was written (or why one was not written), and second that the texts which survive have an oddly symbiotic relationship with each other, and with lost texts. Everything after *The most wonderfull and true storie*, the pamphlet about Darling's dispossession, was a response to something that had already happened, whether that was an interrogatory in court, a text being circulated in manuscript or a book being published. Much of the 'information' we have about Darrell and More thus comes from their enemies, and vice versa, so that we are constantly looking into a mirror, where the text does not faithfully imitate what it sees, but offers an inverted and distorted reflection, with issues of illusion, forgery, theatricality, parody and other inherently literary concepts constantly thrust to the reader's attention. But all this does not mean that the texts are records of fraudulence, or are inherently theatrical because they use theatrical language.

Rather they reflect a world of godly exegesis and argument, and an ongoing verbal battle between the godly and their brethren in the wider church, in which voices merged and diverged in a kind of literary prophesying.

With this in mind, one of the best readings of the texts on the Darrell affair is that of Steven Connor. As a non-specialist in Renaissance literature, Connor has heretically ignored the historical contexts of the pamphlets almost entirely. But what he has done instead of discussing these is to focus on one of the issues that makes it so difficult to offer a definitive account of what any particular text in the controversy 'really means'. Connor has analysed the story of Darrell's dispossessions and the pamphlets that represented them in terms of ventriloquism. The debate during the dispossessions, he argues, was one about voices, about who was speaking, with what authority and with what didactic application. Was Sommers speaking in his own voice, or was Satan speaking through him? What about the dialogues between devils dramatized by Darling, and his ventriloquizing of Christ's voice? Darrell and his friends were, of course, very much at home with the opinion that the devil might hijack the words of men and women, so this reading goes with the grain of godly thinking and not against it. When he first saw Sommers, and the boy told him his name, Darrell had wondered aloud if he was really speaking to him or if it was the devil. When Sommers confessed that the whole matter had been counterfeited, he asked the same question: 'But how shal I know that this is thou William Sommers, which now speakest unto me[?]'. This question could not, of course, be answered in any satisfactory way. Ralph Shute, the vicar of St Peter's church in Nottingham, leapt upon it as 'vain and frivolous'. For, he told his examiners later,

> Somers used his tonge and throat with other parts of his mouth, in as orderly and as naturall an habite at that instant, as any of us all that were present could do: and M[aster] Darrell, could yeeld no other reason to the contrary, but that William Sommers might as well aske of him, whether it were M[aster] Darrell that moved the question.[9]

If it was not Sommers who spoke, it might not be Darrell who spoke either. And Darrell's question was a critical one: how would anyone know? Meaning seemed to recede into nothingness under such extreme strain and the only manageable response seemed to be to conclude that all demonic possession was a mere thespian fiction – which because of Greenblatt's very influential reading has become the default position of literary scholars.[10]

But it is just this search for a *manageable* response that seems to me to be a problem with reading the pamphlets of the Darrell case, and the drama based upon them. It is unhelpful to look for certainty and for readings accessible to the ungodly modern mind in them. The texts talk about something *unmanageable* – hopelessly fugitive and inconceivable even to those who discussed it at most length, a devil inside a human being. Deacon and Walker spent one of their eleven dialogues in *Dialogicall Discourses* discussing what happened to the physical and spiritual substances of the human body, mind and soul if they were invaded by a devil. Was there 'a confusion of substances' (absurd) or 'a rending or separation of substances … a vacuum' (folly, madness to imagine)? Where was the mind, anyway – diffused throughout the body? An imaginary place? Was the devil like wine, which did not (Deacon and Walker said) enter a man's mind itself, but which gave off fumes that did? After a few pages, such discussions led naturally onto the creation of the holy ghost, the nature of the trinity and the size of the devil. The devil was at once circumscribed by God's power and his own essential substance, but also uncontainable, not tied to the normal rules of materiality.[11] These seem to us pointless debates, but their nature is extremely important to an understanding of Renaissance literature. An inability to comprehend and contain was the defining feature of divinity and demonology, which went hand in hand in their attempt to name the unnameable and thus try to contain it. Canonical literature participates in this highly formalized but evasive linguistic dance and much of its power comes from a language that we can no longer speak, because it has no meaning for us. As twenty-first century people, many of us find the language of godly family and society difficult to speak, but the language of possession and dispossession is almost completely dead.

Stuart Clark's work on demonology has shown that it is actually more logical to look at such matters in terms of language systems than it is to read them in any other way. To put it very reductively, because of the binary construction of language, and therefore of ideology, there must be a devil and witches and sabbaths, because there is a God and priests and church services, and vice versa. There is no further need to 'explain' demonology, and other approaches will find themselves examining only epiphenomena – something other than the real subject of the text, and the stories told by early modern people about themselves.[12] Such an approach is that of replacing 'the devil' with 'theatricality', for example. Although it follows the reading of an early modern churchman, Harsnett, it is an ungodly reading, manipulating the language that Harsnett supposedly shared with his fellow ministers to force an identification between polemically opposed concepts: godliness and theatre, sincerity and lies, writing and acting. Where Darrell and his friends heard the devil, we would like to be able to see theatre, or teenage angst or the id, and we think Harsnett or Shakespeare might have had a similar sceptical response. It is certainly not illegitimate to see these things, but it does not get at the unmanageable thing that we cannot comfortably see, which is godliness (and its adversary, the devil), which both Harsnett and Shakespeare could see too, even if Harsnett chose to pretend that in this instance he could not. The only way in which we can access this lost linguistic world is to acknowledge that it is there. Where there is divinity or devilishness for us there is also what contemporaries saw, and what the binary controversy over the Darrell case demonstrates, with all its multivocal and fragmentary polemic: the indeterminacy bred by language and the gap where it cannot suffice to describe experience convincingly, into which Darrell, his friends, patients and their contemporaries kept pouring words for the five years that the controversy lasted in print, in the vain hope of proving something.

This is why Connor's narrowly literary approach is so useful. His essay offers us a description of what the lost linguistic world of possession and dispossession looks like, not what it contains or, historically-speaking, is 'about'. What it looks like is ventriloquial chaos, with an increasing multiplicity of contributors to the pamphlets on dispossession, and thus (I would argue) an increasing pool of possible readings:

> the participants battle over and with their own and each others' voices ... [and] they also cut and splice into their arguments the testimonies of a large and ever-expanding pool of living witnesses and scriptural exegetical authorities.[13]

Whilst this is not a characteristic peculiar to the writings of the Darrell case, the fantastic complexities of the dispute embodied in it do seem to demand such a theoretical reading. In a strikingly multi-layered act of ventriloquism, for example, Darrell asks the reader to suppose for a moment that Sommers had accused not himself but Harsnett of teaching him to counterfeit possession. How would Harsnett prove his innocence? This is Darrell speaking in the voice of Sommers, whom he has just accused of being the mouthpiece of Harsnett, and also of being still possessed and therefore of speaking as the devil:

> admit So[mmers] had accused S. Harshnet instead of J. Dar[rell] and that the accusation were thus: About eight yeares past I dwelling at Langley Abbey with M[aster] Tho[mas] Graye and going on errands now to Ashby a market town there by, now to Lougborrow [Loughborough] an other, mett on a time one M[aster] Harsnet at Ashby, and there the said M[aster] Harsnet perswaded me to counterfeyte to be possessed with the divell ...[14]

Here the rhetorical point being made is that anyone can be misrepresented, and, further, that printing such a misrepresentation is in itself a demonic kind of identity theft, a possession. The linguistic and literary framework in which possession was discussed thus mirrors and mimics its subject: oppositional, binary, ventriloquial.

There is sometimes, even without such overt ventriloquism, a confusion over who is speaking in the pamphlets on the dispossessions. In one passage in his *Detection* of Harsnett's *Discovery*, Darrell quotes from his opponent's book at such length that he has to insert four marginal notes as interjections, and then put his own name at the head of the following paragraph to identify that this is his answer. Suddenly the page of the pamphlet is set out as a play (precisely Harsnett and Greenblatt's point, and a gift for his opponents), and the reader experiences ventriloquism followed immediately by dramatized dialogue between the antagonists: the battle over voices is almost unmanageable, straining at the confines of textual convention. It is as if Darrell wants the exchange to be a verbal confrontation, where the voices are clearly differentiated and he can interrupt at will, just as he could with a possession victim. Here he, irritatedly and ineptly, has to speak for everyone at once. There is indeed a danger in quoting your opponent at too much length. A good number of works from the early modern period survive only because they were disliked enough to be quoted at length in print, and were given significance and preserved by so doing: Reginald Scot's preservation of the pamphlet on the dispossession at the Dutch church in Maidstone, or the survival of the godly transcript of the words of Rachel Pinder in a pamphlet condemning her as a fraud are good examples. Darrell, fascinated by the 'sinnful, shamful, lying and ridiculous' nature of Harsnett's accusations, cannot resist reprinting them, displaying them in all their grotesque glory as part of a point about misrepresentation. But in repeating the arguments against him, he gives new life and language to his opponent, so much so that he is compelled to remind us – and at some level, surely himself – of his separateness, of not being possessed by the voices of others, and of the existence of his own voice which can answer such slander.[15]

A question was begged when Harsnett imitated the godly, or Darrell mimicked Sommers. If it was possible to ventriloquize one's opponent's words, then it would become unclear who was speaking and why. Surely the devil lurked somewhere here, in the space created by human fallibility and the deceits of language, where confusion and illusion would occur? Remember Darrell's insistent use of his own name ('John Darrell, a poore prisoner … Darrell is forsooth a cogger, a cousener, a Jugler …') as if it had been stolen from him by his attackers or by Satan (he came to equate the two as 'accusers of the brethren'). I am not arguing that for the godly demonic possession was 'about' language and was somehow metaphorical, since (as I have said) for the godly the experience of demonic possession was about demonic possession. But like us they experienced the phenomenon through speaking and writing about it, and that is the best and most intimate connection that we have with them. It seems helpful to explore what they said, at least in as far as we can access that through their surviving writings, before taking the word of their opponent that what they are really doing is putting on a deceitful play. When we do look at what they said, we can see a world where the voice is central, and where a naturalized form of expression is prophesying: taking anothers' words and wrestling over them, arguing and sometimes even playing 'devil's advocate', in a way that created confusion, but in the persistent hope of attaining a univocal truth to which all could joyfully submit. If one could not speak to the desired auditory, as Darrell explained in his *True Narration*, writing was the next best option, and the writings of the godly mimic the verbal forms of the movement. They are not plays but godly gatherings in print. So once again in imitating and reviling fellow churchmen we encounter issues of likeness and unlikeness, brotherhood and separation. It is this theme to which I now want to return, because – as if in response to the form of the pamphlet controversy – it is insistently present in the drama springing from the Darrell case.

Like Brother and Brother: *The Comedy of Errors* and *Twelfth Night*

As well as *King Lear*, two of Shakespeare's comedies, *The Comedy of Errors* and *Twelfth Night*, refer explicitly and at some length to exorcism. In her analysis of these two plays Donna B. Hamilton argues that in his depictions of demonic possession Shakespeare is not thinking about theatre, but about a less fashionable subject: the unity of the English church. In other words, he is thinking rather more like the godly than we might have imagined. In the earlier play, written before Darrell had come to public notice – although after the Wright dispossession – Hamilton suggests that part of what is at issue is the divisions within English Christianity, worked through in metaphors and homologies in a way that offers hope of reunion to all those who are willing to remember that they are part of the same family. It has often been noticed that the play is full of ecclesiological language, and it ends as its characters all go into a church together. The play has obvious classical origins, in reworking Plautus's *Menaechmi*, but it combines Plautine with Pauline sources, with its setting in Ephesus recalling Paul's epistle to the Ephesians. This epistle was a battleground for early modern religious controversialists, as were the acts and writings of the apostles generally, as we have seen. But it was an especially important book because not only did it contain some key injunctions and metaphors (such as putting on the armour of God) but it also dealt with demoniacs, the relationship between the apostles and devils, and with church government. Setting the action of *The Comedy of Errors* in Ephesus (not Epidamnum, as in the original) and introducing a suspected demonic possession (instead of madness) was bound to bring some of these references to the minds of the audience, and one of its first audiences – perhaps the first – would have found its concerns precisely echoing their own.

The Comedy of Errors seems to have been a Christmas play, and it was certainly performed at Gray's Inn on 28 December 1594 – where its highly politically-aware and religiously-charged audience would have been ideally placed to receive it. It is a play that deals with issues of freedom, tyranny, jurisdiction and order, the rights of a variety of different subjects (husbands, wives, trading partners – whether goldsmith and merchant or courtesan and client – officers and 'strangers'), and it is framed by a simple choice that preoccupied Shakespeare often in his work: justice or mercy? For lawyers it could not have been more apposite. But for *godly* lawyers, it was especially so, because it was also about separation and reunion, of brothers, parents and children. As we have seen, these images were common in controversialist writing and may have been recognizable to the metaphorically-minded. More ambitiously, however, Hamilton also argues that because of the rhetoric of marriage and fidelity that so often characterized discussions of the church, it would have been possible to see in Antipholus of Ephesus's wife Adriana many of the characteristics attributed to the Elizabethan church hierarchy, whilst her husband appears as a nonconformist, like the nonconforming godly. If this homology held, then Adriana's unfounded jealousy, like the constant anxiety of the Queen and her bishops about nonconformist ministers, could be seen to be the main problem in her relationship with her husband, not any actual infidelity on his – or their – part. It takes the intervention of the Abbess, a figure of wisdom and unity in the play who is the mother, wife and surrogate mother of five of the play's characters, and will be the mother-in-law of two others, to resolve matters in a slippage into a related metaphor, that of the mother church. She must rebuke Adriana and reconcile everyone, undoing thereby the separation brought about before the start of the play by the shipwreck that initially scattered her – the church's – family. Hilaire Kallendorf, whilst she finds Hamilton's wider argument 'a "stretch"' suggests that the Abbess can even be seen as a kind of exorcist, healing the supposed demoniac, and eventually the family, with her 'holy prayers'.[16]

The supposed demonic possession of Antipholus of Ephesus and his servant Dromio at the end of the play, suggests Hamilton, is thus part of a wider discussion of the demonizing of nonconformity in the church. Without any attempt to understand the position of Antipholus and Dromio, Adriana and her friends label them 'mad' and in need of exorcism. The godly were often likened by conformist writers to madmen, most notably to William Hacket, who had begun as a godly nonconformist and ended with a belief that God was telling him to overthrow the Queen and spring Cartwright from jail. Behind Hacket, and behind the disorder of Antipholus and Dromio, seems to lurk anabaptist violence and revolution. Hence the play's two 'demoniacs' are bound and imprisoned, as, curiously, is the man who attempts to exorcize them. Hamilton devotes little discussion to the exorcist Dr Pinch, but he is a schoolmaster and clearly more than a mere cunning-man. Kallendorf sees him as having both Catholic and Protestant attributes, but he is most like a Catholic priest, calling on the holy saints' names to force the supposed devil out.[17] Yet he too is bound, and also singed, drenched in mire and attacked with scissors. Violence, sums up Hamilton, is unleashed on everyone because of Adriana's refusal to trust her husband, and this persecutory impulse intensifies around the supposedly possessed. But in a play notable for its mutual recrimination, where violence of words and behaviour is always a threat, there is a didactic resolution for the audience in the closing couplet, which echoes the vocabulary of the godly: 'we came into the world like brother and brother, / Now let's go hand in hand, not one before another'. Peace and unity is achieved through brotherhood, and there are even two sets of twins, emphasizing further, Hamilton argues, the likenesses between apparently dissimilar sectarian interests within the church. If all can treat each other well, and if the authorities will be merciful to all, happiness can be achieved.[18]

Whether one accepts the specifics of Hamilton's argument or not, it does seem that Shakespeare associated possession and exorcism strongly with the separation of members of a family, and with disunity and strife in the wider polity, because exactly the same configuration appears in *Twelfth Night* (and, as we have seen, in *King Lear*). By the time that Shakespeare wrote *Twelfth Night*, the Darrell affair was almost over, but its echoes are clearly visible in the play.[19] The ambitious puritan Malvolio's resemblance to godly agitators was first noticed in 1845 and explored further by two scholars in the 1950s, G. B. Harrison, who mentioned briefly the evident resemblance of Malvolio to Darrell in his edition of the play, and J. L. Simmons, who, although he did not mention Darrell, explored the characterization of the steward in the light of anti-godly polemic by Bancroft, Sutcliffe and others. For Simmons, Malvolio was most like Hacket, or his associates Coppinger, Arthington and Wigginton: strongly associated with ideas of the godly as crazed and disorderly rebels. Among the main points of his argument was the fact that Bancroft had been particularly angered by the way that such men did not seem to him to be interested in the true meaning of scriptural passages but 'impose a meaning upon them ... not a yeelding to the wordes, but a kind of compulsion'. Malvolio's reading of the love letter that he believes to be from his employer Olivia similarly reveals his determination to justify his imaginings: 'if I could make that resemble something in me', he yearns. Like a godly reader, he then obeys 'every point of the letter' according to his misreading. Bancroft also said in his Paul's Cross sermon of 1589 (published shortly afterwards) that 'selfe-love ... did build the city of the divel' and Malvolio is accused by Olivia of being 'sick of self love'. There is even a reference to Martin Marprelate's pamphlets, in the statement made about Malvolio's own letter that 'a madman's epistles are no gospels', as well as Sir Andrew's attack on Malvolio with the phrase 'Pistol him!'.[20]

In 1990 Winfried Schleiner recognized Darrell's dispossessions in Malvolio's plight at the end of *Twelfth Night*. Fooled by the fraudulent letter into behaving like a madman, Malvolio is imprisoned by his fellow servants and his employer's kinsman, whom he has offended, and treated to a fake 'exorcism' by another enemy, Feste, Olivia's fool. Most obviously, here was a demoniac who was not really possessed being ministered to by a fool dressed as a curate, who asked the question 'do you but counterfeit?' of his patient. As Schleiner noted, the words 'dissemble' and 'counterfeit', which occur in the 'possession' scene (Act IV, Scene ii), were both loaded with significance by the pamphlet war over Darrell's activities, and whilst it is impossible to prove that Shakespeare had read any of these pamphlets before he read Harsnett's *Declaration* sometime in or after 1603, it is a fair – indeed, necessary – supposition that he knew of the case through these or by word of mouth.[21] Elements of Darrell very clearly appear in both Feste and Malvolio, and as the latter, he may be represented as having been falsely imprisoned and abused by cynical jailers. Once again, the dramatist seemed to have returned to issues of fellow-feeling in religious politics, but in a much bitterer, more pointed way than *The Comedy of Errors*. Like the earlier comedy, *Twelfth Night* was performed at the Inns of Court, where law student John Manningham rightly called it 'much like' *The Comedy of Errors* when he saw it first performed in February 1602.[22] But *Twelfth Night* is more politically ambitious, stepping outside the family imagery of the earlier play to offer a model of a noble lady's household as the state itself, which at first encourages and then betrays the godly.

According to Hamilton, who extends Schleiner's analysis substantially, Olivia's household can be read as homologous to Elizabeth's realm: an absolute dictatorship yet one where the mistress is curiously passive. In this realm is an ambitious godly subject, who believes that he can woo its mistress and master her. Echoes of the Essex rebellion seem to be making themselves felt here, as well as Darrell. But although the godly Malvolio is a victim, as Hamilton notes, he is unlikeable and cannot be the play's hero no matter how much sympathy is created for his plight. So although the play clearly re-imagines the fall of a Darrell-like godly man, Hamilton suggests that its rhetoric is kept away from particular historical events and confessional alternatives, and is therefore more interestingly focused on the systems of power-relations by which an established sect represses another. That said, Hamilton offers an assertive reading of Malvolio as a stereotypical godly caricature, which cannot help reminding us of Darrell as he was seen by his opponents:

> like the puritan who plans to achieve pre-eminence in the church, Malvolio dreams of being Toby's superior, works away at a self-serving interpretation of an obscure text, [and] reads the words that instruct him to pursue the 'trick of singularity' ...[23]

The play is full of language that connects Malvolio to Darrell, in particular in Act IV, Scene ii, although the epithets and names that echo writings on his trial are curiously scattered and confused in applying to different characters. For example, having had Malvolio imprisoned like Darrell on suspicion that he is mad or possessed or both, and intending to treat him to what Hamilton calls 'a mocking parody of an ecclesiastical trial', Feste the fool is seen dressing himself in the gown of a curate in order to visit the 'demoniac', remarking 'I will dissemble myself in't and I would I were the first that ever dissembled in such a gown'. As Greenblatt says, 'if the jibe had a specific reference for the play's original audience, it would be to the puritan Darrel[l]'.[24] Now Darrell (at least as he was portrayed by his opponents) is Feste, a dissembling fool dressed as a curate. But in an additional twist, as Schleiner noticed, Feste may be named after Festus, the wise judge who chose to release the apostle Paul/Malvolio/Darrell from prison. Festus was mentioned by the editor of *The Triall of Maist. Dorrell* in his appeal to Popham, urging him to behave similarly towards Darrell. Immediately Feste has begun his exorcizing act, Sir Toby remarks that he 'counterfeits well'. Festus/Feste/Darrell is now a counterfeit: justice to the godly is conflated with folly and deceit. And of course a further contradictory similarity with Darrell's case is woven awkwardly into the play: as Hamilton says, 'disagreeable as Malvolio may be, he is innocent of that of which he is being accused'. Yet this Festus will not release him.[25]

Malvolio's accusers are motivated solely by malice, even though the audience can understand their *animus*, and they, as well as Darrell, are represented by a fool in curate's robes. Feste is now analogous to Bancroft and Harsnett. In this role, he will continue to fault, imprison and abuse his victim for as long as he can, baffling him with obvious lies and nonsensical claims, such as that his prison has 'windows transparent as barricadoes'. Malvolio responds in the vein of Darrell: 'there was never man thus abused'. He asks for ink, paper and light, begging, as Darrell did with Elizabeth, to be allowed to tell his story to 'my lady'. And in the light of my account of Darrell's release, Toby, whom Hamilton has likened to Marprelate's drunken bishops, also suddenly bears a further similarity to the ecclesiastical authorities when they found themselves needing to be merciful to Darrell in December 1599:

> I would we were well rid of this knavery. If he may be conveniently delivered, I would he were, for I am now so far in offence with my niece that I cannot pursue with any safety this sport to the upshot.[26]

If Olivia is homologous with Elizabeth, then there might be an implication that Whitgift, Bancroft and Harsnett were indeed in trouble before they chose to let Darrell out. The reading can easily become over-literal, but the energy of the plot surrounding Malvolio's imprisonment, and the specific linguistic echoes, establish clearly that the notorious Darrell affair lies somewhere in its origins.

In its totality, although its significances shift and reform themselves as we watch – just as they do in the pamphlets which constitute the story of Darrell

– the episode can be read as a devastating attack on the High Commission and Darrell's accusers. This is the more remarkable because the play makes it clear that the playwright, cast and audience are reluctantly offering sympathy to someone (Malvolio or Darrell) who could under most other circumstances be portrayed as their natural enemy. With this in mind, Hamilton suggests a further significance in the transfer to the church authorities of many of Darrell's attributes as a dispossessor. Whilst Malvolio is seen to be nonconforming and rebellious, like Darrell, Essex and the godly, he is also deliberately deluded and lured by others into expressing that rebelliousness openly. Once drawn into the open by a fabricated text (Maria's letter purporting to come from Olivia) and by play-acting (Maria, Toby and Fabian's response to his changed behaviour), he can be attacked with all the force that his adversaries wish to unleash on him. Hamilton accordingly argues that

> Shakespeare focuses not on puritanism or on madness or on exorcism, but on the extent to which authority will fabricate in order to protect itself, thus laying bare the strategies of containment, suppression, demonising and scapegoating that the ecclesiastical officials had been using – against Darrell in this instance, but, by implication, against all nonconformists.[27]

As in *The Comedy of Errors*, it is the authorities and not the 'nonconformists' themselves who insist on the reality of demonic possession and demand an exorcism. The nonconformists are the victim of this insistence, which, unlike that in the earlier play, is cynical and fraudulent. These ideas, as we saw earlier in the chapter, would recur in *King Lear* with even more force, this time with Catholic exorcists occupying the place of Darrell in drawing the attention of Shakespeare's audience to the persecutory histrionics of the state church.

Twelfth Night, meanwhile, ends with a separation. References to puritanism and the separatist heresy Brownism have been swirling disconnectedly throughout the play, but Malvolio does in fact alienate himself from the established order and will not be reconciled. He even promises revenge, an ominous foreboding of coming events that seems again to hark back to Essex's leaving court and returning to march on London. What will the puritan's revenge be here?[28] In Darrell's case it was a written revenge. But others responded differently with an actual separation from the family of the church, as we saw in Chapters 2 and 5, and Hamilton sums up *Twelfth Night*'s contribution to this *topos*. When everyone else in the play is forming a big, happy family, reuniting with siblings and twins, marrying and forging new ties of friendship, Malvolio stands aside. Thus the play is:

> targeting the degree to which church politics, and especially the machinery of the ecclesiastical court system, were responsible for a social order which, instead of inviting unity, was forcing people to various forms of dissociation.[29]

More even-handedly, John D. Cox sees in *Twelfth Night* 'strategic satire aimed at both religious extremes'.[30] But in both arguments, comic resolution can only come with a rediscovery of the brotherhood and familial relationships that seem to lie at the heart of Shakespeare's interest in religious politics. Where extremists will not acknowledge such connections, as in *King Lear*, metaphorical exorcisms do not bring unity, and separation and civil strife is the result. Darrell wrote at the end of the last work of the controversy over his dispossessions that 'it is the rebell that makes civil war: the faithful subjects wepons are not against the peace but for the peace'.[31] Dangerous energies were at work in the Darrell controversy that would one day lead to an actual civil war, and Shakespeare's two plays about brother- and sisterhood and the reunion of families seem to dramatize concerns early in the seventeenth century about separation as a product of injustice and extremism.

Sympathy for the Devil: *The Devil is an Ass*

There were, of course, more cynical ways of reading the Darrell affair. We have examined some of the issues of metatheatricality and the politics of separation in Shakespeare's plays, but Ben Jonson, who also read the literature of the Darrell affair, had a much more straighforwardly satirical approach to his sources in his 1616 play *The Devil is an Ass*. Jonson drew primarily on Harsnett's *Discovery of the Fraudulent Practices*, which more explicitly than his *Declaration* linked godly dispossession with trickery. For Jonson, the faking of possession was a kind of crowning con-artistry, cony-catching *par excellence*, chosen as the last trick set up by the projector Merecraft in the last play that Jonson would write for a decade. Merecraft's profession, that of the projector, combined the roles of corrupt political lobbyist and common cony-catcher, and so when he mentions John Darrell and his dispossessions, we know that Jonson is associating Darrell with both of these worlds. Merecraft advises greedy, wealthy clients on a range of matters centring on how to obtain favour in government circles for projects that he devises for his dupes. These schemes, he explains, will lead to the granting of monopolies and patents to the clients, as well as earning them vast sums of money and titles. But his whole operation is a fraud. Some of the projects are ludicrous (a scheme to set up a government office for the better testing and regulation of toothpicks) whilst some seem relatively plausible (reclaiming 'drowned' land from the sea and marshes, and leasing it out). None of them, however, result in monopolies, wealth or honour for their investors, because Merecraft has no intention of promoting any such schemes. He is simply looking for money and whatever political or personal advantage he can obtain in the short term. For Jonson, Merecraft is like Darrell because Jonson has been reading Harsnett's *Discovery* and sees Darrell through Harsnett's eyes as a moneygrubber and place-seeker. It would be a natural step, therefore, for the projector, a similar self-promoter, to stage a possession and dispossession.

Merecraft's entirely earthy and worldly cast of mind is emphasized from his first introduction of the idea of faking a possession. Without explaining to the audience what Merecraft is discussing, Jonson has him walk into Act V, Scene iii of the play telling Fabian Fitzdottrel, who will act out the possession, that:

> It is the easiest thing, sir, to be done,
> As plain as fizzling: roll but wi' your eyes,
> And foam at th'mouth. A little castle-soap
> Will do't, to rub your lips: and then a nutshell,
> With tow and touchwood in it to spit fire.
> Did you never read, sir, little Darrel's tricks,
> With they boy o'Burton, and the seven in Lancashire,
> Sommers at Nottingham? All these do teach it.[32]

This fakery with its soap borrowed from William Sommers, says Merecraft, will be as easy as 'fizzling', the art of breaking wind silently. His discussion is all about the physical details of feigning possession, and offers no hint of any spiritual aspect to the phenomenon.[33]

But his worldliness is actually rather surprising: given Jonson's previous record of deriding the godly, and his source, it is odd that Merecraft and Fitzdottrel have no sectarian motive for their scam. They are not troublesome puritans, like Jonson's previous creations Tribulation Wholesome, Ananias or Zeal-of-the-Land Busy. They are in fact irreligious in the extreme, and when we first meet Fitzdottrel he is desperate to strike a deal with the devil that will enable him to become a treasure hunter, and thus find buried hoards of money. Treasure hunting was explicitly forbidden in the contemporary laws against witchcraft and conjuration, and it is also a surprise that Jonson does not take his comedy down this route, since it has great potential for cony-catching plots. However, he has a different target in mind with his introduction of a faked demonic possession: the malicious accusation of witches. This reflected recent events. Firstly, there was the scandal of the Essex divorce case and the poisoning of Sir Thomas Overbury. Frances Howard, Countess of Essex, had arranged a divorce from her husband, son of the executed second Earl, on the grounds that he had been bewitched and so had proved unable to consummate the marriage. Subsequently, she had sought to marry her lover, Robert Carr, Earl of Somerset, and when Overbury had opposed the match he had been killed. Carr and Howard were found guilty of inspiring the crime, but those executed for it were members of a community of fortune-tellers, astrologers and makers of charms and potions (therefore, 'witches') that the Countess had gathered around her. One of these, Anne Turner, was said to have compounded the poison, as well as more innocent activities like making a yellow starch for ruffs and other fashion items – which, as we shall see, is explicitly alluded to in *The Devil is an Ass*. It may be that this was one of the reasons that the play ran into political trouble shortly after its first performance.[34]

A second context was the affair of John Smyth, a Leicester demoniac and nephew of the godly preacher Henry Smyth, who had accused six women of witchcraft earlier in 1616.[35] After some of them had been executed on 18 July, the King exposed the boy as a fraud whilst he was on a visit to the city, suggesting that Smyth had accused them maliciously.[36] In the play, we see this device in action: if Fitzdottrel can accuse his wife and her friends of bewitching him, he can also claim that he was not in his right mind when he signed away his estate to their use, which he did as part of a virtuous attempt by his wife's admirer Wittipol to protect her from Fitzdottrel wasting her inheritance. If Fitzdottrel can get his wife and Wittipol imprisoned and executed, he and Merecraft can regain the money – and then Merecraft, the real controller of the situation, can proceed to bilk Fitzdottrel of the rest of it. There is thus no confessional or sectarian motive in Jonson's account of the uses of counterfeiting possession: it is all about delusion and fraud. The godly are not explicitly attacked, therefore, in *The Devil is an Ass*, although they are associated with the criminals and reprobates who participate in the same counterfeiting activity as they allegedly do, in a casual way that is in itself insulting. The idea of vice and devilment is also used in the play in a way that casually dismissed the godly dispossessors' view of the world, as one in which the devil roamed in some hard-to-imagine physical manifestation, waiting to entrap men and women into sin, and in which he could enter even their living bodies if he chose.[37]

The devil of the title, Pug, begins the play with precisely these notions: that he is a very dangerous and important creature indeed. He begs Satan to be allowed a trip to earth to work evil among humans as a relief from the pains of hell and an opportunity to serve the state of hell. But Satan is sceptical. Pug's 'main achievements' so far have been causing sows to abort their litters – apparently, he can enter the bodies of pigs, like the Gadarene swine – and upsetting the horses of farmers' wives on their way to market. Pug pleads to be allowed to take a Vice with him, one of the old stage incarnations of sin, such as 'Fraud, / Or Covetousness, or Lady Vanity'. But Satan is even more unimpressed with this suggestion. 'As vice stands in this present year?' he questions Pug incredulously:

> ... they are other things
> That are received now upon earth for Vices,
> Stranger and newer ... We strive still to breed
> And rear 'em up new ones; but they do not stand
> When they come there ...
> And it is feared they have a stud o' their own

Will put down ours ...
They have their Vices there most like to Virtues.[38]

In a world where competition rules everything, humans have become better than devils at inventing new vices, and threaten their monopoly. Those who appear virtuous and noble are not so, and the upper levels of English society are too sinful for the devil to be able to add anything to their imagination.

Thus whilst Jonson echoes the godly in his perception that sin is everywhere in the world, he makes a joke of the physical devils themselves. Pug is routinely humiliated: forced to inhabit the body of a hanged cutpurse because he has no substance of his own, beaten, deceived, stolen from and finally jailed awaiting sentence of death. In a parody of the ending of Christopher Marlowe's *Dr. Faustus*, he laments the slow passage of time before he can return to hell to learn his punishment from Satan and bear his ridicule for being such a poor agent of hell. Most ironically, when Pug offers Fitzdottrel help in counterfeiting his possession, he does not offer (is not able to offer?) to possess him in reality, but says that he can teach him tricks, such as how to make his belly seem to swell, how to roll his eyes, foam and 'feign six voices'. But Fitzdottrel angrily rejects his suggestion. Even though Pug has revealed to him that he is 'the very Devil', Fitzdottrel does not believe him and reviles him, in a clear Harsnettian echo, as a 'counterfeit wretch'.[39] And what is Pug's response? Does he afflict Fitzdottrel, possess him against his will, call down curses on him, tear him into pieces? No – he is arrested by the constable and dragged away. It is difficult to imagine a more comprehensive rebuttal of godly claims about demonic possession.

But alongside this persistent slighting of the discourse of godly demonologists is another absence – a most un-Jonsonian lack of sententiousness. By the end of the play Satan's assessment of humankind is somewhat different than it was in Act I, Scene i. Some people are able to outdo devils in wickedness, certainly: 'most have proved the better fiends'. But some of the play's characters were able to resist the temptation to sin: Pug missed an opportunity to forward an adulterous love affair, and Wittipol and Mrs Fitzdottrel eventually proved virtuous enough to resolve to keep their relationship a non-sexual one. Wittipol was also able to resist the lure of securing her estate for himself, as was his friend Manly, and the denouement of the play comes in an unexpected burst of virtue: Fitzdottrel gives up his counterfeit possession and instead says that he will 'defy' the devil and 'have faith against him'. The good are not pure, and the bad are not punished: compare Celia in *Volpone* with Mrs Fitzdottrel, and the sentencing of Voltore, another counterfeit demoniac, with the redemption of Fitzdottrel, and it can be seen that a very different point is made in a very different play.[40] Jonson's conclusion, spoken by Manly, is an unusually charitable one:

> It is not manly to take joy, or pride
> In human errors. We do all ill things:
> They do 'em worst that love 'em, and dwell there,
> Till the plague comes. The few that have the seeds
> Of goodness left will sooner make their way
> To a true life by shame, than punishment.[41]

The play ends with the sinful dismissively forgiven, even ignored, in a way that suggests Jonson was continuing an already noticeable move away from Juvenalian tone, and did not intend his play to be judgmental.[42] *The Devil is an Ass* is a curiously non-binary and unclosed play, which is especially surprising given that one of its sources was Harsnett's supremely polemical *Discovery*.

Harsnett and Jonson would normally be expected to have a great deal in common in both their attitude to the godly and their enjoyment of abuse aimed at them. They shared a position on the 'ungodly' side of the religious spectrum, and also a delight in language. Both writers have a characteristic love of lists, nicknames, insults, humour, the spatter of carefully-directed invective and the pithy put-down of the contemptible opponent. It is an excessive, roistering mode of expression that is aesthetically, as well as polemically, anti-godly. Here is Harsnett's description in his *Declaration* of a godly exorcist who has decided that his patient, 'a knavish boy ... or an idle girle', is bewitched:

> some idle, adle [addled], giddie, lymphaticall, illuminate dotrel, who being out of credite, learning, sobriety, honesty, and wit, wil take this holy advantage to raise the ruines of his desperate decayed name, and for his better glory will be-pray the jugling drab, and cast out Mopp the devil.

It is hard not to believe that Fitzdottrel's name comes from this passage as the offspring (the prefix 'Fitz' usually meaning illegitimate son) of the Darrell-figure here.[43] For comparison of the rhetoric, here is Jonson on Zeal-of-the-Land Busy in *Bartholomew Fair*:

> A notable hypocritical vermin it is ... One that stands upon his face more than his faith, at all times; ever in seditious motion, and reproving for vain-glory; of a most lunatic conscience and spleen, and affects the violence of singularity in all he does ... denies all antiquity; defies any other learning than inspiration; and what discretion soever years should afford him, it is all prevented in his original ignorance.[44]

Bartholomew Fair was written a mere two years before *The Devil is an Ass* but there is no godly buffoon or hypocrite in the latter, although the plot offers an open invitation to Jonson to write one. In creating a Vice called 'Fraud' of which no other comparable example is known, he once again seems to hint at an element in the play which never developed, a commentary on Darrell's alleged fraudulence but one from which the playwright unexpectedly backed away.[45]

Jonson seems, therefore, to have used Harsnett's work to glean technical details of the symptoms of possession, rather than as an inspiration for the play as a whole as an assault on religious extremism. The counterfeit possession, whilst it is the climax of the play, only occupies about one and a half scenes. And the play's ending seems almost to reprove Harsnett's glee in destroying Darrell: 'it is not manly to take joy, or pride / In human errors. We do all ill things.' Perhaps it is worth remembering that by the time Darrell was released, Jonson himself was in prison for the murder during a fight of Gabriel Spencer, and knew only too well his own sins and those of his profession.[46] In any case, by 1603 Harsnett's rhetoric carried a surprising and interesting suggestion of uncertainty about Darrell. The careful reader will have noticed that in his description of the Darrell-like godly dispossessor in the *Declaration*, Harsnett called this man a 'dotrel'. The dotterel is a farmland bird that was thought to be so stupid – or innocent – that it could be caught by simply walking up to it mimicking its movements. If Darrell is now a dotterel, then it is hard to see him simultaneously as a cunning fraud. Clearly Harsnett wishes the reader to continue to believe in his fraudulence, alongside that of the Catholic exorcists who are his main target, and so this unexpected slippage of rhetoric is an oddity. But perhaps it betrays what Darrell had always suspected: that Harsnett did not in his heart believe him to be guilty. Jonson used Harsnett as a source, but his response – especially to this passage – seems to have picked up on this uncertainty, and been therefore at odds with the chaplain's usually savage rhetoric of blame.

So if Jonson's concern is not to attack the godly, why does he include a fake demoniac in *The Devil is an Ass*? In part the answer seems to lie in his interest in genre and language, the relationship between these and human corruption. This concern – a feature of all Jonson's plays – can be seen most clearly in the possession scene itself.[47] The 'possessed' Fitzdottrel speaks in riddling rhymes and repetitions

> My wife is a whore, I'll kiss her no more: and why?
> Mayst not thou be a cuckold, as well as I?

These remind the audience of the couplets in which the old stage Vice speaks earlier in the play:

> What is he calls upon me and would seem to lack a Vice?
> Ere his words be half spoken, I am with him in a trice.

The possession and the Vice are thus linked by their language patterns in a rather antiquated theatricality, which highlights their obvious artifice and so

their inability to be taken seriously by the supposedly sophisticated modern
audience. As Satan points out, the Vice might have been acceptable in 1560,
but not 1616. Jonson is interested in the genre of the 'devil play, or interlude',
and how such devices represent human motivation, as much as in actually
performing that representation himself.[48] The sense that the possession is not
remotely credible, and is composed of snippets of playing and poetry which
interest the dramatist in their own right is made even clearer when Fitzdottrel
mocks those stood around his bed, including the lawyer and magistrate Sir Paul
Eitherside: 'Knight, shite, Poule [Paul], jowl, owl, foul, troule, bowl'. Sir Paul
comments that this is 'Crambe, another of the devil's games', which refers to
the rhyming word-game crambo.

The interpretations of Fitzdottrel's words and actions are also shown to be
a kind of game of charades, with the watchers having to read signs and words
given to them by the 'possessed'. Fitzdottrel mimes something which Sir Paul
reads as 'the taking of tobacco, with which the Devil / Is so delighted' and
when he coughs or hesitates, this is interpreted as calling 'for hum' (a strong
ale). Moralizing what he has read, Sir Paul addresses the audience as well as the
cast: 'You takers of strong waters and tobacco, / Mark this'. When Fitzdottrel
cries 'yellow, yellow …', Sir Paul responds excitedly, recalling Anne Turner,
'That's starch! The Devil's idol of that colour. / He [Fitzdottrel] ratifies it with
clapping of his hands.' This exchange prompts reflections on the stage and on
language itself: 'How the Devil can act!' and 'He is the master of players! …
And poets too! You heard him talk in rhyme!' On one hand this can be read as
a moment of anti-godly satire, recalling their suspicion that the 'abuses' of the
theatre and literature were prompted by the antichrist. But if it is compared
with the lengthy and uproarious attack on the godly embodied in the dialogue
of Zeal-of-the-Land Busy and the puppet player in *Bartholomew Fair*, its mild-
ness is very noticeable. Busy is utterly defeated in disputation by a puppet,
which finally responds to his attack on the 'profanations' of the stage by forcing
him humiliatingly to inspect its lack of genitalia – thus refuting the puritan
argument against players that it is sinful for the sexes to dress in each others' clothing.[49] Compared with this, whilst Jonson reproduces accurately and
amusingly Darrell and his friends' interpretation of Sommers's sin-acting and
Darling's rhyming, it is dismissed as a kind of 'crambo' or game, a folly rather
a fraud. Again, Jonson has softened his moralistic tone, but he has softened
Harsnett's even further.

Perhaps Jonson was losing his edge: Dryden called his later plays 'dotages'
and C. H. Herford and Percy Simpson regard *The Devil is an Ass* as 'palpably
thin' and 'a little dull'.[50] But maybe *The Devil is an Ass* is simply a work reflecting without righteous anger on the events of Darrell's dispossessions and trial,
and finding them rather ridiculous and sad than matters for bitter condemna-
tion. By 1616 it was all a very long time ago.

The Last Word

So what happened to Darrell after he had beaten off Deacon and Walker, and ended his career as an illegal author? It was widely believed that he must have died, either in prison or shortly after his release.[51] But on 8 May 1607 the churchwardens of Teversal in Nottinghamshire, Richard Ball and William Howson, presented to the archdeaconry court at Nottingham:

> Mr. John Dorrell and his wyfe and daughter and his maid servante and Alice Simson servant to John Bradshawe for not receavinge the communion at Easter laste paste.[52]

Darrell had returned to Nottinghamshire and was once again living with his family and in relative affluence, since they could afford to employ a servant. Clearly the family were being brought up to be godly too. R. A. Marchant, who discovered this presentment, suggests that the fact that Darrell was not receiving communion at his parish church means that he might have 'contemplated becoming a Separatist'. This is a striking suggestion in the light of what we have seen of the importance of separatism – both as a reality and metaphorically – in writings of and about the godly. But it seems more likely that Darrell was receiving communion somewhere else, where the minister's opinion was more to his liking. This might have been at Greasley or Sutton in Ashfield. Both were favourite churches with the godly, who travelled there from as far away as Mansfield.[53] And later the same year, the churchwardens of both Greasley and Sutton in Ashfield presented themselves to the archdeaconry court for allowing Darrell to preach in their churches without exhibiting (or, in fact, possessing) a licence to preach.[54] Darrell was being welcomed in godly circles, but some of their members then felt compelled to seek punishment for their disobedience in hosting him.

These were also separatist circles. In 1606 there was a conference at the house of Lady Bowes, twenty years after her interest in Darrell was marked by his gift to her of his manuscript on Katherine Wright. Arthur Hildersham attended, as did many eminent godly ministers.[55] There is no record of Darrell being there, but he must have known of the event. The meeting was to discuss separation, and ministers were asked to make their positions clear. Hildersham was for staying within the Church of England and it seems likely that Darrell shared his views. But it was clear that great changes were taking effect in the Midlands community of godly. Tussle with Bancroft was a thing of the past: he was Archbishop of Canterbury now, and some ministers were not interested in continuing a fight for the Church's soul. In an admission of failure that was also, after the manner of the unputdownable godly, supremely self-confident, they went home and set up their own churches. A steady trickle of godly left for the Low Countries and the new world and in this climate of disunity Darrell felt compelled to write again. For the first time in his life he published an authorized book, which was also his last. *A Treatise of the Church* was entered in the Stationers' Register on 4 April 1617.[56] Although its author signed himself 'John Dayrell', the Stationers' Register calls him 'master Darrell' (and since they mentioned authors' names only infrequently, there is a suggestion that, like 'Mr. Greenham' and 'Mr. Perkins', this author was something of a celebrity). Meanwhile, Bishop Joseph Hall, a scholar of Ashby Grammar School and someone well acquainted with Arthur Hildersham, William Bradshaw and probably Darrell himself, refers to him as 'Dayrel'.[57] The spelling is immaterial: this is our man. His book was described in the Register as being titled 'The Church of Englande is the true Church', which is a succinct summary of its argument.

As the records of presentation to the church courts in 1607 show, it is unlikely that Darrell had become a craven conformist, repudiating his previous views. In fact, he was arguing the same thing that he had tried to demonstrate with his dispossessions. But in a climate where the poles of the theological debate were now Arminianism and separation, rather than mere nonconformity, he was now ideally placed to put into print the arguments of the moderate godly against the separatists. He was about fifty-five years old, and in a very different position from his younger, noisier self. In the quieter middle ground of the church, he had moved towards acceptance as it had moved towards him. He was now out of the public eye, and had apparently remained quiet and reasonably conformable for at least ten years. Darrell's new and final book was thus an assertion of maturity, of judgment and experience, and it established publicly his regained place within his church: alongside supportive brethren, and in an effort to retain the fellowship of those brothers who had responded differently to persecution than he had. In his *Treatise*, bizarrely, he could thus find common ground even with Harsnett. The church could afford to license his voice where it had once silenced it. And as the godly regrouped and responded to the new conservative drive in the church and government in the 1630s and 1640s, Darrell's work enjoyed an after-life. His final appearance in print was a republication of his account in *A True Narration* of Sommers's dispossession as *A True Relation of The grievous handling of William Sommers of Nottingham* in 1641.[58] Once again he was cast in a revolutionary light, months before the raising of the King's standard in the key town of Nottingham triggered the Civil War. It is a clear indicator of the swirling energies of highly-localized repression and radicalism in the pamphlets of the Darrell dispossessions, and of their importance to the political, cultural and literary history of early modern England.

NOTES

The following abbreviations are used in the notes:

AAOD   John Darrell, *An Apologie or Defence of the Possession of William Sommers* (?Amsterdam, 1598).

ABA   Anon., *A Brief Apologie proving the possession of William Sommers* (Middelburg, 1599).

ABN   Anon., *A Breife Narration of the possession, dispossession, and repossession of William Sommers* (?Amsterdam, 1598).

ATN   John Darrell, *A True Narration of the Strange and Grevous Vexation by the Devil of 7 Persons in Lancashire and William Sommers of Nottingham* (n.p., 1600).

Detection   John Darrell, *A Detection of that Sinnful, Shamful, Lying and Ridiculous Discours of Samuel Harshnet* (n.p., 1600).

DFP   Samuel Harsnett, *A Discovery of the Fraudulent Practices of John Darrel* (London, 1599).

DNB   *Dictionary of National Biography.*

EPI   Samuel Harsnett, *A Declaration of Egregious Popish Impostures* (London, 1603) in F. W. Brownlow (ed.), *Shakespeare, Harsnett and the Devils of Denham* (Newark and London, University of Delaware Press, Associated University Presses, 1993).

NA   Nottinghamshire County Council, Nottinghamshire Archives.

Replie   John Darrell, *The Replie of John Darrell to the Answer of John Deacon and John Walker* (n.p., 1602).

Survey   John Darrell, *A Survey of Certaine Dialogical Discourses* (n.p., 1602).

Treatise   John Darrell, *A Treatise of the Church* (London, 1617).

Triall   Anon., *The Triall of Maist. Dorrell* (Middelburg, 1599).

Introduction

1. *ABN*, D.
2. *ATN*, C.
3. Matthew Sutcliffe, *An Answer to a Certain Libel* (London, 1592), A3v., p. 201.
4. *DFP*, J.
5. *DNB*.
6. Geneva Bible, 'This kind can by no other means come forth but by prayer and fasting'.
7. Keith Thomas, *Religion and the Decline of Magic* (1971; London, Peregrine, 1978), p. 575; British Library, Harley MS 590, ff. 6–63, and Lansdowne MS 101, ff. 165–75; Thomas Freeman, 'Demons, Deviance and Defiance, John Darrell and the Politics of Exorcism in Late Elizabethan England' in Peter Lake and Michael Questier (eds), *Conformity and Orthodoxy in the English Church c. 1560–1660* (Woodbridge, Boydell Press, 2000), p. 39; for Parkhurst see also Matthew Reynolds, *Godly Reformers and their Opponents in Early Modern England: Religion in Norwich c. 1560–1643* (Woodbridge, Boydell Press, 2005), *passim*; *ATN*, Dv., F2v.; *DFP*, C4v.; Reginald Scot, *The Discoverie of Witchcraft* (London, 1584), book 7, chs 1–2, gives a full account from a lost pamphlet on the Westwell case.
8. Joseph Goadby, *Memoirs of the Reverend Arthur Hildersham* (Bingham, 1819), pp. 12, 20.
9. John Dryden, 'Absolom and Achitophel' in M. H. Abrams and Stephen Greenblatt (eds), *The Norton Anthology of English Literature*, 7th edn, 2 vols (New York and London, W. W. Norton, 2000), vol. 1, pp. 2077–99, ll. 69–76.
10. Dryden, 'Absolom and Achitophel', ll. 529, 586.
11. Peter Heylyn, *Aerius Redivivus, or, The History of the Presbyterians* (Oxford, 1670), A–Av.
12. A phrase allegedly used by the Queen to her Archbishop Edwin Sandys (Albert Peel (ed.), *The Seconde Parte of a Register: being a Calendar of Manuscripts under that title intended for publication by the Puritans about 1593*, 2 vols (Cambridge, Cambridge University Press, 1915), vol. 1, p. 224).
13. Knollys to Burghley, 13 June 1584, quoted in M. M. Knappen, *Tudor Puritanism: A Chapter in the History of Idealism* (Chicago, University of Chicago Press, 1939), p. 275.
14. Diarmaid MacCulloch, *The Later Reformation in England 1547–1603* (Basingstoke, Macmillan, 1990), p. 40.
15. Elizabeth was Supreme Governor, replacing the title Supreme Head – a fine distinction that quieted some godly concerns whilst raising others (J. E. Neale, *Elizabeth I and Her Parliaments 1559–1581* (London, Jonathan Cape, 1953), p. 75.
16. MacCulloch, p. 40.
17. Ireton to Anthony Gilby, May 1576, quoted in Patrick Collinson, *The Religion of Protestants: The Church in English Society 1559–1625* (Oxford, Clarendon, 1982), p. 130.
18. MacCullough, p. 44.
19. Neale, *1559–1581*, pp. 2, 270.

20. John Dykstra Eusden, *Puritans, Lawyers and Poltics in the Early Seventeenth Century* (New Haven, Archon/Yale University Press, 1968), p. viii.

21. When tested, this was also the verdict of the common law courts (Cawdry 1591 (5 Coke, f. 8); Knappen, p. 273; W. J. Sheils, *The Puritans in the Diocese of Peterborough 1558–1610* (Northampton, Northamptonshire Record Society, 1979), p. 64).

22. Knappen, pp. 270–2; J. E. Neale, *Elizabeth I and Her Parliaments 1584–1601* (London, Jonathan Cape, 1957), p. 22.

23. Patrick Collinson, *The Elizabethan Puritan Movement* (London, Jonathon Cape, 1967), pp. 209–11; Collinson, *Godly People: Essays on English Protestantism and Puritanism* (London, Hambledon, 1983), p. 8.

24. MacCulloch, p. 50.

25. See Collinson, *The Elizabethan Puritan Movement*, pp. 220–31.

26. Sheils, pp. 52–8.

27. Collinson, *The Elizabethan Puritan Movement*, p. 217.

28. MacCulloch, pp. 56–7.

29. Knappen, p. 301.

30. Samuel Clarke, *A General Martyrologie ... Whereunto is added the lives of thirty two English Divines* (London, 1677), p. 13.

31. Rosemary O'Day, 'Ecclesiastical Patronage, Who Controlled the Church' in Felicity Heal and Rosemary O'Day (eds), *Church and Society in England: Henry VIII to James I* (London and Basingstoke, Macmillan, 1977), p. 138.

32. Albert Peel (ed.), *Tracts Ascribed to Richard Bancroft* (Cambridge, Cambridge University Press, 1953), p. xvii.

33. MacCulloch, p. 58.

34. For David Loades's useful definition of separatism see MacCulloch, p. 154.

35. MacCulloch, p. 59.

36. Ibid., p. 61.

37. 'Martin' is now widely believed to have been the Midland gentleman Job Throckmorton, operating with a group of fellow conspirators from his Warwickshire estate, with key supporters and presses in Northamptonshire and Manchester (Leland H. Carlson, *Martin Marprelate, Gentleman: Master Job Throkmorton Laid Open in his Colors* (San Marino, Huntington Library, 1981)).

38. John Donne, 'Satire III' in John Carey (ed.), *John Donne, Selected Poetry* (Oxford, Oxford University Press, 1996), p. 7.

39. *Detection*, pp. 63–4, 32.

40. See below for discussion of all of these: Walker's book *Unclean Spirits: Possession and Exorcism in the Late Sixteenth and Early Seventeenth Centuries* (London, Scolar, 1981) was a breakthrough with its serious consideration of exorcism in its European context, whilst Freeman's article is easily the best account to date. See also Philip C. Almond, *Demonic Possession and Exorcism in Early Modern England: Contemporary Texts and their Cultural Contexts* (Cambridge, Cambridge University Press, 2004). Rickert's book has been criticized for its errors, but Rossell Hope-Robbins's allegation that she had no doctoral qualification is untrue (Rossell Hope-Robbins, review of Corinne Holt Rickert, *The Case of John Darrell, Minister and Exorcist* (Gainesville, University of Florida Press, 1962), *Renaissance News*, 16 (1963), pp. 28–30, and it must be said that Robbins's own account of Darrell is

even more inaccurate (*The Encyclopaedia of Witchcraft and Demonology* (London, Spring, 1959), pp. 118–19).

41. Patrick Collinson and John Craig (eds), *The Reformation in English Towns 1500–1640* (Basingstoke, Macmillan, 1998), p. 1; see for example Alan Everitt, *The Community of Kent and the Great Rebellion* (Leicester, Leicester University Press, 1966) and *The Local Community and the Great Rebellion* (London, Historical Association, 1969).

42. Alexandra Walsham, *Providence in Early Modern England* (Oxford, Oxford University Press, 1999), pp. 53–6.

1 A Literary Geography of Exorcism

1. Henry is always referred to as 'Dorrell', but I have adopted 'Darrell' for his son as this was the way he spelled his own name most often. Henry may have attended Trinity College, Cambridge, as a sizar in 1554 (J. and J. A. Venn (eds), *Alumni Cantabrigienses*, 4 vols (Cambridge, Cambridge University Press, 1927).

2. Chambers brass, St Peter's church; Henry Dorrell married Elizabeth Walker, presumably a remarriage after the death of John Darrell's mother. NA, Mansfield St Peter's Parish Register, 16 December 1566; National Archives, E 134/MISC/2457 (Eliz I), E 133/3/563 (Eliz I), E 134/20 and 21 Eliz/Mich 6, E 134/21 Eliz/East 17 and E 211/496 (23 Eliz). See also NA, Mansfield Manorial Court Rolls, DD/P//17/3 and 5.

3. National Archives, E134/MISC/2457, E133/3/563, E134/21 Eliz/East17, E134/20&21 Eliz/Mich6; NA, DD/4P/79/48–51.

4. Christine M. Newman, '"An Honourable and Elect Lady", The Faith of Isabel, Lady Bowes' in Diana Wood (ed.), *Life and Thought in the Northern Church c. 1100–1700: Essays in Honour of Claire Cross* (Woodbridge, Boydell Press, 1999), p. 415; *DNB*; John Twigg, *A History of Queens' College Cambridge 1448–1986* (Woodbridge, Boydell Press, 1987), pp. 89–90, 450, 96; J. H. Gray, *The Queens' College of St. Margaret and St. Bernard in the University of Cambridge*, rev. edn (1899; Cambridge, Cambridge University Press, 1926), p. 107.

5. Peter Lake, *Moderate Puritans and the Elizabethan Church* (Cambridge, Cambridge University Press, 1982), pp. 36–8; letter to Burghley, 11 June 1570, quoted in Gray, p. 103.

6. Gray, pp. 104–6, 110; Twigg, pp. 39–40, 68–71, 81, 84, 140, 91, 98; *Detection*, pp. 31, 75.

7. *DFP*, D4v.; *Detection*, pp. 29–30, 75; Peel (ed.), *Tracts Ascribed*, p. 57.

8. Bulwell Parish Register begins in 1621; Mansfield, St Peter's Register. R. A. Marchant's suggestion that Darrell may have 'had to break off his legal education because of the death of his father' can be seen to be wrong in the light of this new information (R. A. Marchant, 'John Darrell – Exorcist', *Transactions of the Thoroton Society*, 64 (1960), p. 48; NA DD/P/17/7. Darrell may have had a step-brother, Rowland (St Peter's Register, 15 September 1569). Joyce is described in the parish register as 'widowe Waulby', suggesting that she was the last of John

and Joan Darrell's parents to die. This may help explain why they felt able to leave Mansfield in 1592.

9. *AAOD*, I4v.; William Horner Groves, *The History of Mansfield* (Nottingham, 1894), p. 218; Nottingham University Library, Department of Manuscripts and Special Collections, AN/IM201/17; Marchant, *The Puritans and the Church Courts in the Diocese of York* (London, Longman, 1960), entry for Brittain, pp. 134–5, 170; NA, Parish Register 15041.

10. NA, 'Transcriptions of Proceedings in the Court of the Archdeaconry of Nottingham 1565–1675', vol. 1, pp. 38–9 (June 1574).

11. *ATN*, A4v.; Eckington Court Rolls, East Sussex Record Office, Gage of Firle Papers, SAS/G3/25 and 26, transcribed in H. J. H. Garratt, *Eckington, The Court Rolls, vol. 3: 1506–1589* (Huddersfield, H. J. H. Garratt, 2003), pp. 120, 141, 143, 151, 159, 172, 191, 238, 239, 247.

12. Garratt, pp. 191, 197, 200; *DFP*, Qq-Qqv.; *ATN*, 2A4v. ('The Doctrin of … Possession'); *Triall*, pp. 17–18; Lambeth Palace Library, Fairhurst Papers, MS 3470, f. 200.

13. *DFP*, Qq2; NA, 157DD/P/42, 157DD/P/CD/116, 157DD/P/43/6. He leased Cutthorpe Hall from the Foljambes (Sheffield Archives, Broomhead Hall Deeds, BHD/311); NA, 157DD/P/51/17 and 18, 157DD/P/113/10; *DFP*, C; *ATN*, B4; *Triall*, p. 18.

14. Nottingham University Library, Department of Manuscripts and Special Collections, AN/IM 201/14; *Detection*, p. 193. Isabel's last husband would be John, Lord Darcy of Aston.

15. *AAOD*, E4; he was also rector of Winsthorpe (NA, 'Transcriptions', vol. 1, p. 20 (15 April 1573)).

16. *DFP*, Qq3v.; *EPI*, p. 301; *ATN*, F2; *DFP*, Qq2–Qq2v.; *Detection*, pp. 189–190, 193, marginal note, p. 169; Peter Heylyn, *Miscellaneous Tracts* cited in Benjamin Brook, *Lives of the Puritans* (London, 1813), p. 119. The Crosses were married the month after the Darrells (Mansfield St Peter's Register, 22 February 1583/4) and Isabel Crosse was questioned by Harsnett at the time of Darrell's trial. Darrell knew of this, suggesting continued contact. The Loades' were also young, there is no record of their marriage at Mansfield, but they had several children there from 1584.

17. *Detection*, pp. 189–92; *DFP*, Qq2v.–Qq3; *Triall*, pp. 20, 21.

18. Newman, pp. 407–19; see Richard Galis, *A Brief Treatise* (London, 1579) or Mary Moore, *Wonderfull News from the North* (London, 1650). Galis, however, was imprisoned sometime after he had attempted to have his suspect committed.

19. *DFP*, Rr3v.; *Detection*, p. 190.

20. John Strype, *The Life and Acts of the Most Reverend Father in God John Whitgift* (London, 1718), pp. 492–5; John Pocklington, *Altare Christianum* (London, 1637), pp. 153–4.

21. Cornelius Brown, *Lives of Nottingham Worthies* (London, 1882), p. 128; John Nichols, *The History and Antiquities of the County of Leicester*, 4 vols (1804; Wakefield, S. R. Publishers/Leicester County Council, 1971), vol. 3, p. 627 – like Hutchinson, whom he cites, Nichols confuses him with the Catholic Thomas Darrell, which adds to his *animus*; Thomas Bailey, *Annals of Nottinghamshire*, 4

vols (London, Simpkin, Marshall, n.d.), vol. 2, p. 527; *DNB*; Marchant, 'John Darrell – Exorcist', p. 50; Barbara Rosen, *Witchcraft in England 1558–1618* (1969; Amherst, University of Massachusetts Press, 1999), p. 234, n. 4; Brook, p. 117; Walker, p. 52.

22. NA, DD/FJ/4/12/13; Newman, p. 410; Lambeth Palace Library, Shrewsbury and Talbot Papers, MS 710, f. 35, N 121, H 77, O 36, H 917; see George Gifford, *A Dialogue of Witches* (London, 1593). Gifford's work was published later, but Foljambe might have been reading Reginald Scot's recent *The Discoverie of Witchcraft*. Scot spoke from a vigorously Protestant position, although there is evidence that he was actually a Familist (David Wootton, 'Reginald Scot/Abraham Fleming/The Family of Love' in Stuart Clark (ed.), *Languages of Witchcraft: Narrative, Ideology and Meaning in Early Modern Culture* (Basingstoke, Macmillan, 2001), pp. 119–38); Michael Austin, *A Stage or Two Beyond Christendom: A Social History of the Church of England in Derbyshire* (Cromford, Scarthin Books, 2001), p. 77, n. 1.

23. *DFP*, Rr., Rr.2.

24. *Detection*, pp. 174, 191; *Triall*, p. 18.

25. *Triall*, pp. 92–8; the Maidstone pamphlet is now lost but survives in part in Scot, book 7, ch. 3. The pamphlet on Herison is also lost (*Detection*, p. 89). See also John Fisher, *The Copy of a Letter Describing the wonderful woorke of God in delivering a Mayden within the City of Chester* (London, 1564); Anon., *A Booke Declaring the Fearfull Vexasion of one Alexander Nyndge, at Herringswell, Suffolk* (London, 1573), Anon., *A true and most Dreadfull discourse of a woman possessed with the Devill, at Ditchet, Somerset* (London, 1584). It is not clear why Herringswell and Ditchet might have been significant, and like Wright's case their dispossessions passed without any controversy being recorded at the time.

26. Although, with more information, Wright's dispossession might be linked tentatively to the political troubles of Chesterfield, discussed further in Chapter 3; Peel (ed.), *Tracts Ascribed*, pp. xvi–xvii; *DFP*, C4v.–D; *AAOD*, C3v., I4v.

27. Adrian Prockter and Robert Taylor (eds), *The A–Z of Elizabethan London* (Lympne, Harry Margary/Guildhall Library, 1979); *ABN*, B2.

28. Peel (ed.), *Tracts Ascribed*, pp. 47, 57.

29. *AAOD*, I; *DFP*, Ev.; *Detection*, pp. 31–3.

30. Kristen Poole, *Radical Religion from Shakespeare to Milton: Figures of Nonconformity in Early Modern England* (Cambridge, Cambridge University Press, 2000) explores such representations of the godly as greedy, carnal and generally excessive; *DFP*, D4v.

31. *DFP*, Bbv.; *ABA*, B6. Although see Peter Clark's 'The Alehouse and Alternative Society' in Donald Pennington and Keith Thomas (eds), *Puritans and Revolutionaries, Essays in Seventeenth-Century History Presented to Christopher Hill* (Oxford, Clarendon, 1978), pp. 47–72.

32. Nichols, vol. 3, part 2, p. 612; Kenneth Hillier, *The Book of Ashby de la Zouch* (Buckingham, Barracuda, 1984); Arthur Hildersham, *Lectures upon the Fourth of John* (London, 1629), A2–A2v.; *DNB*; Claire Cross, *The Puritan Earl: The Life of Henry Hastings, Earl of Huntingdon 1536–1595* (London, Macmillan, 1966), pp. 132–9; C. W. Foster (ed.), *The State of the Church in the Reigns of Queen Elizabeth*

and King James as Illustrated by Documents Relating to the Diocese of Lincoln, vol. 1 (Horncastle, Morton/Lincoln Record Society, 1926), p. 216. Like Hildersham, Brinsley later became involved with the exorcism of Sommers and tried to give evidence for Darrell at the resultant Commission (*ABN*, A3).

33. *DFP*, N3v.–N4v., M2v. Whilst it might be possible that Darrell travelled to Mansfield to petition the Manorial Court, he is not described as being from another place.

34. *Detection*, pp. 69–78; for Brackenbury's rabbits see also Lambeth Palace Library, Shrewsbury and Talbot Papers, MS 700, f. 65.

35. St Helen's Parish Register, Leicestershire Record Office; *DFP*, N4.

36. Collinson, *The Elizabethan Puritan Movement*, p. 212; *DNB*.

37. Hildersham had plenty of experience of parental bereavement to draw on. In the period of Darrell's residence, the Hildershams had had two children and buried three. St Helen's Parish Register, Leicestershire Record Office.

38. George More, *A True Discourse concerning the certaine Possession and Dispossession of 7 persons in one Familie in Lancashire* (n.p., 1600), E4v.; *Detection*, pp. 26, 28.

39. Lambeth Palace Library, Fairhurst Papers, MS 3470, f. 201.

40. *AAOD*, I3; More, A4, F3; *ATN*, I2; *Detection*, A2v., pp. 21, 174; *Triall*, A4v., pp. 44, 50, *Detection*, p. 71; *ABN*, A3v., Clarke, p. 191.

41. *DFP*, B2 – the description of this book differs from that of *The most wonderfull and true storie*, which Harsnett describes explicitly as 'published in print and … commonly sold and called for' (Bv.); *Detection*, p. 55; More, E.6v.

42. *Detection*, pp. 18, 40; Rickert, p. 21, n. 8, where Dickons appears as 'Deacon' and is later confused with the John Deacon who wrote against Darrell; *DNB*; Christopher Haigh, *Reformation and Resistance in Tudor Lancashire* (Cambridge, Cambridge University Press, 1975), p. 54, and 'Puritan Evangelism in the Reign of Elizabeth I', *English Historical Review*, 92:362 (January 1977), pp. 30–58 ; see Oxenbridge's afterword advertisement in [Jesse Bee *et al.*], *The most wonderfull and true storie* (London, 1597); Edward Arber (ed.), *A Transcript of the Registers of the Company of Stationers in London. 1554–1640*, 5 vols (1875–94; Gloucester, MA, Peter Smith, 1967), vol. 3, p. 23; Thomas Freeman believes that the work was printed but all copies are lost (p. 34); More, A2v., E6v., and More then says that the team at Lambeth Palace 'have the storie of this matter in Lancashire penned by Mai[ster] Dickoms [*sic*]'.

43. More, A2–A2v., E5v.–E6v.

44. *Detection*, p. 169; *ABN*, Cv.; *DFP*, B3v., C; Clarke, p. 190; Freeman, *passim*; More, D–Dv.

45. More, A3. Several George Mores graduated from Cambridge and Oxford in the period but it is unclear whether any of them are Darrell's collaborator (Venn and Venn); *Replie*, A2v.; see *Triall*, A3v. for 'Mistr[ess] Moore'.

46. *AAOD*, D4v., E4; Jonathan Lumby, *The Lancashire Witch-Craze: Jennet Preston and the Lancashire Witches 1612* (Preston, Carnegie, 1995), p. 120.

47. More, A6–A7.

48. More, A7–A8; Charlotte Fell Smith, *John Dee 1527–1608* (London, Constable, 1909), p. 269; the Hardmans have not been traced, but Ellen Holland was probably a dependent of Richard Holland, a Justice of the Peace from a Protestant

family and associate of Alexander Reddish (Haigh, *Reformation and Resistance*, p. 46; Greater Manchester County Record Office, Egerton Family Papers, E4/24/7c; Manchester University, John Rylands Library, Crutchley Muniments, CRU/16, 19, 64, 68); Walker, p. 58.

49. More, A8v.–Bv.; Palmer was curate from December 1596 – see John Eglington Bailey (ed.), *Diary for the Years 1595–1601 of Dr. John Dee* (n.p., Kessinger, 2006), pp. 40, 45, 55, 57, 61; and Lancashire Record Office, Kenyon of Peel Papers, DDKE/acc7840 HMC/f.182d; Fell Smith, p. 268.

50. For Assheton's connections with Hopwood and the Reddishes see Manchester University, John Rylands Library, Clowes Deeds, CLD/3, and Crutchley Muniments, CRU/589; for Hopwood, see Lancashire Record Office, Hopwood Manuscripts, DDHP 39/2, 39/4; and on his religious views see Kenyon of Peel Papers, DDKE/acc7480 HMC/f. 23, f. 103d, f. 108d, f. 112 and 112d, f. 113d, f. 115, f. 119; Eglington Bailey (ed.), pp. 45, 49, 58, 79, 85; More, B2–B2v.

51. For the text of the 1563 Witchcraft Act see Marion Gibson (ed.), *Witchcraft and Society in England and America 1550–1750* (London, Cornell University Press/ Continuum, 2003), pp. 3–5.

52. *ATN*, A4v.; *Detection*, p. 26; Walkden had been Dee's servant since 1592 and was entrusted with such duties as financial and scholarly errands, the care of Dee's family on journeys and escorting the mapmaker Christopher Saxton on his survey of Manchester – see Eglington Bailey (ed.), pp. 17, 26, 27, 31, 36, 55, 60, 62, 69, 89.

53. Haigh, *Reformation and Resistance*, pp. 1, 46, 51, 53–4; Thomas Potts, *The Wonderfull Discoverie of Witches* (London, 1612), Bv.; Eglington Bailey (ed.), pp. 8–9, note. See also R. C. Richardson, *Puritanism in North West England: A Regional Study of the Diocese of Chester* (Manchester and Towota, NJ, Manchester University Press and Rowman and Littlefield, 1972).

54. *Detection*, p. 63; More, D2v.

55. More, D6–D7v.; *Detection*, pp. 65, 169.

56. More, A3; *Triall*, p. 16; Haigh, 'Puritan Evangelism', p. 33.

2 Spreading the Word

1. *ABN*, A3v.; [Bee *et al.*], A3, A4v. (although Darling also seemed to be trying to suggest that he was having a 'good possession' in which God, the holy spirit or an angel spoke through him, which caused confusion (Walker, p. 56)); Staffordshire Record Office, D(W)1734/2/3/14, Stapenhill Field Book.

2. 'Burton-upon-Trent: Established Church', *A History of the County of Staffordshire, Volume 9, Burton-upon-Trent* (2003), pp. 107–30. URL: http://www.british-history.ac.uk/report.asp?compid=12339. Date accessed, 1 December 2005.

3. *Detection*, p. 63; Staffordshire Record Office, D603/E/1/104; D603/E/1/94 (Leases, renewed 1614, 1623); D603/E/1/116 (Lease to Mary Toone, 1635/6); 'Burton-upon-Trent: Economic History', *A History of the County of Staffordshire, Volume 9, Burton-upon-Trent* (2003), pp. 53–84. URL: http://www.british-history. ac.uk/report.asp?compid=12335. Date accessed, 1 December 2005; http://www.

burton2000.org.uk/history/greensmiths/gmills6.htm. Date accessed 25 December 2005; D(W) 1734/213/18 (fishing rights); D603/E/1/93 (Lease, renewed 1614); Richard Stone, *Burton Upon Trent: A History* (Chichester, Phillmore, 2004), pp. 45–6; *Triall*, p. 55.

4. Staffordshire Record Office, Burton St Modwen Parish Register, 11 October, marriage to Elizabeth Dutton; Thomas Dutton had been the bailiff for at least thirty years – see for example D(W)1734/3/4/29, D(W)1734/2/3/18, D(W)1734/2/3/26 for his official and business dealings. Toone's reputation apparently survived his nephew's disgrace, for a warrant of 1610 names him as 'Mr. Toone', a man trusted by magistrates to reconcile neighbours in lieu of arrest (Staffordshire Record Office, D.4219/7/2).

5. *ATN*, A4v.–B; it has proved impossible so far to reconstruct the Darling-Walkden family completely, the parish registers from Clifton Campville (about eight miles from Burton) begin only in the 1650s, and Darling's birth is not recorded at Burton. His mother was Walkden's daughter, as the identification of Richard Walkden as his cousin demonstrates. For Walkden see Birmingham City Archives, MS3069/Acc 1926–021/328962 (dealings with William Caldwall and others) and Anthony G. Petti (ed.), *Roman Catholicism in Elizabethan and Jacobean Staffordshire* (Stafford, Staffordshire Record Society, 1979), pp. 25, 30. Some of the Darlings lived at Clifton, and from there William Darling went to Emmanuel College, Cambridge, in 1580. He was later vicar of Ashby in one of Hildersham's absences, and died in 1612 as vicar of Packington-on-the-Heath (Venn and Venn).

6. *Detection*, p. 173.

7. *Detection*, pp. 182–5, 172–3; Burton St Modwen Parish Register, baptism October 1584; Staffordshire Record Office, D603/E/1/1, D603E/1/7, D(W)1734/2/3/21a; Burton St Modwen Parish Register; http://www.british-history.ac.uk/report. asp?compid=12335.

8. [Bee *et al.*], D; Staffordshire Record Office, D(W)1734/2/1, bundle 107–73, contains an unnumbered and undated document naming Horabin as an innholder; his son Thomas's godparents were William Caldwall and Katherine Dethick, Burton St Modwen Parish Register, baptism July 1585; he had some renown as a surgeon, drawing patients from as far away as Worcestershire and Yorkshire (http://www. british-history.ac.uk/report.asp?compid=12335); Staffordshire Record Office, D603/ E/1/37, D(W)1734/2/1/107–73, D(W)1734/2/3/21a, D(W)1734/2/1/107–73; *DNB*.

9. *DFP*, MM4; [Bee *et al.*], F, Dv.; Staffordshire Record Office, 268/M/T/27; *DNB*; Staffordshire Record Office, Stapenhill Field Book, 20 April 1575, D(W)1734/2/3/14, D(W)1734/2/3/18 and leases from an undated late sixteenth-century rental, D(W)1734/2/3/21a.

10. Clarke, p. 47; Staffordshire Record Office, D(W)1734/3/3/280.

11. Especially in his collaboration with Arthur Hildersham, *A direction for the weaker sort of Christian ... Whereunto is adjoined a verie profitable treatise* (London, 1609; still in print 1636) and *English Puritanisme* (1605).

12. [Bee *et al.*], C, D2v.–D3; Staffordshire Record Office, D603/A/2/65; Oswald Hull, *South Derbyshire and Its People: A History* (Derby, Derbyshire County Council, 2004), pp. 24, 173; Manchester University, John Rylands Library,

Crutchley Muniments, CRU/534, Marriage Settlement of Katherine Gresley and Francis Dethicke, 10 August 1596; Derbyshire Record Office, D5710; John Rylands Library, CRU/672, CRU/557, Dethick-Reddish documentation. After Humphrey Dethick's death Elizabeth married Sir Humphrey Ferrers (CRU/747; British Library, Stowe MS 150, f. 198, Reddish to Ferrers), becoming the 'Lady Ferrers' of Samuel Clarke's life of Bradshaw (Clarke, pp. 43–8, 58–9, 122).

13. Harsnett mentions Charles's participation in the plot (*EPI*, pp. 206–8). The plot revolved around an expected French invasion in support of Mary, Queen of Scots. See also *DNB*.

14. Stone, pp. 53–4; *DNB* – the fleet sailed on 3 June. Lambeth Palace Library, Fairhurst Papers, MS 4370, ff. 217–18v.

15. *DFP*, title page, G4v.; Lambeth Palace Library, Fairhurst Papers, MS 4370, ff. 200–1.

16. Stone, p. 77; http://www.british-history.ac.uk/report.asp?compid=12335.

17. See National Archives, E134/25&26 Eliz/Mich3 (1583), E134/23 Eliz/East13 (1581), E134/18&19 Eliz/Mich8 (1576) and E134/28 Eliz/East19 (1586).

18. http://www.british-history.ac.uk/report.asp?compid=12335.

19. National Archives, E134/32&33 Eliz/Mich3.

20. http://www.british-history.ac.uk/report.asp?compid=12339; Burton St Modwen Parish Register; Stone, p. 39.

21. Clarke, p. 51; Ian Atherton and David Como, 'The Burning of Edward Wightman: Puritanism, Prelacy and the Politics of Heresy in Early Modern England', *English Historical Review*, 120:489 (December 2005), p. 1220.

22. [Bee *et al.*], E4v.

23. Saunders was the husband of Alice Toone, possibly Robert Toone's sister. They were married at Clifton Campville in 1575 (International Genealogical Index; no source given); it has not been possible to trace Bee with certainty, except as a juror in the manorial court on one of the few occasions for which records survive (1595–6, Staffordshire Record Office, D(W)1734/2/1/111). The Bees seem to have come from Stapenhill.

24. It is not clear if Denison is the same man who later became an eminent preacher (*DNB*). It is not impossible that his views changed from godly to Anglican (Harsnett went on a similar journey); [Bee *et al.*], A2v.

25. *DNB*; Christopher Hill, *Society and Puritanism in Pre-Revolutionary England* (London, Secker and Warburg, 1964), *Puritanism and Revolution* (1958; London, Penguin, 1988), *The World Turned Upside Down* (1972; London, Penguin, 1991). Peel (ed.), *The Seconde Parte*, vol. 1, pp. 117, 153, 188, 228; Richard Bancroft, *Dangerous Positions* (London, 1593), p. 9, *A Survey of the Pretended Holy Discipline* (London, 1593), pp. 22–38; Sutcliffe, p. 37; William Bradshaw and Arthur Hildersham, *English Puritanisme* (1605) in Lawrence A. Sasek (ed.), *Images of English Puritanism: A Collection of Contemporary Sources 1589–1646* (Baton Rouge and London, Louisiana State University Press, 1989), p. 89; Peel (ed.), *Tracts Ascribed*, pp. 12, 77–8, 93.

26. *DFP*, Mmv.–Mm2.

27. Heylyn, p. 348.

28. Henry Goodcole, *The wonderfull discoverie of Elizabeth Sawyer, a Witch* (London, 1621), D.
29. Peel (ed.), *The Seconde Parte*, vol. 2, pp. 259–60. Dated January 1587/8.
30. Atherton and Como suggest a date of about 1600 for Wightman's career as an alehouse-keeper, which was linked to financial difficulties in the clothing trade (p. 1227); http://www.british-history.ac.uk/report.asp?compid=12339.
31. Burton St Modwen Parish Register, marriage 2 September 1593; son John christened 8 December 1594.
32. [Bee *et al.*], E4.
33. *DFP*, Mm2–Mm2v.
34. *Detection*, p. 172.
35. *DNB*; Atherton and Como, pp. 1215–16, 1229–35, 1243–6.
36. F. W. Brownlow, *Shakespeare, Harsnett and the Devils of Denham* (Newark and London, University of Delaware Press, Associated University Presses, 1993), pp. 175–6; Rickert, pp. 42–3; Susan Doran, *Elizabeth I and Religion 1558–1603* (London and New York, Routledge, 1994), p. 30; Laurence Chaderton's order for exercises is a good example – see Lake, *Moderate Puritans*, pp. 37–8.
37. *DNB*; Doran, p. 20; Margaret Aston, 'Puritans and Iconoclasm 1560–1660' in Christopher Durston and Jacqueline Eales (eds), *The Culture of English Puritanism 1560–1700* (Basingstoke, Macmillan, 1996), p. 106; Brownlow, p. 44.
38. Peter Lake, *Anglicans and Puritans? Presbyterianism and English Conformist Thought from Whitgift to Hooker* (London, Unwin Hyman, 1988), p. 128.
39. Walsham, *Providence*, pp. 53–6.
40. Tom Webster, *Godly Clergy in Early Stuart England: The Caroline Puritan Movement c. 1620–1643* (Cambridge, Cambridge University Press, 1997), p. 50.
41. Although there is an argument that these tend also to plurality of voices because, as proponents of a party viewpoint, discussion and shared reading of arguments was almost inevitable.
42. Ian Green, *Print and Protestantism in Early Modern England* (Oxford, Oxford University Press, 2000), pp. 6–7.
43. G. Co. did not claim authorship of *A Breife Narration* but A. Ri. seems to attribute it to him (see below); *Triall*, B. *Triall* has been optimistically attributed to James Balmford (the Lambeth Palace Library and British Library catalogues agree, but not the *Short Title Catalogue*).
44. Arber (ed.), vol. 3, p. 53v.
45. *Triall*, A3v., B2.
46. Ibid., pp. 21, 69; *DNB*.
47. *Triall*, pp. 30, 45, 55.
48. Ibid., pp. 61–2.
49. Ibid., pp. 82–3.
50. Ibid., pp. 87–8. A. Ri. also said that the 'this Collector' (his new name for the original author of the *Triall*) had now died, and he attributed to this man also the authorship or editorship of *A Breife Narration* (calling him in this capacity 'the Narrator') and also the publication of Darrell's *Apologie*, or possibly the edited version of it, *A Brief Apologie*, which contains similar legal arguments (*Triall*, p. 89; *ABA*, A2, A4–A4v., B7v.). Venn and Venn list a number of A. Ri.s and G.

Co.s, but none are ideal candidates. Freeman suggests that G. Co. might be a Nottinghamshire cleric, although the author of the main part of the *Triall* is a lawyer (pp. 45, 49). What one believes their/his profession and history to be is partly dependent on the distinctions between author, publisher, editor, narrator and collector, which are left very unclear, so that it is impossible to reconstruct precisely who wrote what.

51. *Triall*, A2.
52. Heylyn, title page, pp. 272, 277–9, 348–9, 352.
53. Daniel Neal, *The History of the Puritans or Protestant Non-Conformists*, 2nd edn (London, 1732), p. 585, A2, p. xvi; Atherton and Como, p. 1218.
54. Clarke, pp. 33–4.
55. Collinson, *The Religion of Protestants*, p. 188.
56. Clarke, p. 32.

3 The Possession of William Sommers

1. David Marcombe, 'The Last Days of Lenton Priory' in Wood (ed.), p. 304; *ABN*, A2v.; John Heskay's will, 29 September 1558, Prerogative Court of York (copy at Nottingham High School, transcript by Marilyn Clark); Charles Deering, *The History of Nottingham* (1751; Nottingham, S. R. Publishing, 1970), pp. 154, 159; A. W. Thomas, *A History of Nottingham High School* (Nottingham, J. and H. Bell, 1958), pp. 82–3.
2. NA, CA 2758a; Nottingham High School 'Accounts of the Nottingham Free Grammar School 1577–1699', 1598, 1599, 1600; for school finances see William Page (ed.), *The Victoria History of the County of Nottingham, vol. 2* (London, Constable, 1910), pp. 225–6.
3. NA, CA 396b Box A, CA 3347; St Peter's Register, 22 May 1601, 1 September 1570, 19 December 1573, 6 April 1578, 27 January 1583 (marriage to Anne James), CA 4635b, CA 3377; *DFP*, Nv.; NA, Parish Records of St Mary's, 4615A.
4. NA, Parish Records of St Mary's, 4615b and 4612; Deering, pp. 106–7; Alfred Stapleton, *The Churches and Monasteries of Old and New Nottingham* (Nottingham, Haubitz, 1903), pp. 21–2; NA, Parish Records of St Mary's, 4614, CA 7484, CA 4626b, Parish Records of St Mary's, 4615A.
5. NA, CA 396n Box A, Parish Records of St Mary's, 4615A, CA 402b Box A, CA 407b; Sally Kersting, 'Churchwardens of St Peter's 1559–1991' in Peter Hoare, *The Rectors of St. Peter's Church, Nottingham, 1241–1991* (Nottingham, St Peter's Parochial Church Council, 1992), pp. 49–50; Jackson was a tough customer, hardened perhaps in particular by the deaths of three of his children within a week in 1587 (NA, St Peter's Register, 15 January, 24 January 1587). His second son Luke (baptized 18 October 1582) became a London girdler and founded a Nottingham charity (Deering, p. 141).
6. NA, CA 4928, CA 2175, CA 2174, CA 4918 Box B, CA 5319, CA 5335 Box B, CA 2374, CA 5466a, CA 4916 Box B, CA 5320, CA 2175. Details of the topography of early modern Nottingham are from Deering's *History of Nottingham*, for which he interviewed Nottingham's oldest inhabitants in the 1740s.

7. NA, CA 4931 Box B, Chamber Estate Lease, 17 November 1606, for twenty-one years.

8. NA, CA 3020; see also W. H. Stevenson and James Raine (eds), *Records of the Borough of Nottingham*, 9 vols (London, 1889), vol. 4, pp. 253, 215, 189, 237–8, ix, xi, xiii, 191.

9. Philip Riden and John Blair (eds), *History of Chesterfield*, 5 vols (Chesterfield, Borough of Chesterfield, 1980), vol. 5, pp. 54–70.

10. NA, CA 2174, CA 2175, CA 5461/1–2, CA 5468, CA 2175, CA 7484; Lucy Hutchinson, *Memoirs of the Life of Colonel Hutchinson* (MS 1671; London, Dent, 1995); NA, St Mary's Register, 19 August, November 1579 (date unclear), 28 August 1583; in 1603–4 Millington represented the burgesses in discussions with the Corporation and signed documentation with his mark; Stevenson and Raine (eds), vol. 4, p. 270; NA, CA 3376, partly printed in Stevenson and Raine (eds), vol. 4, pp. 245–8.

11. NA, CA 3020, CA 5466b, CA 2558a; for further agitations involving Millington see CA 3347, CA3974 and Stevenson and Raine (eds), vol. 4, pp. 278–81; Deering, pp. 278–85; Stevenson and Raine (eds), vol. 4, pp. xvii–xviii. For 'the triumph of oligarchy' in post-reformation towns, and an argument that in less conservative towns this was *strengthened* by attempts to impose godly discipline, see Robert Tittler, *The Reformation and the Towns in England: Politics and Political Culture c. 1540–1640* (Oxford, Clarendon, 1998), pp. 9–19, 182–209.

12. *DFP*, Pv.–P3; neither the Webbs nor Porter have yet been identified in the borough records; *Detection*, p. 31; *DFP*, D4v.; NA, CA 4635b, St Peter's Register, 14 January 1578/9; NA, CA 2374, shows the property in either Smith's Row or Rotten Row but Deering (p. 7) explains that the corn market was to the north, whilst Rotten Row was a horse market; Pie also leased the right from the Bridge Estate to cut gorse on Hunger Hill; NA, CA 4614, 4615a, 4615b; Stevenson and Raine (eds), vol. 4, p. 254.

13. Donna B. Hamilton, *Shakespeare and the Politics of Protestant England* (New York and London, Harvester Wheatsheaf, 1992), pp. xii, 7; Susan Brigden, 'Youth and the English Reformation', *Past and Present*, 95 (1982), pp. 39, 43, 46. For a summary of the debate see Margo Todd (ed.), *Reformation to Revolution: Politics and Religion in Early Modern England* (London and New York, Routledge, 1995), pp. 1–3.

14. Samuel H. Beer, 'Christopher Hill, Some Reminiscences' in Pennington and Thomas (eds), p. 3; Collinson, *The Elizabethan Puritan Movement*, p. 211; NA, CA 3020; Sheils, p. 121 and *passim*.

15. NA, CA 3014, CA 3015, CA 3019, 3022; Paul Seaver, *The Puritan Lectureships: The Politics of Religious Dissent 1560–1662* (Stanford, Stanford University Press, 1970), p. 101; Hutchinson gives an unflattering account of him as a Jonsonian 'Sir Politic Wouldbe', pp. 169–75.

16. NA, 'Transcriptions', vol. 2, p. 169 (7 May 1595); e.g. *ABN*, E – both are also neighbours of Bonner; Hutchinson, p. 179; Durston and Eales (eds), p. 10.

17. But as Durston and Eales point out, the practice of such naming was rare outside the south-east (p. 23) and Anker or Anchor may have been a family name (moth-

er's maiden name or other). The rest of the Jacksons bore standard Christian names (NA, St Peter's Parish Register).

18. NA, 'Transcriptions', vol. 2, p. 169 (14 May 1595) – this was not a personal gift, since money from commuted penances was put into the fund; see also J. C. F. Hood, *An Account of St. Mary's Church Nottingham* (Nottingham, Cooke and Vowles, 1910), pp. 40–1; Deering, p. 107; 'Transcriptions', vol. 1, p. 56 (16 May 1587); the Assize records do not survive for this period; *Triall*, p. 65; Stapleton, p. 21; *Triall*, p. 44; *Detection*, p. 120; *ATN*, C4.

19. Anne Porter had a sister named Mary Millwood (*ATN*, B4); *ABN*, C3; Nottingham University Library, Department of Manuscripts and Special Collections, AN/IM 201/58; Darrell, *Detection*, p. 28; St Mary's Parish Register, 17 January 1581 and 8 May 1597.

20. *DFP*, D4; *ATN*, B4. Darrell spent time with John Beresford at Whittington, who also knew Sommers at Nottingham before Darrell's arrival. Darrell prints the letter of invitation, *Detection*, p. 27, saying it was written by one 'Syr Evan as they call him' (Barnaby Evans?) for Mrs Wallis; NA, 'Transcripts', vol. 1, pp. 54/35–54/36; *Detection*, pp. 28–9. Ireton was rector of Kegworth (Foster, p. 108).

21. *DFP*, O; for the Pickerings, see my *Reading Witchcraft* (London and New York, Routledge, 1999); NA, 'Transcriptions', vol. 1, pp. 175 (17 June 1595) and 91 (5 June 1592); Nottingham University Library, Department of Manuscripts and Special Collections, AN/IM 201/22; NA, CA3016; Stevenson and Raine (eds), vol. 4, p. 277.

22. Elizabeth Milner married Henry Sommers on 18 January 1574 (NA, St Peter's Register); William Sommers was bailed by his uncle Randolph Milner (*DFP*, V3) when accused as a witch; Robert Cowper married Elizabeth Sommers on 23 April 1593; Robert Cowper junior married Mary Sommers on 28 April 1595 (St Mary's Register); *DFP*, Kk2v.

23. NA, Parish Records of St Mary's, 4613, 4614, 4615a, 4615b; for example, in the 1580s he kept the register (Stevenson and Raine (eds), vol. 4, p. 224) and signed presentments to the Archdeacon's Court (e.g. Nottingham University Library, Department of Manuscripts and Special Collections, AN/PB 293/7/20); Cowper was still clerk at his death in June 1622 (John. T. Godfrey, *Notes on the Parish Registers of St. Mary's Nottingham 1566–1812* (Nottingham, Saxton, 1901), p. 16); *Triall*, p. 24; Mary and William had more than one step-sister, also to be provided for (*DFP*, V2v.).

24. *DFP*, N4v.–O, M2, N4v.; *Detection*, p. 88.

25. *Detection*, pp. 86–7.

26. Lambeth Palace Library, Fairhurst Papers, MS3470, f. 202; *Detection*, p. 166; *Triall*, p. 63; Peter Lake with Michael Questier, *The Anti-Christ's Lewd Hat: Protestants, Papists and Players in Post-Reformation England* (New Haven and London, Yale University Press, 2002), p. 473.

27. *ATN*, B4; *DFP*, O; *ATN*, B4v.–C; *DFP*, F3, N2v.; *ABN*, E; Nottingham's fairs are now amalgamated into the Goose Fair (thanks to John Swain for explaining this).

28. Sommers's symptoms were described in Syr Evan's letter (*Detection*, pp. 27–8); More, B4v.–B5; *DFP*, A3.

29. Stephen Greenblatt, *Shakespearean Negotiations: The Circulation of Social Energy in Renaissance England* (Oxford, Clarendon Press, 1988), p. 109, although Greenblatt does not suggest there is anything distinctively godly in this; Cassanda Willoughby, in W. H. Stevenson, *HMC Report on the Manuscripts of Lord Middleton, Preserved at Wollaton Hall* (London, HMSO, 1911), p. 580; Atkinson was also assessed for the subsidy of 1598 at the second highest rate, in Bonner's ward (NA, CA 7484); Nottingham University Library, Department of Manuscripts and Special Collections, Mi.F.10/4.

30. Stevenson, pp. 151–2; NA, 'Transactions', vol. 1, p. 20.

31. Lake with Questier, p. 473.

32. *DFP*, H–Hv., Q3.

33. Marchant, *The Puritans*, entry for Aldred; *ABN*, E; *DFP*, D4v., R4v.; Small was a wealthy man and a neighbour of Clark and Anchor Jackson in St Peter's parish when he was assessed for the subsidy in 1598 (NA, CA 7484); *DFP*, G4–G4v.

34. *ATN*, C2; *Detection*, p. 166; *ABN*, E; *ATN*, C2v.; *DFP*, R3v., Qv., Q4.

35. *Detection*, p. 112; *DFP*, Q4–Q4v., R4. One later account calls him 'Assistant Curate', which makes him sound more permanent than he probably was (Hood, p. 81); *DFP*, C4; Seaver, pp. 42–3.

36. *AAOD*, I4; *DFP*, S2–S3, O3v. Unfortunately none of these texts survive. It is not clear where they might have been kept, but records of the Quarter Sessions for this period are missing, and there is no record of the examinations of the 'witches' or Sommers in the Mayor's Books. Possibly, like Sommers's apprenticeship papers, these items were given to Samuel Harsnett at a later date (*DFP*, N4), but if so he made no use of them in his books; *DFP*, T3.

37. *DFP*, F3. It is not clear how closely related Alice and William Freeman were. Marchant calls her his 'niece' ('John Darrell – Exorcist', p. 51); *DFP*, A2v.; D. J. Lamburn, 'Digging and Dunging: Some Aspects of Lay Influence in the Church in Northern Towns' in Wood (ed.), pp. 368–71.

38. *DFP* O4; Stevenson and Raine (eds), vol. 4, p. 275. Groves was said to make charms from extracts of St John's gospel and sell them for ten shillings a piece. Many Sessions records are lost, including that of 1597–8; *Detection*, pp. 109–10.

39. *DFP*, Ss4v.; *Detection*, pp. 119–20, 121, 127.

40. Marchant, *The Puritans*, p. 136, and entry for Hallam; A.C. Wood, *A History of Nottinghamshire* (Nottingham, Thoroton Society, 1947), p. 163, n.1; *Detection*, p. 107; *DFP*, T4v., Kk2v.

41. *DFP*, Hh; *Detection*, pp. 112, 113. In 1603 John Parker actually did leave twenty shillings to the minister of St Mary's on condition that he preached a sermon on Christian love and charity every Good Friday, which suggests the continued factionalism in the town (John Throsby, *The History and Antiquities of the Town and County of the Town of Nottingham* (Nottingham, 1795), p. 49); *DFP*, T4v.–V2.

42. *Detection*, p. 132; *DFP*, Aa, Bbv.

43. *DFP*, Cc, B4; *Detection*, p. 117; Brown was also a nonconformist (see Foster (ed.), p. cxxvii).

44. *DFP*, Ddv., B4v., Dd2v.–Dd4.

45. *DFP*, Dd2v., Tt; *Detection*, p. 110; Marchant, 'John Darrell – Exorcist', p. 52; *DNB*; *DFP*, B4v.; Walker, p. 62; *Triall*, pp. 59–60; *ABN*, B2.

46. NA, CA7626 Box B; *Detection*, p. 144; Hutchinson, p. 148; *AAOD*, K3; *ABN*, A4–A4v.; *AAOD*, L3.
47. *DFP*, B3; it was not until 1617 that Nottingham followed the example of other Corporations and appointed a salaried preacher, who was kept in place by pressure from Lord Zouch (among others) in 1623 (Seaver, pp. 94, 98).

4 Authority and Subversion in Possession Narratives

1. *DFP*, C2v.; Peel (ed.), *The Seconde Parte*, vol. 1, pp. 213, 215, 217.
2. Ibid., vol. 2, p. 230; Freeman, p. 42; *DFP*, I4, I2v., K3v.
3. Paul Griffiths, *Youth and Authority: Formative Experiences in England 1560–1640* (Oxford, Clarendon, 1996), p. 9; Knappen, p. 262; see also Brigden, *passim*.
4. Quoted in Patrick Collinson (ed.), *The Puritan Character: Polemics and Polarities in Early Seventeenth-Century English Culture*, ed. Karen E. Rowe (Los Angeles, William Andrews Clark Memorial Library, 1989), p. 4.
5. Griffiths, p. 34; Patrick Collinson, *The Birthpangs of Protestant England* (Basingstoke, Macmillan, 1998), p. 36; Henry Smith, *Sermons* (London, 1599), quoted in Knappen, p. 268.
6. Peel (ed.), *The Seconde Parte*, vol. 2, pp. 228, 211.
7. Lake with Questier, p. 57.
8. Lawrence Stone, *The Family, Sex and Marriage in England 1500–1800* (London, Penguin, 1977), pp. 121, 123. Linda Pollock first challenged Stone's views in *Forgotten Children: Parent-Child Relations from 1500–1800* (Cambridge, Cambridge University Press, 1983), but see also Ralph Houlbrooke, *The English Family 1450–1700* (London, Longman, 1984) and Keith Wrightson, *English Society 1580–1680* (London, Hutchinson, 1982).
9. Darren Oldridge, *The Devil in Early Modern England* (Stroud, Sutton, 2000), pp. 119–20.
10. J.A. Sharpe, 'Disruption in the Well-Ordered Household, Age, Authority, and Possessed Young People' in Paul Griffiths, Adam Fox and Steve Hindle (eds), *The Experience of Authority in Early Modern England* (Basingstoke, Macmillan, 1996), p. 188.
11. Ibid., pp. 188, 198.
12. *ATN*, A2v., Bv., B2–B2v.; More, B5–B5v., A8, C3, B6–B7, C7.
13. C. John Sommerville, *The Discovery of Childhood in Puritan England* (Athens, GA, University of Georgia, 1992); Griffiths, pp. 1–2, 59.
14. Robert Muchembled, 'Satanic Myths and Cultural Reality' in Bengt Ankarloo and Gustav Henningsen (eds), *Early Modern European Witchcraft: Centres and Peripheries* (Oxford, Clarendon, 1993), pp. 150–1.
15. Robin Briggs, *Witches and Neighbours: The Social and Cultural Context of European Witchcraft* (London, HarperCollins, 1996), pp. 321–5, offers a measured analysis of the usefulness of such functionalist models of power. On the relationship between state and witch-hunt, see also Christina Larner, *Witchcraft and Religion*, ed. Alan Macfarlane (Oxford, Blackwell, 1984) and Norman Cohn, *Europe's*

Inner Demons: The Demonization of Christians in Medieval Christendom, rev. edn (London, Pimlico, 1993).

16. Lana Condie, 'The Practice of Exorcism and the Challenge to Clerical Authority', *Access: History*, 3:1 (Summer 2000), pp. 98–9.

17. Alexandra Walsham, '"Frantick Hacket", Prophecy, Sorcery, Insanity and the Elizabethan Puritan Movement', *The Historical Journal*, 41:1 (March 1998), pp. 27–66.

18. *Triall*, p. 88.

19. *Detection*, pp. 89–90; Anon., *The most strange and admirable discoverie of the three Witches of Warboys* (London, 1593), A3, Hv. See Sharpe, 'Disruption', p. 200, for another four-year delay in accusing witches.

20. *The most strange and admirable discoverie*, A3–A3v.

21. Ibid., A3v.–A4.

22. Ibid., B.

23. See Anon., *The Witches of Northamptonshire* (London, 1612).

24. *The most strange and admirable discoverie*, B2.

25. Ibid., F4.

26. Ibid., L2–L2v.

27. Ibid., L, F4; for a similar reading see Rebecca Louise Mullins, 'Children of Disobedience: Aspects of Possession in Early Modern England' (MA thesis, University of York, 1997), p. 44.

28. Rosen, p. 286, n. 36.

29. *The most strange and admirable discoverie*, D4v.–Ev.

30. Ibid., Ov.

31. *Detection*, pp. 21–2.

32. Anon., *The Examination and Confession of certaine Wytches* (London, 1566); Rosen, p. 72.

33. Lambeth Palace Library, Fairhurst Papers, MS 3470, ff. 200–1.

34. [Bee *et al.*], A3v.

35. Ibid., A3v.

36. Ibid., A4v.–B.

37. Ibid., Bv.–B3v.

38. *Detection*, p. 40.

39. Sarah Williams (ed.), *Letters Written by John Chamberlain* (London, Camden Society, 1861), pp. 178–9; J. Bruce (ed.), *Diary of John Manningham* (London, Camden Society, 1868), p. 169.

40. *DFP*, Pp4v.

41. Foster, pp. 363–6; Edward Fairfax, 'A Discourse of Witchcraft' (British Library, Add. MS 32496), printed in William Grainge (ed.), *Daemonologia* (Harrogate, 1882).

42. Sharpe, 'Disruption', p. 205; Fairfax in Grainge (ed.).

43. Gendered aspects of possession and witchcraft cases have been discussed by Deborah Willis, *Malevolent Nurture: Witch-Hunting and Maternal Power in Early Modern England* (Ithaca and London, Cornell University Press, 1995); Lyndal Roper, *Oedipus and the Devil: Witchcraft, Sexuality and the Devil in Early Modern Europe* (London and New York, Routledge, 1994); Frances Dolan, *Dangerous*

Familiars: Representations of Domestic Crime in England 1550–1700 (Ithaca and London, Cornell University Press, 1994); and most recently in Sarah Ferber's *Demonic Possession and Exorcism in Early Modern France* (London and New York, Routledge, 2004). See also Deirdre O'Callaghan, 'Vexed and Volatile Bodies: the Drama of Possession and Exorcism in Late Elizabethan England – the John Darrell Cases' (MA thesis, University of Melbourne, 1998).

44. Fairfax in in Grainge (ed.).
45. Ibid., p. 77.
46. Griffiths, p. 66.
47. William Shakespeare, *Twelfth Night*, ed. Bruce R. Smith (Boston and New York, Bedford/St Martin's, 2001), IV.ii.104–8.
48. Thomas, *Religion and the Decline of Magic*, pp. 645–6; J. A. Sharpe, *Instruments of Darkness: Witchcraft in England 1550–1750* (London, Hamish Hamilton, 1996), pp. 126, 164; and Alison Findlay, 'Sexual and Spiritual Politics in the Events of 1633–4 and *The Late Lancashire Witches*' in Robert Poole (ed.), *The Lancashire Witches: Histories and Stories* (Manchester, Manchester University Press, 2002), pp. 146–65.
49. Thomas Heywood and Richard Brome, *The Late Lancashire Witches* (London, 1634), I.i.269.
50. Ibid., I.i.274–80.
51. Findlay, p. 160.
52. *The Late Lancashire Witches*, I.i.285–7.
53. Ibid., I.i.266–331.
54. Findlay, pp. 160–1.
55. On the entertainment value of the play see Diane Purkiss, *The Witch in History* (London and New York, Routledge, 1996), pp. 231–49.
56. *Detection*, pp. 19, 62, 172; *ATN*, M3–Nv.; *Treatise*, no sig. 2v.
57. John Swan, *A True and Breife Report, of Mary Glovers Vexation* (London, 1603), pp. 22, 23, 35, 47, 53, 66.
58. John F. H. New, *Anglican and Puritan: The Basis of their Opposition* (London, A. and C. Black, 1964); Lake with Questier, p. 475.

5 Dialogicall Discourses and Summarie Answeres

1. Lake, *Anglicans and Puritans*, pp. 239–40.
2. Bancroft, *Dangerous Positions*, cited in Hamilton, p. 74.
3. Peel (ed.), *Tracts Ascribed*, p. 73; *Detection*, p. 169, *AAOD*, B3; e.g. 1 Timothy 5:1–2, 2 Thessalonians 1:3.
4. John Smyth, preacher at Gainsborough, furnishes a good example. He separated from the Church of England in about 1607, covenanting with a congregation there and deciding to emigrate to Holland. Then he separated from them to become an anabaptist, baptizing himself into his own new church. When this church split, Smyth joined with the Dutch Mennonites, renouncing his self-baptism in 1610 (B. R. White, *The English Separatist Tradition: From the Marian Martyrs to the Pilgrim Fathers* (Oxford, Oxford University Press, 1971), pp. 121–40).

5. Ibid., pp. 121–40.
6. *Triall*, D8v.
7. Ibid., pp. 15, 64; *Detection*, pp. 14, 28.
8. Ibid., pp. 124–5; *Triall*, pp. 43, 67–8.
9. Ibid., p. 70; *Detection*, p. 185.
10. *Triall*, pp. 22, 45; *Detection*, pp. 178, 179.
11. *ABN*, A3v.; *Detection*, pp. 15–16, 94.
12. *Detection*, A2, p. 13; *ATN*, C4; Thomas Fuller, *The History of the Worthies of England* (London, 1662), p. 112; Doran, p. 43.
13. Walker, p. 66; *DNB*.
14. *Triall*, pp. 68–9, 45; *Detection*, pp. 15–16; George W. Keeton, *Shakespeare's Legal and Political Background* (London, Pitman, 1967), pp. 3–12; B. J. Sokol and Mary Sokol, *Shakespeare's Legal Language: A Dictionary*, 2nd edn (London and New York, Continuum, 2004); Marchant, *The Puritans*, pp. 5–8; *Triall*, p. 63. I am especially indebted to Thomas Freeman for discussion of several points of technical and chronological significance in this chapter.
15. Bradshaw in Sasek (ed.), p. 91.
16. *Triall*, p. 47; *ABN*, B2.
17. *ABA*, A2; *Triall*, A2.
18. *DFP*, B3v., C, Cv.; *DNB*.
19. In his translation of Michel Marescot, *A True Discourse upon the Matter of Martha Brossier* (London, 1599), A2; *Detection*, pp. 68, 77–8; 169; *DFP*, D4v.; More, E5.
20. *DFP*, Cv.–C3v.; *ABA*, A2v.–A3; *AAOD*, A3; Swan, A3, in Michael Macdonald, *Witchcraft and Hysteria in Elizabethan London: Edward Jorden and the Mary Glover Case* (London and New York, Tavistock Routledge, 1991); *ABN*, B4v.; *Detection*, p. 115.
21. *Triall*, p. 71; *Detection*, p. 18.
22. *Detection*, A2v.; *AAOD*, A2.
23. *ATN*, no sig. v., sig. **; *AAOD*, A3v.
24. Freeman, p. 45; the narrator cites numerous theological works, and is concerned to confute atheists; *ABN*, B2. Although its title page is dated 1598, the *Breife Narration* must have been published in January–March 1598/9, because its prefacer says the trial has been going on for a year (A4). For the narrator's identity see *Triall*, p. 89, where he is described as 'the Narrator, Publisher of [Darrell's] apologie, and this Collection … they be all one (as some may suppose, and I have heard presumptions given so to thinke)'.
25. Darrell had read both *ABN* and *ABA* by the time he wrote his *Detection* (p. 19); *Detection*, p. 77: 'my *Apology* I made since my departure from Ashby [Michaelmas] … 99'.
26. *ABA*, title page, A3v.–A4v.
27. Freeman, p. 46; although the work may have been delayed at the press, it was common practice to modify any out-of-date information with a note from an editor or publisher (as with the *Triall* or George More's book) if this had happened. The absence of this in the *Brief Apologie* suggests that it did indeed appear before the close of the trial.

28. *AAOD*, A2–B3.
29. Freeman, p. 49, n. 73; *Triall*, D8v., F, F5.
30. Peel (ed.), *Tracts Ascribed*, pp. 12, 77–8, 93; contrary to Rickert's suggestion, no further books are known to have been published on the case during its first (pre-Deacon and Walker) phase (Rickert, p. 67) and it is likely that these remained in manuscript; *Triall*, A2v.
31. *Triall*, B2v., p. 81.
32. The identification of Whitgift's hand is by E. G. W. Bill.
33. *Triall*, p. 76.
34. *Detection*, B; *Triall*, pp. 79, 45–6.
35. *ATN*, E4, Rv. (Darrell kept in touch with Darling's state of health, reporting in 1600 on his continued 'pristine estate'); *Triall*, p. 90; More, F3.
36. Freeman, p. 46; *Detection*, A2v.
37. *EPI*, p. 331.
38. Hamilton suggests that Whitgift and Bancroft's order of 1 June 1599 forbidding satire and restricting the authority to license histories is related to the illegal pro-Darrell works (p. 92); Freeman, p. 46.
39. Arber (ed.), vol. 3, p. 53v.; Freeman, p. 46; although as Thomas Freeman has rightly pointed out to me, dates in the Stationers' Register may not be those of the actual appearance of texts; Marchant, who first noticed that Darrell had actually been released, erroneously placed this event in 1601 (Marchant, 'John Darrell – Exorcist', p. 54).
40. *Triall*, p. 90; by 'committed', the editor must mean 're-committed'.
41. *DNB*; *Detection*, p. 77.
42. *DNB*.
43. *DFP*, Hh4v., V4, Ii2; *ATN*, *–**v.; *Detection*, p. 114; *DFP*, T4, Dd4v.–Ee2.
44. *Replie*, A2v. – it is not clear whether Darrell sold up at Ashby and left with his family, or whether he went into hiding alone but, given the tight time-scale, the latter seems more likely; John Deacon and John Walker, *A Summarie Answere to al the Material Points in any of Master Darel his Bookes* (London, 1601), F4–F6v.; Harsnett too seemed to have an idea of where Darrell might have been, implying that he was in London when he was writing *Egregious Popish Impostures* in 1602–3 (*EPI*, p. 331: 'if they want devils in Italy to exorcise … let them come but over into London in England, and wee have ready for them Darrells wife, Moores minion …' and the men involved in the Mary Glover case). It is not clear how specific or serious this reference is intended to be, but Mistress Moore is named by Swan amongst the dispossessors (Av.). For the Northwich case see also Jacqueline Eales, 'Thomas Pierson and the Transmission of Moderate Puritan Tradition', *Midland History*, 20 (1995), pp. 75–102.
45. J. Dover Wilson, 'Richard Schilders and the English Puritans', *Transactions of the Bibliographical Society*, 11 (1909), pp. 65–134, although he does not mention those publications from the Darrell controversy now attributed to Schilders by the *Short Title Catalogue*; *ATN*, R2v.
46. Freeman, pp. 44, 50 (order recorded by the Stationers' Company on 29 October 1600); *Short Title Catalogue*; *ABN*, A3v.
47. *ABA*, A4v.

48. *AAOD*, Bv., *Detection*, A.
49. *Triall*, F; Clarke, p. 32; *Detection*, A3, Bv.; *AAOD*, A4.
50. William Salt Library, Salt MSS. 438.
51. Marchant, *The Puritans*, pp. 144–5 and entry for Deacon; NA, 'Transcriptions', vol. 2, p. 154.
52. Marchant, *The Puritans*, entry for Walker; Brownlow, p. 71.
53. Walker, p. 66; G. L. Kittredge, *Witchcraft in Old and New England* (Cambridge, MA, Harvard University Press, 1929), p. 299; Marchant, *The Puritans*, p. 144.
54. John Deacon and John Walker, *Dialogicall Discourses of Spirits and Divels* (London, 1601), A2v.–A4, av.; Freeman, p. 52.
55. Deacon and Walker, *Dialogicall Discourses*, A5–A5v, no sig. 1v.
56. *Replie*, D (Leviticus 19:17, which is rather more equivocal in the Authorised Version).
57. Macdonald, p. xxii; *Survey*, A4v., B, L3v. He also says that, whilst he will not give Deacon and Walker the answers 'which you deserve to heare, and to lay you open in your colours', he wonders how they dare draw the attention of the land's chief judges to themselves (ibid., A4).
58. Ibid., A2–A4.
59. Deacon and Walker, *A Summarie Answere*, *3–*3v.; *Replie*, A2–C; Revelation 12:10.
60. *EPI*, pp. 221, 250, 309, 331. Harsnett also attacked Joan Darrell and Mrs More. On Harsnett's intent to smear Darrell by publishing on Catholic rites see Brownlow, pp. 74–5.

6 The Madman in the Wilderness

1. Peel (ed.), *The Seconde Parte*, vol. 2, pp. 241–9; Greenblatt, *Shakespearean Negotiations*, pp. 94–128, 'Loudun and London', *Critical Inquiry*, 12:2 (Winter 1986), pp. 326–46, and 'Exorcism into Art', *Representations*, 12 (Autumn 1985), pp. 15–23.
2. More, D4; Lewis Theobald, *The Works of Shakespeare*, 7 vols (London, 1733), vol. 5, p. 164; Kenneth Muir, 'Samuel Harsnett and *King Lear*', *Review of English Studies*, new series, 2 (1951), pp. 11–21.
3. Greenblatt, *Shakespearean Negotiations*, pp. 118–19, 121, 123–8; *Triall*, A4v.; Amy Wolf, 'Shakespeare and Harsnett: "Pregnant to Good Pity?"', *Studies in English Literature 1500–1900*, 38:2 (Spring 1998), p. 252; Barber quoted in John L. Murphy, *Darkness and Devils: Exorcism and King Lear* (Athens, OH, and London, Ohio University Press, 1984), p. 85.
4. Ibid., p. 85; Brownlow, p. 53, n. 2, pp. 60–1. Harsnett describes him as 'no minister' only in the early part of his career (*DFP*, B) and it would have been impossible for Darrell to sustain a claim to be a minister and preacher under the scrutiny of Whitgift and Hutton if he had not been so. Their suspension and deprivation of him effectively confirms that he correctly calls himself a minister in all five of his books, and refers to his own ordination in 1589 in *AAOD* (I4v.).

5. Hilaire Kallendorf, *Exorcism and Its Texts: Subjectivity in Early Modern literature of England and Spain* (Toronto, Buffalo and London, University of Toronto Press, 2003), pp. 127–8, 133–9, 199. See also the critique offered by Thomas Healy, *New Latitudes: Theory and English Renaissance Literature* (London, Edward Arnold, 1992), pp. 72–4.

6. *ATN*, I4.

7. Brownlow, p. 12.

8. *Detection*, A3, C2.

9. Many thanks to Laura Salisbury for directing me to Connor's book, Steven Connor, *Dumbstruck: A Cultural History of Ventriloquism* (Oxford, Oxford University Press, 2000); *DFP*, Bb2–Bb2v.

10. Although in a book forthcoming with Boydell and Brewer Jan Frans van Dijkhuizen argues for a number of different readings, focusing especially on the self and the practice of taking illusion seriously. He also offers readings of over a dozen other plays which refer to demonic possession in the period (*Devil Theatre: Demonic Possession and Exorcism in English Drama 1558–1642*). For Shute see Hoare, p. 16.

11. Deacon and Walker, *Dialogicall Discourses*, D7–E3.

12. Stuart Clark, *Thinking with Demons: The Idea of Witchcraft in Early Modern Europe* (Oxford, Clarendon, 1997).

13. Connor, p. 148.

14. *Detection*, pp. 84–5, 158–9.

15. Ibid., p. 68.

16. Hamilton, pp. 59–85; Kallendorf, p. 42.

17. Hamilton, p. 79; Kallendorf, pp. 40–1. It is not clear why binding a demoniac in a dark room is seen as specifically Protestant.

18. Hamilton, pp. 74, 80; William Shakespeare, *The Comedy of Errors*, ed. Stanley Wells (London, Penguin, 2005), IV.iv.49–55, 103–10, V.i.169–77. Pinch charges the devil in the name of the saints in a Catholic way.

19. Although Hamilton believed, like many other scholars, that Darrell probably died in about 1602 (p. 87).

20. Peter Milward, 'Shakespeare and Elizabethan Exorcism', *English Literature and Language*, 17 (1981), p. 48; J. L. Simmons, 'A Source for Shakespeare's Malvolio: The Elizabethan Controversy with the Puritans', *Huntington Library Quarterly*, 36 (1973), pp. 181–201; Bancroft, *A Survey*, pp. 415–16, and *A Sermon Preached at Paules Crosse* (London, 1589), p. 21; *Twelfth Night*, II.v.100, V.i.271, II.v.37; G. B. Harrison (ed.), *Complete Works of Shakespeare* (New York, n.p., 1952), p. 847; Hamilton, p. 97.

21. There has been a long argument over Feste's use of the phrase 'bibble babble', which may be drawn from either More or Darrell's account of the Lancashire seven, but it was a fairly common phrase (Winfried Schleiner, 'The Feste-Malvolio Scene in *Twelfth Night* against the Background of Renaissance Ideas about Madness and Possession', *Deutsche Shakespeare Gesellschaft West Jahrbuch* (1990), pp. 55–6, Hamilton, p. 101).

22. Quoted in Bruce R. Smith, 'Introduction' to *Twelfth Night*, ed. Smith, p. 2.

23. Hamilton, p. 97; see also Leonard Tennenhouse, *Power on Display: The Politics of Shakespeare's Genres* (New York and London, Methuen, 1986), pp. 61–8.

24. Hamilton, p. 100; Greenblatt, *Shakespearean Negotiations*, p. 115.

25. Schleiner, p. 54; *Twelfth Night*, IV.ii.3, 16.

26. *Twelfth Night*, IV.ii.29, 36, 89, 51–3; Hamilton, p. 95.

27. Hamilton, p. 100.

28. *Twelfth Night*, II.iii.115, III.iii.24.

29. Hamilton, pp. 88–9; see also Cristina Malcolmson, '"What You Will": Social Mobility and Gender in *Twelfth Night*' (1991) in R. S. White, *Twelfth Night: Contemporary Critical Essays* (Basingstoke, Macmillan, 1996), p. 179.

30. John D. Cox, *The Devil and the Sacred in English Drama 1350–1642* (Cambridge, Cambridge University Press, 2000), p. 154.

31. *Replie*, P2v.

32. Ben Jonson, *The Devil is an Ass*, ed. Peter Happé (Manchester, Manchester University Press, 1994), V.iii.1–8.

33. There are other echoes too, identified in Happé's edition, p. 214, n. 35, p. 216, n. 67 and p. 221, n. 144, although p. 215, n. 50 confuses the devil's torments with tests of the possessed.

34. Happé, 'Introduction' to Ben Jonson, *The Devil is an Ass*, ed. Happé, pp. 1, 3, 14; Beatrice White, *A Cast of Ravens: The Strange Case of Sir Thomas Overbury* (London, John Murray, 1965); Anne Somerset, *Unnatural Murder: Poison at the Court of James I* (London, Weidenfeld and Nicolson, 1997).

35. Walker, pp. 81–3; G. L. Kittredge, 'King James I and *The Devil is an Ass*', *Modern Philology*, 9 (1911), pp. 195–209; and Leah Marcus, *The Politics of Mirth* (Chicago, University of Chicago Press, 1986), p. 91.

36. Julie Sanders, 'A Parody of Lord Chief Justice Popham in *The Devil is an Ass*', *Notes and Queries*, new series, 44:4 (1997), pp. 528–30; Robert C. Evans, 'Contemporary Contexts of Jonson's *The Devil is an Ass*', *Comparative Drama*, 26:2 (1992), pp. 140–76.

37. Deacon and Walker's *Dialogicall Discourses* offers an overview of theories about the devil's nature, material substance and capabilities.

38. *The Devil is an Ass*, I.i.41–2, 80, 100–9, 121.

39. Ibid., V.v.14, 29.

40. Ben Jonson, *Volpone* in *Ben Jonson: Five Plays*, ed. G. A. Wilkes (Oxford, Oxford University Press, 1988), V.xii.22–31; his punishment is the loss of his professional standing and banishment (126–8).

41. *The Devil is an Ass*, V.viii.139, 141, 169–74.

42. G. A. Wilkes, 'Introduction' to *Five Plays*, p. xii.

43. *EPI*, pp. 308–9.

44. Ben Jonson, *Bartholomew Fair* in *Five Plays*, I.iii.119–28.

45. *The Devil is an Ass*, ed. Happé, p. 59, nn. 41–3.

46. John Cordy Jeaffreson (ed.), *Middlesex County Records*, old series, 4 vols (1886; London, Greater London Council, 1972), vol. 1, p. 249 (indictment 22 September 1598).

47. As Jonson put it, 'where soever manners and fashions are corrupted, language is …' (quoted in Happé, p. 8).

48. M. J. Kidnie, 'Introduction' to *Ben Jonson: The Devil is an Ass and Other Plays* (Oxford, Oxford University Press, 2000), p. xxii, Happé, p. 4.
49. *Bartholomew Fair*, V.v.
50. Kidnie, p. xxx; C. H. Herford and Percy Simpson, *Ben Jonson*, 11 vols (Oxford, Clarendon, 1925), vol. 1, p. 70, vol. 2, p. 160.
51. See for example Macdonald, p. xxii.
52. Nottingham University Library, Department of Manuscripts and Special Collections, AN/PB 293/7/31. Teversal parish records for the period are lost.
53. Marchant, 'John Darrell – Exorcist', p. 54; Marchant, *The Puritans*, p. 171.
54. Nottingham University Library, Department of Manuscripts and Special Collections, A24, ff. 26, 34.
55. *DNB*.
56. Arber (ed.), vol. 3, p. 280v.
57. Here Darrell mentions his contacts with separatists such as John Smyth and situates himself in the north of England, presumably the north Midlands (*Treatise*, A–A2v.); Philip Wynter (ed.), *The Works of the Right Reverend Joseph Hall*, 10 vols (Oxford, 1863), vol. 8, pp. 209–10.
58. *A True Relation of The grievous handling of William Sommers of Nottingham* (London, 1641); Thomas, *Religion and the Decline of Magic*, p. 580; it is not (yet) known when or where Darrell died.

WORKS CITED

Primary Sources

Anon., *The Examination and Confession of certaine Wytches* (London, 1566).

—, *A Booke Declaringe the Fearfull Vexasion of one Alexander Nyndge, at Herringswell, Suffolk* (London, 1573).

—, *A true and most Dreadfull discourse of a woman possesed with the Devill, at Ditchet, Somerset* (London, 1584).

—, *The Most strange and admirable discoverie of the three Witches of Warboys* (London, 1593).

—, *A Breife Narration of the possession, dispossession, and repossession of William Sommers* (?Amsterdam, 1598).

—, *A Brief Apologie proving the possession of William Sommers* (Middelburg, 1599).

—, *The Triall of Maist. Dorrell* (Middelburg, 1599).

—, *The Witches of Northamptonshire* (London, 1612).

Arber, Edward (ed.), *A Transcript of the Registers of the Company of Stationers in London. 1554–1640*, 5 vols (1875–94; Gloucester, MA, Peter Smith, 1967).

Bailey, John Eglington (ed.), *Diary for the Years 1595–1601 of Dr. John Dee* (n.p., Kessinger, 2006).

Bancroft, Richard, *A Sermon Preached at Paules Crosse* (London, 1589).

—, *Dangerous Positions* (London, 1593).

—, *A Survey of the Pretended Holy Discipline* (London, 1593).

[Bee, Jesse, et al.], *The most wonderfull and true storie* (London, 1597).

Bradshaw, William, and Arthur Hildersham, *English Puritanisme* (n.p., 1605).

—, *A direction for the weaker sort of Christian ... Whereunto is adjoined a verie profitable treatise* (London, 1609).

Brook, Benjamin, *Lives of the Puritans* (London, 1813).

Bruce, J. (ed.), *Diary of John Manningham* (London, Camden Society, 1868).

Carey, John (ed.), *John Donne, Selected Poetry* (Oxford, Oxford University Press, 1996).

Clarke, Samuel, *A General Martyrologie … Whereunto is added the lives of thirty two English Divines* (London, 1677).

Darrell, John, *An Apologie or Defence of the Possession of William Sommers* (?Amsterdam, 1598).

—, *A Detection of that Sinnful, Shamful, Lying and Ridiculous Discours of Samuel Harshnet* (n.p., 1600).

—, *A True Narration of the Strange and Grevous Vexation by the Devil of 7 Persons in Lancashire and William Sommers of Nottingham* (n.p., 1600).

—, *The Replie of John Darrell to the Answer of John Deacon and John Walker* (n.p., 1602).

—, *A Survey of Certaine Dialogical Discourses* (n.p., 1602).

—, *A Treatise of the Church* (London, 1617).

—, *A True Relation of The grievous handling of William Sommers* (London, 1641).

Deacon, John, and John Walker, *Dialogicall Discourses of Spirits and Divels* (London, 1601).

—, *A Summarie Answere to al the Material Points in any of Master Darel his Bookes* (London, 1601).

Fairfax, Edward, 'A Discourse of Witchcraft' in William Grainge (ed.), *Daemonologia* (Harrogate, 1882).

Fisher, John, *The Copy of a Letter Describing the wonderful woorke of God in delivering a Mayden within the City of Chester* (London, 1564).

Foster, C. W. (ed.), *The State of the Church in the Reigns of Queen Elizabeth and King James as Illustrated by Documents Relating to the Diocese of Lincoln, vol. 1* (Horncastle, Morton/Lincoln Record Society, 1926).

Fuller, Thomas, *The History of the Worthies of England* (London, 1662).

Galis, Richard, *A Brief Treatise* (London, 1579).

Gifford, George, *A Dialogue of Witches* (London, 1593).

Goadby, Joseph, *Memoirs of the Reverend Arthur Hildersham* (Bingham, 1819).

Goodcole, Henry, *The wonderfull discoverie of Elizabeth Sawyer, a Witch* (London, 1621).

Harsnett, Samuel, *A Dicovery of the Fraudulent Practices of John Darrel* (London, 1599).

—, *A Declaration of Egregious Popish Impostures* (London, 1603).

Heylyn, Peter, *Aerius Redivivus, or, The History of the Presbyterians* (Oxford, 1670).

Heywood, Thomas, and Richard Brome, *The Late Lancashire Witches* (London, 1634).

Hildersham, Arthur, *Lectures upon the Fourth of John* (London, 1629).

Hoare, Peter, *The Rectors of St. Peter's Church, Nottingham, 1241–1991* (Nottingham, St Peter's Parochial Church Council, 1992).

Hutchinson, Lucy, *Memoirs of the Life of Colonel Hutchinson* (MS 1671; London, Dent, 1995).

Jeaffreson, John Cordy, *Middlesex County Records*, old series, 4 vols (1886; London, Greater London Council, 1972).

Jonson, Ben, *Bartholomew Fair* in *Ben Jonson: Five Plays*, ed. G. A. Wilkes (Oxford, Oxford University Press, 1988).

—, *The Devil is an Ass*, ed. Peter Happé (Manchester, Manchester University Press, 1994).

—, *Volpone* in *Five Plays*.

Kersting, Sally, 'Churchwardens of St. Peter's 1559–1991' in Hoare, pp. 49–50.

Marescot, Michel, *A True Discourse upon the Matter of Martha Brossier*, trans. Abraham Hartwell (London, 1599).

Moore, Mary, *Wonderfull News from the North* (London, 1650).

More, George, *A True Discourse concerning the certaine Possession and Dispossession of 7 persons in one Familie in Lancashire* (n.p., 1600).

Neal, Daniel, *The History of the Puritans or Protestant Non-Conformists*, 2nd edn (London, 1732).

Peel, Albert (ed.), *The Seconde Parte of a Register: being a Calendar of Manuscripts under that title intended for publication by the Puritans about 1593*, 2 vols (Cambridge, Cambridge University Press, 1915).

—, *Tracts Ascribed to Richard Bancroft* (Cambridge, Cambridge University Press, 1953).

Pocklington, John, *Altare Christianum* (London, 1637).

Potts, Thomas, *The Wonderfull Discoverie of Witches* (London, 1612).

Scot, Reginald, *The Discoverie of Witchcraft* (London, 1584).

Shakespeare, William, *The Comedy of Errors*, ed. Stanley Wells (London, Penguin, 2005).

—, *Twelfth Night*, ed. Bruce R. Smith (Boston and New York, Bedford/St Martin's, 2001).

Smith, Henry, *Sermons* (London, 1599).

Stevenson, W. H., *HMC Report on the Manuscripts of Lord Middleton, Preserved at Wollaton Hall* (London, HMSO, 1911).

Stevenson, W. H., and James Raine (eds), *Records of the Borough of Nottingham*, 9 vols (London, 1889).

Strype, John, *The Life and Acts of the Most Reverend Father in God John Whitgift* (London, 1718).

Sutcliffe, Matthew, *An Answer to a Certain Libel* (London, 1592).

Swan, John, *A True and Breife Report, of Mary Glovers Vexation* (London, 1603).

Williams, Sarah (ed.), *Letters Written by John Chamberlain* (London, Camden Society 1861).

Secondary Sources

Abrams, M. H., and Stephen Greenblatt, *The Norton Anthology of English Literature*, 7th edn, 2 vols (New York and London, W. W. Norton, 2000).

Almond, Philip. C., *Demonic Possession and Exorcism in Early Modern England: Contemporary Texts and their Cultural Contexts* (Cambridge, Cambridge University Press, 2004).

Aston, Margaret, 'Puritans and Iconoclasm 1560–1660' in Durston and Eales (eds), pp. 92–121.

Atherton, Ian, and David Como, 'The Burning of Edward Wightman: Puritanism, Prelacy and the Politics of Heresy in Early Modern England', *English Historical Review*, 120:489 (December 2005), pp. 1215–50.

Austin, Michael, *A Stage or Two Beyond Christendom: A Social History of the Church of England in Derbyshire* (Cromford, Scarthin Books, 2001).

Bailey, Thomas, *Annals of Nottinghamshire*, 4 vols (London, Simpkin, Marshall, n.d).

Beer, Samuel H., 'Christopher Hill, Some Reminiscences' in Pennington and Thomas (eds), pp. 1–21.

Brigden, Susan, 'Youth and the English Reformation', *Past and Present*, 95 (1982), pp. 37–67.

Briggs, Robin, *Witches and Neighbours: The Social and Cultural Context of European Witchcraft* (London, HarperCollins, 1996).

Brown, Cornelius, *Lives of Nottingham Worthies* (London, 1882).

Brownlow, F. W., *Shakespeare, Harsnett and the Devils of Denham* (Newark and London, University of Delaware Press, Associated University Presses, 1993).

Carlson, Leland H., *Martin Marprelate, Gentleman: Master Job Throkmorton Laid Open in his Colors* (San Marino, Huntington Library, 1981).

Clark, Peter, 'The Alehouse and Alternative Society' in Pennington and Thomas (eds), pp. 47–72.

Clark, Stuart, *Thinking with Demons: The Idea of Witchcraft in Early Modern Europe* (Oxford, Clarendon, 1997).

Cohn, Norman, *Europe's Inner Demons: The Demonization of Christians in Medieval Christendom*, rev. edn (London, Pimlico, 1993).

Collinson, Patrick, *The Elizabethan Puritan Movement* (London, Jonathan Cape, 1967).

—, *The Religion of Protestants: The Church in English Society 1559–1625* (Oxford, Clarendon, 1982).

—, *Godly People: Essays on English Protestantism and Puritanism* (London, Hambledon, 1983).

—, *The Birthpangs of Protestant England* (Basingstoke, Macmillan, 1988).

—, *The Puritan Character: Polemics and Polarities in Early Seventeenth-Century English Culture*, ed. Karen E. Rowe (Los Angeles, William Andrews Clark Memorial Library, 1989).

Collinson, Patrick, and John Craig (eds), *The Reformation in English Towns 1500–1640* (Basingstoke, Macmillan, 1998).

Condie, Lana, 'The Practice of Exorcism and the Challenge to Clerical Authority', *Access: History*, 3:1 (Summer 2000), pp. 93–102.

Connor, Steven, *Dumbstruck: A Cultural History of Ventriloquism* (Oxford, Oxford University Press, 2000).

Cox, John D., *The Devil and the Sacred in English Drama 1350–1642* (Cambridge, Cambridge University Press, 2000).

Cross, Claire, *The Puritan Earl: The Life of Henry Hastings, Earl of Huntingdon 1536–1595* (London, Macmillan, 1966).

Deering, Charles, *The History of Nottingham* (1751; Nottingham, S. R. Publishing, 1970).

Dictionary of National Biography (Oxford, Oxford University Press, 2004).

Dolan, Frances, *Dangerous Familiars: Representations of Domestic Crime in England 1550–1700* (Ithaca and London, Cornell University Press, 1994).

Doran, Susan, *Elizabeth I and Religion 1558–1603* (London and New York, Routledge, 1994).

Dover Wilson, J., 'Richard Schilders and the English Puritans', *Transactions of the Bibliographical Society*, 11 (1909), pp. 65–134.

Durston, Christopher, and Jacqueline Eales (eds), *The Culture of English Puritanism 1560–1700* (Basingstoke, Macmillan, 1996).

Eales, Jacqueline, 'Thomas Pierson and the Transmission of Moderate Puritan Tradition', *Midland History*, 20 (1995), pp. 75–102.

Eusden, John Dykstra, *Puritans, Lawyers and Politics in the Early Seventeenth Century* (New Haven, Archon/Yale University Press, 1968).

Evans, Robert C., 'Contemporary Contexts of Jonson's *The Devil is an Ass*', *Comparative Drama*, 26:2 (1992), pp. 140–76.

Everitt, Alan, *The Community of Kent and the Great Rebellion* (Leicester, Leicester University Press, 1966).

—, *The Local Community and the Great Rebellion* (London, Historical Association, 1969).

Fell Smith, Charlotte, *John Dee 1527–1608* (London, Constable, 1909).

Ferber, Sarah, *Demonic Possession and Exorcism in Early Modern France* (London and New York, Routledge, 2004).

Findlay, Alison, 'Sexual and Spiritual Politics in the Events of 1633–4 and *The Late Lancashire Witches*' in Robert Poole (ed.), *The Lancashire Witches: Histories and Stories* (Manchester, Manchester University Press, 2002), pp. 146–65.

Freeman, Thomas, 'Demons, Deviance and Defiance, John Darrell and the Politics of Exorcism in Late Elizabethan England' in Peter Lake and Michael Questier (eds), *Conformity and Orthodoxy in the English Church c. 1560–1660* (Woodbridge, Boydell Press, 2000), pp. 34–63.

Garratt, H. J. H., *Eckington, The Court Rolls, vol. 3: 1506–1589* (Huddersfield, H. J. H. Garratt, 2003).

Gibson, Marion (ed.), *Reading Witchcraft* (London and New York, Routledge, 1999).

—, *Witchcraft and Society in England and America 1550–1750* (Ithaca and London, Cornell University Press/Continuum, 2003).

Godfrey, John. T., *Notes on the Parish Registers of St. Mary's Nottingham 1566–1812* (Nottingham, Saxton, 1901).

Gray, J. H., *The Queens' College of St. Margaret and St. Bernard in the University of Cambridge*, rev. edn (1899; Cambridge, Cambridge University Press, 1926).

Green, Ian, *Print and Protestantism in Early Modern England* (Oxford, Oxford University Press, 2000).

Greenblatt, Stephen, 'Exorcism into Art', *Representations*, 12 (Autumn 1985), pp. 15–23.

—, 'Loudun and London', *Critical Inquiry*, 12:2 (Winter 1986), pp. 326–46.

—, *Shakespearean Negotiations: The Circulation of Social Energy in Renaissance England* (Oxford, Clarendon Press, 1988).

Griffiths, Paul, *Youth and Authority: Formative Experiences in England 1560–1640* (Oxford, Clarendon, 1996).

Haigh, Christopher, *Reformation and Resistance in Tudor Lancashire* (Cambridge, Cambridge University Press, 1975).

—, 'Puritan Evangelism in the Reign of Elizabeth I', *English Historical Review*, 92:362 (January 1977), pp. 30–58.

Hamilton, Donna B., *Shakespeare and the Politics of Protestant England* (New York and London, Harvester Wheatsheaf, 1992).

Happé, Peter, 'Introduction' to Ben Jonson, *The Devil is an Ass*, ed. Peter Happé (Manchester, Manchester University Press, 1994).

Harrison, G. B. (ed.), *Complete Works of Shakespeare* (New York, n.p., 1952).

Healy, Thomas, *New Latitudes: Theory and English Renaissance Literature* (London, Edward Arnold, 1992).

Herford, C. H., and Percy Simpson, *Ben Jonson*, 11 vols (Oxford, Clarendon, 1925).

Hill, Christopher, *Society and Puritanism in Pre-Revolutionary England* (London, Secker and Warburg, 1964).

—, *Puritanism and Revolution* (1958; London, Penguin, 1988).

—, *The World Turned Upside Down* (1972; London, Penguin, 1991).

Hillier, Kenneth, *The Book of Ashby de la Zouch* (Buckingham, Barracuda, 1984).

Hood, J. C. F., *An Account of St. Mary's Church Nottingham* (Nottingham, Cooke and Vowles, 1910).

Hope-Robbins, Rossell, *The Encyclopaedia of Witchcraft and Demonology* (London, Spring, 1959).

—, Review of Corinne Holt Rickert, *The Case of John Darrell, Minister and Exorcist*, *Renaissance News*, 16 (1963), pp. 28–30.

Horner Groves, William, *The History of Mansfield* (Nottingham, 1894).

Houlbrooke, Ralph, *The English Family 1450–1700* (London, Longman, 1984).

Hull, Oswald, *South Derbyshire and Its People: A History* (Derby, Derbyshire County Council, 2004).

Kallendorf, Hilaire, *Exorcism and Its Texts: Subjectivity in Early Modern Literature of England and Spain* (Toronto, Buffalo and London, University of Toronto Press, 2003).

Keeton, George W., *Shakespeare's Legal and Political Background* (London, Pitman, 1967).

Kidnie, M. J., 'Introduction' to *Ben Jonson, The Devil is an Ass and Other Plays* (Oxford, Oxford University Press, 2000).

Kittredge, G. L., 'King James I and *The Devil is an Ass*', *Modern Philology*, 9 (1911), pp. 195–209.

—, *Witchcraft in Old and New England* (Cambridge, MA, Harvard University Press, 1929).

Knappen, M. M., *Tudor Puritanism: A Chapter in the History of Idealism* (Chicago, University of Chicago Press, 1939).

Lake, Peter, *Moderate Puritans and the Elizabethan Church* (Cambridge, Cambridge University Press, 1982).

—, *Anglicans and Puritans? Presbyterianism and English Conformist Thought from Whitgift to Hooker* (London, Unwin Hyman, 1988).

Lake, Peter, with Michael Questier, *The Anti-Christ's Lewd Hat: Protestants, Papists and Players in Post-Reformation England* (New Haven and London, Yale University Press, 2002).

Lamburn, D. J., 'Digging and Dunging: Some Aspects of Lay Influence in the Church in Northern Towns' in Wood (ed.), pp. 365–80.

Larner, Christina, *Witchcraft and Religion*, ed. Alan Macfarlane (Oxford, Blackwell, 1984).

Lumby, Jonathan, *The Lancashire Witch-Craze: Jennet Preston and the Lancashire Witches 1612* (Preston, Carnegie, 1995).

MacCulloch, Diarmaid, *The Later Reformation in England 1547–1603* (Basingstoke, Macmillan, 1990).

Macdonald, Michael, *Witchcraft and Hysteria in Elizabethan London: Edward Jorden and the Mary Glover Case* (London and New York, Tavistock Routledge, 1991).

Malcolmson, Cristina, '"What You Will": Social Mobility and Gender in *Twelfth Night*' (1991) in R. S. White, *Twelfth Night: Contemporary Critical Essays* (Basingstoke, Macmillan, 1996), pp. 160–93.

Marchant, R. A., 'John Darrell – Exorcist', *Transactions of the Thoroton Society*, 64 (1960), pp. 47–55.

—, *The Puritans and the Church Courts in the Diocese of York* (London, Longman, 1960).

Marcombe, David, 'The Last Days of Lenton Priory' in Wood (ed.), pp. 295–313.

Marcus, Leah, *The Politics of Mirth* (Chicago, University of Chicago Press, 1986).

Milward, Peter, 'Shakespeare and Elizabethan Exorcism', *English Literature and Language*, 17 (1981), pp. 33–45.

Muchembled, Robert, 'Satanic Myths and Cultural Reality' in Bengt Ankarloo and Gustav Henningsen (eds), *Early Modern European Witchcraft: Centres and Peripheries* (Oxford, Clarendon, 1993).

Muir, Kenneth, 'Samuel Harsnett and *King Lear*', *Review of English Studies*, new series, 2 (1951), pp. 11–21.

Mullins, Rebecca Louise, 'Children of Disobedience: Aspects of Possession in Early Modern England' (MA thesis, University of York, 1997).

Murphy, John L., *Darkness and Devils: Exorcism and King Lear* (Athens, OH, and London, Ohio University Press, 1984).

Neale, J. E., *Elizabeth I and Her Parliaments 1559–1581* (London, Jonathan Cape, 1953).

—, *Elizabeth I and Her Parliaments 1584–1601* (London, Jonathan Cape, 1957).

New, John F. H., *Anglican and Puritan: The Basis of their Opposition* (London, A. and C. Black, 1964).

Newman, Christine M., '"An Honourable and Elect Lady", The Faith of Isabel, Lady Bowes' in Wood (ed.), pp. 407–19.

Nichols, John, *The History and Antiquities of the County of Leicester*, 4 vols (1804; Wakefield, S. R. Publishers/Leicester County Council, 1971).

O'Callaghan, Deirdre, 'Vexed and Volatile Bodies: the Drama of Possession and Exorcism in Late Elizabethan England – the John Darrell Cases' (MA thesis, University of Melbourne, 1998).

O'Day, Rosemary, 'Ecclesiastical Patronage, Who Controlled the Church' in Felicity Heal and Rosemary O'Day (eds), *Church and Society in England: Henry VIII to James I* (London and Basingstoke, Macmillan, 1977), pp. 137–55.

Oldridge, Darren, *The Devil in Early Modern England* (Stroud, Sutton, 2000).

Page, William (ed.), *The Victoria History of the County of Nottingham, vol. 2* (London, Constable, 1910).

Pennington, Donald and Keith Thomas (eds), *Puritans and Revolutionaries: Essays in Seventeenth-Century History Presented to Christopher Hill* (Oxford, Clarendon, 1978).

Petti, Anthony G. (ed.), *Roman Catholicism in Elizabethan and Jacobean Staffordshire* (Stafford, Staffordshire Record Society, 1979).

Pollock, Linda, *Forgotten Children: Parent-Child Relations from 1500–1800* (Cambridge, Cambridge University Press, 1983).

Poole, Kristen, *Radical Religion from Shakespeare to Milton: Figures of Nonconformity in Early Modern England* (Cambridge, Cambridge University Press, 2000).

Prockter, Adrian, and Robert Taylor (eds), *The A–Z of Elizabethan London* (Lympne, Harry Margary/Guildhall Library, 1979).

Purkiss, Diane, *The Witch in History* (London and New York, Routledge, 1996).

Reynolds, Matthew, *Godly Reformers and their Opponents in Early Modern England: Religion in Norwich c. 1560–1643* (Woodbridge, Boydell Press, 2005).

Richardson, R. C., *Puritanism in North West England: A Regional Study of the Diocese of Chester* (Manchester and Towota, NJ, Manchester University Press and Rowman and Littlefield, 1972).

Rickert, Corinne Holt, *The Case of John Darrell, Minister and Exorcist* (Gainesville, University of Florida Press, 1962).

Riden, Philip, and John Blair (eds), *History of Chesterfield*, 5 vols (Chesterfield, Borough of Chesterfield, 1980).

Roper, Lyndal, *Oedipus and the Devil: Witchcraft, Sexuality and the Devil in Early Modern Europe* (London and New York, Routledge, 1994).

Rosen, Barbara, *Witchcraft in England 1558–1618* (1969; Amherst, University of Massachusetts Press, 1999).

Sanders, Julie, 'A Parody of Lord Chief Justice Popham in *The Devil is an Ass*', *Notes and Queries*, new series, 44:4 (1997), pp. 528–30.

Sasek, Lawrence A. (ed.), *Images of English Puritanism: A Collection of Contemporary Sources 1589–1646* (Baton Rouge and London, Louisiana State University Press, 1989).

Schleiner, Winfried, 'The Feste-Malvolio Scene in *Twelfth Night* against the Background of Renaissance Ideas about Madness and Possession', *Deutsche Shakespeare Gesellschaft West Jahrbuch* (1990), pp. 48–57.

Seaver, Paul, *The Puritan Lectureships: The Politics of Religious Dissent 1560–1662* (Stanford, Stanford University Press, 1970).

Sharpe, J. A., 'Disruption in the Well-Ordered Household, Age, Authority, and Possessed Young People' in Paul Griffiths, Adam Fox and Steve Hindle (eds), *The Experience of Authority in Early Modern England* (Basingstoke, Macmillan, 1996), pp. 187–212.

—, *Instruments of Darkness: Witchcraft in England 1550–1750* (London, Hamish Hamilton, 1996).

Sheils, W. J., *The Puritans in the Diocese of Peterborough 1558–1610* (Northampton, Northamptonshire Record Society, 1979).

Simmons, J. L., 'A Source for Shakespeare's Malvolio: The Elizabethan Controversy with the Puritans', *Huntington Library Quarterly*, 36 (1973), pp. 181–201.

Smith, Bruce R., 'Introduction' to *Twelfth Night* (Boston and New York, Bedford/St Martin's, 2001).

Sokol, B. J., and Mary Sokol, *Shakespeare's Legal Language: A Dictionary*, 2nd edn (London and New York, Continuum, 2004).

Somerset, Anne, *Unnatural Murder: Poison at the Court of James I* (London, Weidenfeld and Nicolson, 1997).

Sommerville, C. John, *The Discovery of Childhood in Puritan England* (Athens, GA, University of Georgia, 1992).

Stapleton, Alfred, *The Churches and Monasteries of Old and New Nottingham* (Nottingham, Haubitz, 1903).

Stone, Lawrence, *The Family, Sex and Marriage in England 1500–1800* (London, Penguin, 1977).

Stone, Richard, *Burton Upon Trent: A History* (Chichester, Phillmore, 2004).

Tennenhouse, Leonard, *Power on Display: The Politics of Shakespeare's Genres* (New York and London, Methuen, 1986).

Theobald, Lewis, *The Works of Shakespeare*, 7 vols (London, 1733).

Thomas, A. W., *A History of Nottingham High School* (Nottingham, J. and H. Bell, 1958).

Thomas, Keith, *Religion and the Decline of Magic* (1971; London, Peregrine, 1978).

Throsby, John, *The History and Antiquities of the Town and County of the Town of Nottingham* (Nottingham, 1795).

Tittler, Robert, *The Reformation and the Towns in England: Politics and Political Culture c. 1540–1640* (Oxford, Clarendon, 1998).

Todd, Margo (ed.), *Reformation to Revolution: Politics and Religion in Early Modern England* (London and New York, Routledge, 1995).

Twigg, John, *A History of Queens' College Cambridge 1448–1986* (Woodbridge, Boydell Press, 1987).

van Dijkhuizen, Jan Frans, *Devil Theatre: Demonic Possession and Exorcism in English Drama 1558–1642* (Woodbridge, Boydell and Brewer, forthcoming)

Venn, J., and J. A. Venn (eds), *Alumni Cantabrigienses*, 4 vols (Cambridge, Cambridge University Press, 1927).

Walker, D. P., *Unclean Spirits: Possession and Exorcism in the Late Sixteenth and Early Seventeenth Centuries* (London, Scolar, 1981).

Walsham, Alexandra, '"Frantick Hacket", Prophecy, Sorcery, Insanity and the Elizabethan Puritan Movement', *The Historical Journal*, 41:1 (March 1998), pp. 27–66.

—, *Providence in Early Modern England* (Oxford, Oxford University Press, 1999).

Webster, Tom, *Godly Clergy in Early Stuart England: The Caroline Puritan Movement c. 1620–1643* (Cambridge, Cambridge University Press, 1997).

White, Beatrice, *A Cast of Ravens: The Strange Case of Sir Thomas Overbury* (London, John Murray, 1965).

White, B. R., *The English Separatist Tradition: From the Marian Martyrs to the Pilgrim Fathers* (Oxford, Oxford University Press, 1971).

Willis, Deborah, *Malevolent Nurture: Witch-Hunting and Maternal Power in Early Modern England* (Ithaca and London, Cornell University Press, 1995).

Wolf, Amy, 'Shakespeare and Harsnett, "Pregnant to Good Pity?"', *Studies in English Literature 1500–1900*, 38:2 (Spring 1998), pp. 251–64.

Wood, A. C., *A History of Nottinghamshire* (Nottingham, Thoroton Society, 1947).

Wood, Diana (ed.), *Life and Thought in the Northern Church c. 1100–1700: Essays in Honour of Claire Cross* (Woodbridge, Boydell Press, 1999).

Wootton, David, 'Reginald Scot/Abraham Fleming/The Family of Love' in Stuart Clark (ed.), *Languages of Witchcraft: Narrative, Ideology and Meaning in Early Modern Culture* (Basingstoke, Macmillan, 2001), pp. 119–38.

Wrightson, Keith, *English Society 1580–1680* (London, Hutchinson, 1982).

Wynter, Philip (ed.), *The Works of the Right Reverend Joseph Hall*, 10 vols (Oxford, 1863).

Websites

'Burton-upon-Trent: Established Church', *A History of the County of Staffordshire, Volume 9, Burton-upon-Trent* (2003), pp. 107–30. URL: http://www.british-history. ac.uk/report.asp?compid=12339. Date accessed: 1 December 2005.

'Burton-upon-Trent: Economic History', *A History of the County of Staffordshire, Volume 9, Burton-upon-Trent* (2003), pp. 53–84. URL, http://www.british-history.ac.uk/ report.asp?compid=12335. Date accessed: 1 December 2005.

http://www.burton2000.org.uk/history/greensmiths/gmills6.htm. Date accessed: 25 December 2005.

INDEX

Works appear directly under title and also under author, if known. JD is John Darrell.